THE
8-WEEK
CHOLESTEROL
CURE COOKBOOK

Also by Robert E. Kowalski

THE *8*-WEEK CHOLESTEROL CURE

CHOLESTEROL & CHILDREN

THE 8-WEEK CHOLESTEROL CURE COOKBOOK

More than 200 Delicious Recipes Featuring the Foods Proven to Lower Cholesterol

ROBERT E. KOWALSKI

HARPER & ROW, PUBLISHERS, NEW YORK
1817

GRAND RAPIDS, PHILADELPHIA, ST. LOUIS, SAN FRANCISCO, LONDON, SINGAPORE, SYDNEY, TOKYO

FIRST EDITION

Designed by Barbara Du Pree Knowles

LIBRARY OF CONGRESS CATALOGING-IN-PUBLICATION DATA

Kowalski, Robert E.
    The 8-week cholesterol cure cookbook: more than 200 delicious recipes
featuring the foods proven to lower cholesterol / Robert E. Kowalski.—
1st ed.
      p. cm.
    Includes index.
    ISBN 0-06-016095-0
    1. Low-cholesterol diet—Recipes.   I. Title.   II. Title: Eight-
week cholesterol cure cookbook.
  RM237.75.K679 1989   88-45896
  641.5'6311—dc20

89 90 91 92 93 CC/RRD 10 9 8 7 6 5 4 3 2 1

I dedicate this book to my mother, Helen, who encouraged my interest in cooking when I was just a child. She put up with me in the kitchen when I was more hindrance than help. An essential ingredient for any recipe is love, and there was plenty of that in our house throughout my childhood.

Acknowledgments

The recipe for preparing this book calls for a generous mixing of the talents of many people. My thanks as always to my agent, Clyde Taylor, who guided the project along from the beginning. To Michele Urvater, for her culinary skills in recipe development. To my editors, Larry Ashmead and Margaret Wimberger; Margaret showed extraordinary patience on this one. And to Jennifer Jensen, R.D., for her able assistance and patience in doing the nutritional analyses of the recipes.

Contents

Part One

INTRODUCTION: DECLARING WAR ON CHOLESTEROL

Welcome to a most unusual cookbook, one that quite literally could help save your life. This is not another low-fat, low-calorie cookbook. God knows the world has enough of those, and many of them are quite good. Each of the recipes in this book contains foods that have the ability to actually lower your cholesterol level and to protect you from heart disease. And, if that isn't enough to entice you, eating these special foods will help you to maintain your weight, or even to lose a few pounds if necessary, as well.

In the past we have heard only negatives when it came to following a heart-healthy diet. Don't eat this. Avoid that. The advice from well-meaning dietitians seemed to be, if a food tastes good, spit it out since it can't be good for you.

But what we've been learning in the past few years is that what you do eat is as important as what you avoid when it comes to protecting yourself from heart disease. A lot of what was accepted as gospel truth not long ago has been shown now to be incorrect. For example, even though salmon is a very fatty fish, it's actually a wise choice for a heart-healthy diet. If you've been avoiding such shellfish delicacies as oysters and scallops because you think they have too much cholesterol, you can now think again. You might equate red meat with heart attacks, but now I can show you how to enjoy red meat every week without putting yourself at risk. The same is true for cheese and egg noodles. I'll teach you how to prepare recipes that will make your mouth water and your cholesterol drop.

For those of you who are not familiar with *The 8-Week Cholesterol Cure,* here is a brief introduction to my history with cholesterol and heart disease.

Even though I had been writing about health and medical issues for more than twenty years, cholesterol and heart disease remained just one more area of research to me until it became a matter of life and death. First, I had a family history of heart disease, having lost my dad to a massive heart attack when he was just fifty-seven years old. Others in my family were also afflicted. Even then, I was not prepared for the heart attack that struck when I was only thirty-five years old. By the age of forty-one, I had undergone two coronary bypass surgeries. After the second one, I knew cholesterol was the culprit and something had to be done about it.

Unsatisfied by the options of either cholesterol-reducing drugs or a severely restricted diet, I turned to the medical literature for clues to another approach. Trained in both journalism and medical physiology, I had easy access to all that had been written about cholesterol and heart disease.

To save my own life, I developed what is now known as "The 8-Week Cholesterol Cure." It worked for me by lowering my own cholesterol from a dangerously high 284 mg/dl down to a safe 169 mg/dl, without drugs and without deprivation. And it has worked for thousands of others who have read the book and followed my program. At the core of my program are foods and vitamins that I learned can dramatically lower cholesterol levels.

Today cholesterol is a household word. Just a few years ago, people couldn't even pronounce it, and many wondered whether all the fuss about it wasn't much ado about nothing. That all changed in August, 1987, when the National Cholesterol Education Panel, a prestigious group of experts representing the National Institutes of Health and twenty of the nation's top medical organizations, including the American Heart Association and the American Medical Association, told America that cholesterol levels for all men and women, regardless of age, should be no higher than 200 mg/dl.

The National Cholesterol Education Program has subsequently spread the word to both the public and physicians that everyone should have a cholesterol test, everyone should know his or her numbers, and if those levels are too high, something should be done about it.

We all have good reason for concern. Nearly 66 million Americans have one or more forms of heart or blood-vessel disease. This year as many as 1.5 million of us will have heart attacks, and more than 500,000 will die. Heart disease remains the nation's number one killer, claiming nearly one of every two men and women. Those 1989 American Heart Association statistics are shocking: nearly half of all Americans will die of heart disease.

But there is good news, too. Heart disease is, to a large extent, a preventable disorder. We can accurately predict just who will perish, based on their risk factors. Certain factors cannot be altered: family history of heart disease, advanced age, and male sex all put one at undeniable risk. But we can most definitely control the other factors: high cholesterol levels, high blood pressure, and cigarette smoking are the "Big Three" that can be changed. And we can also take charge of contributing factors, including a sedentary lifestyle, Type A behavior patterns (marked especially by anger and hostility), obesity, and, to a very large extent, diabetes.

While all these risk factors contribute significantly to heart-disease mortality, the focus today remains on cholesterol. We have proof positive that reducing cholesterol levels can slash heart-attack and death rates. *For every 1 percent cut in cholesterol, we achieve a 2 percent drop in heart-disease risk.*

Many authorities believe that, while a cholesterol level of 200 mg/dl is a good start, we should shoot for even lower numbers. Dr. William Castelli, director of the famed Framingham Heart Study, has stated that he has never seen a heart attack in a person whose cholesterol level was under 155 mg/dl. One of the pioneers in establishing the link between cholesterol and heart disease, Dr. Jeremiah Stamler of Northwestern University, maintains that between 160 and 180 mg/dl there is little if any risk of heart disease, but that after 180 the risk increases gradually, and that after 200 the risk goes up significantly. Moreover, if one looks at the incidence of heart disease in populations around the world, one finds that the lower the cholesterol levels the lower the heart-disease rates.

Another reason for wanting to get cholesterol levels as low as possible comes from research into the potential for reversing heart disease. Investigators have found that only when cholesterol counts drop to the 160 level or below can one expect either to stop the progress of the disease or actually to reverse it.

We also have to consider the different kinds of cholesterol in our blood. A finger-prick test, such as is done in supermarkets and shopping malls, gives a count of total blood cholesterol. A more thorough analysis, which can be done in hospital or clinical laboratories, reveals the amounts of the different kinds of cholesterol.

These types are based on the size and density of the chemical carriers, known as lipoproteins, that move cholesterol through the bloodstream to and from the liver where it is produced. Low-density-lipoprotein (LDL) cholesterol has been termed "bad" cholesterol because this is the type that is deposited in arteries, resulting in heart disease. High-density-lipoprotein (HDL) cholesterol, on the other hand, has been called "good" cholesterol because it is carried away from the artery walls and back to the liver for disposal. We want to keep LDLs down and HDLs up.

How do we accomplish these goals? The American Heart Association has proposed that Americans should eat no more than 30 percent of calories as fat. (The average American consumes 40 percent of calories as fat.) That's excellent advice for the general population, but for those with already elevated cholesterol levels this recommendation alone isn't enough. The AHA Prudent Diet will achieve, on average, a 10 percent cholesterol reduction. If one starts out with a cholesterol level of 260, for example, a 10 percent reduction brings the individual down to 234, leaving him or her still at risk. Even squeezing a bit more fat from the diet will not likely bring the count to under 200, where it belongs.

On the other hand, severely restricted diets such as that proposed in the Pritikin Program can achieve remarkable cholesterol reductions. But there are problems with these plans. Reducing fat intake to the recommended 7 to 10 percent of total intake, especially for a lifetime, is difficult if not impossible for most men and women. Few of us are willing to give up all our favorite foods for the rest of our lives. This just isn't a practical approach. Moreover, extremely low-fat diets reduce the levels not only of the bad LDL cholesterol but of the good HDL cholesterol as well.

Authorities advocate drugs if diet alone cannot reduce cholesterol levels sufficiently. Two such drugs, colestipol and cholestyramine, are called bile-sequestering agents because they grab onto the bile acids in the intestine and prevent them from being reabsorbed into the bloodstream by carrying them out of the body in the bowel movement. Since bile acids are made from cholesterol, the body must draw some cholesterol out of the blood in order to make more of those acids, which are needed in digestion. Over time the cholesterol levels in the blood drop.

But cholesterol-lowering drugs are expensive and must be taken for a lifetime. They are also extremely unpleasant to swallow, and can cause some adverse reactions.

Imagine my dilemma, then, when faced with the urgent need to reduce my own cholesterol level. Then imagine my delight at finding that certain foods actually lower the amount of cholesterol in the blood in exactly the same way as the drugs. Those foods, including oat bran and oatmeal, dried beans and peas, barley, corn bran, certain fruits and vegetables, and rice bran, all contain soluble fiber, which, like the drugs, binds onto bile acids in the digestive tract and literally carries the cholesterol right out of the body. We'll be discussing these foods in detail in this book.

But, whatever the benefits of these foods, most people aren't very familiar with cooking dried beans and peas, or rice bran, or barley. In fact, when I first wrote *The 8-Week Cholesterol Cure,* very few had even heard of oat bran, much less rice bran. I included some recipes in that book, but a gap remained. I realized that people need to learn a lot more about those cholesterol-lowering foods and how they can be used on a daily basis. And, even though I've been cooking as a hobby since I was just thirteen years old, I too wanted to learn more about cooking with those foods.

I was delighted, then, to be introduced to Michele Urvater by my editor at Harper & Row, Margaret Wimberger.

Michele began her cooking career as a chef in the New York restaurant Ruskay's. In 1976 she established her own cooking school, listed in the *New York Times* as "one of the premier schools in the city." Since closing the school in 1981, Michele has been involved in virtually all aspects of professional cooking and is today a cooking consultant and frequent contributor to food magazines. She is the editor of *The Culinary Institute of America's Cookbook* (Harper & Row, 1990). She also wrote *Fine Fresh Fast Food* (Irena Chalmers Cookbooks, 1982) and served as recipe consultant for the popular *Reader's Digest* cookbook *Eat Well, Be Well.*

Coming even closer to home, Michele's collaboration with David Liederman, a New York cookie mogul and restaurateur, in writing *Cooking the Nouvelle Cuisine in America* (Workman, 1979), led to their developing a best-selling muffin recipe. David's Oat Bran Muffins have gotten widespread acclaim and were publicized in the *New York Times.*

It turned out that Michele was very much interested in working with me to develop some new recipes for a book that would focus exclusively on those foods proven to reduce cholesterol and to protect against heart disease.

After a handshake by telephone, I started to make a "wish list" of all the ways I wanted to cook and bake with those wonderful foods. I suggested to Michele, for example, that guacamole was delicious but high in fat; could she, I wondered, come up with an alternative recipe made with beans and peas? As you'll soon see, she did that and far more.

At the same time Michele was sweating over her New York stove, I experimented with recipes at home in California. After four and a half years, I was hungry for some new oat-bran-muffin recipes. And I was finding all sorts of new food products and equipment that offered lots of promise. Between the two of us, we came up with more than two hundred recipes designed to keep the heart healthy, the stomach content, and the mouth watering. These recipes are designed to fit into my total program for cholesterol reduction. Pick one of the recipes to start with today. Bon appétit!

A DIET
TO LIVE WITH
FOR LIFE

Any successful program to reduce cholesterol must have a good, low-fat, low-cholesterol diet as its foundation. But you can enjoy a wide variety of all kinds of foods and still achieve tremendous success. Importantly, you won't have to totally eliminate certain types of foods, as you do with some fad diets that no one can stay with for long. In fact, you'll probably find that eating the way I propose will keep you more satisfied than your present diet.

The food we eat must provide the nutrients we need for energy, performance of bodily functions, and maintenance and repair. But keeping track of individual nutrients can be confusing. Do you have any idea how much selenium you had today? Or the amount of copper and zinc in last week's menus? No one does, yet it is important that we get enough of those trace minerals, along with the more recognized nutrients such as calcium, protein, and iron.

Recognizing that people couldn't possibly keep track of the many individual nutrients, nutritionists long ago developed an approach that, with modifications, makes as much sense today as it did sixty years ago. This approach is based on the four food groups: meats, fish, and meat alternatives; milk and other dairy foods; fruits and vegetables; and breads and cereals. In addition, we can include a fifth group of other foods that supply little if any nutrition but do provide food satisfaction. Each of these categories of foods tends to supply a group of major nutrients not readily available in any of the other categories. And, when foods from all the groups are consumed on a regular basis, one can be certain of getting enough of both the major and minor nutrients.

The first group is better named the "protein group." It includes meat, fish and seafood, poultry, eggs, and other meat alternatives. Any or all of these will provide protein needed for maintenance and repair of the body. Adults need two servings a day, with a serving of meat measured as 3½ ounces, to satisfy the daily protein requirements. Of course, protein foods supply a number of other nutrients as well.

In selecting foods from the meat group, those conscious of cholesterol will opt for lean cuts of beef, the white meat of poultry, lots of fish and seafood, egg whites and egg substitutes, and other meat alternatives. Happily, the meat alternatives are some of the same foods that also lower cholesterol, as we'll see in detail later on in this book—dried beans and peas, lentils, split yellow and green peas, garbanzos or chickpeas, and so forth. I'll show you how they can be used in entrées, soups, salads, and dips.

The second group is typically a major contributor of fat and cholesterol in the American diet, which is notorious for its high fat content. These are dairy products, which are the main supplier of calcium in the diet, as well as providing substantial protein and a variety of other nutrients. While we never outgrow our need for milk and other dairy foods, we never need the excessive fat and cholesterol that come along with many of them.

Picking foods from this group means opting for the low-fat and nonfat varieties. Start looking at the fat listings on dairy foods to pick those with the least fat. Today you can easily find nonfat yogurt, very-low-fat cottage cheese, and reduced-fat or part-skim cheeses. The best choice in cheese is filled cheese, in which the manufacturer has replaced the butterfat with soybean or other vegetable oil, thus eliminating the cholesterol and the saturated fat and typically cutting down on total fat as well. You can choose a number of brands of these filled cheeses now on the market, but my personal preference is Formagg, made by the Galaxy Cheese Company, which I discuss on page 53. The recipes in this book that call for cheese, all work very well with the Formagg, which is available in a full line of flavors.

Fat presents virtually no problem for the next food group, the fruits and vegetables. Generally speaking, fruits provide the best source of vitamin C, while vegetables supply abundant vitamin A. Adults need at least two servings of fruit each day, and at least two servings of both green and yellow vegetables. The emphasis here is on *at least;* when you cut back on fat, you can enjoy far more food, and fruits and vegetables really fill the bill.

For the most part you can eat fruits and vegetables with no worry about fat. And of course there is no cholesterol since that comes only from animal sources. The only fruits to be somewhat wary of are olives and avocados, which contain a lot of fat and so should be eaten in moderation.

Every mother tells her children, "Eat your vegetables, they're good for you!" Of course we always knew that Mom was right, but now we're learning that she was absolutely on target when it comes to preventing heart disease. Three major recent studies zeroing in on vegetables were reported at the First International Congress on Vegetarian Nutrition held in Washington, D.C., in 1987.

Dr. Michael Burr reported on a study that compared vegetarian and nonvegetarian customers of health-food stores. As health-food store shoppers, it was assumed that both groups would share an interest in healthful eating habits. A total of nearly 11,000 men and women were followed for ten to twelve years.

Death rates from heart disease were significantly lower in the vegetarians than in the nonvegetarians, especially among men. Cholesterol levels were lower in vegetarians, but not tremendously so, and there was no difference in blood pressure readings. Dr. Burr concluded that vegetarianism seems to confer some protection against heart disease, but he remains inconclusive as to "whether this is due to abstinence from meat or to a high consumption of vegetables."

Several studies have shown that Seventh Day Adventists, who avoid meat of all kinds, have a lower rate of heart disease than non-Adventists. Dr. Gary Fraser of Loma Linda University reported his long-term data at the Congress, showing that, indeed, vegetarian Adventists enjoy protection from heart attacks.

In discussing his findings, Dr. Fraser said the lower risk in Adventist men could be owing to their dietary habits, nonsmoking status, possibly better exercise habits, and greater social support. Or could it be the religious practices of the Adventists that protected them, in terms of a sense of community or reduction of stress?

Dr. V. Fonnebo looked at those possibilities with groups of Adventists in Norway. His Tromso Heart Study has become a classic in the field of nutrition and health. To examine the potential role of religion in conferring protection against heart disease, Dr. Fonnebo compared Adventists with equally fervent Baptists. When all other risk factors were taken into consideration, the serum cholesterol levels of the Adventists appeared to be the only factor protecting them from death by heart attack. Dr. Fonnebo concluded that religion is not a factor.

Now you might conclude that it's a simple matter of avoiding saturated fat and cholesterol in the diet of the Adventists. But in fact the Adventists are lacto-ovo vegetarians, consuming quite large quantities of dairy foods and eggs. In some cases, the saturated fat and cholesterol contents of their diets are higher than those in meat eaters. But there remains a big difference in the amount of fruit and vegetables consumed regularly.

No one has the final answer yet, and there may be a number of factors involved. And even the leaders within the Adventist church are trying to persuade their members to cut back significantly on the amount of dairy foods and eggs they consume, regardless of other dietary practices. So don't assume that eating more fruits and vegetables will give you carte blanche to eat all the cheese and butter you want.

But the fact remains that something in the fruits and vegetables does indeed offer some protection against heart disease as well as against other diseases such as cancer. If nothing else, the more fruits and vegetables you eat, the less saturated fat and cholesterol are likely to be in your diet. An apple is a far better snack than a doughnut. And an extra-large salad or serving of vegetables at dinner will help cut back on the serving size of meat on the plate.

I'm far from a vegetarian. In fact, I believe that man was meant to be an omnivore, a creature who eats a little of this and a little of that rather than a meat-eating carnivore or a plant-eating herbivore. It's a question of balance. And certainly we've seen the specific benefits in terms of certain seafood rich in the oils which offer protection to the Eskimos. Many of the meat, fish, and poultry choices available supply us with high-quality protein with far less saturated fat and cholesterol than cheese and eggs. However, I do believe that everyone interested in total health—not just heart disease—ought to eat lots more fruit and vegetables. There's absolutely no down side to eating fruits and vegetables.

All types of fruits and vegetables contain *insoluble* fiber. That fiber, not the soluble type, moves food more quickly through the digestive tract. The short-term benefit is greater bowel movement regularity. The long-term benefit appears to be protection from diseases of the colon such as cancer.

In addition, many kinds of fruits and vegetables are rich in soluble fiber. Take a look at the numbers in the table on page 41. I hasten to point out that we currently have no clinical evidence that the soluble fiber in those foods will directly lower cholesterol levels, however. Until studies are done with human subjects we won't know for sure whether that particular source of soluble fiber is as effective as, say, oat bran or dried beans and peas.

To be effective in jacking up your fruit and vegetable consumption, as well as that of your family, try to be a bit creative. A bowl of limp lettuce leaves with a chunk of tomato doesn't make anyone look forward to the next salad. Go for all the variety you can think of: different kinds of lettuce, shredded carrots, little flowerets of cauliflower and broccoli, artichoke hearts, raisins, jicama, hearts of palm, and so on.

Keep some prepared fruits and vegetables in the refrigerator in bowls or sealed containers so you can grab for them easily. No one wants to start peeling and paring at 10 P.M. for that little snack. Make it convenient.

Finally we come to the breads and cereals group, sometimes called the grain group. Here's where we'll find a lot of beneficial dietary fiber, both soluble and insoluble, along with a wealth of B vitamins. Adults need a minimum of four servings daily. Again, those on low-fat diets will find they can eat a lot more from this group without worrying about weight gain. I delight in amazing my friends with the amounts of pasta I can put away at one sitting, or to finish a big meal and then ask for another basket of bread and rolls. Of course I don't put butter on that bread, so I can eat a lot more.

Baked goods and some cereals, however, can be a significant source of hidden fat in the diet. You'll have to start reading the labels carefully to learn just what you're buying. One brand of rolls, for example, will be made with a bit of corn or soybean oil while another uses animal shortening. No need to tell you which to choose. The same applies to breakfast cereals. It really disturbs me that some manufacturers will make oat-bran cereals with coconut oil, which is a far more saturated form of fat than even lard or butter.

While the foods in those four basic food groups provide all the nutrients we need, other foods supply a lot of calories along with their taste appeal. Those "others," including fats and oils, sugars, alcohol, and salt form a fifth group. We know from a great number of authorities, including the Surgeon General, that we should all eat a lot less of those foods.

First let's consider fats and oils. Recipes taste a whole lot better with them than without them. So the key here must be moderation. Choosing fats and oils to cook and bake with can be difficult, and nutrition labels can be confusing. So let's take a closer look, beginning with a bit of basic chemistry.

All fats and oils are composed of varying combinations of individual molecules termed fatty acids. Depending on the composition of those molecules, the fats are termed saturated, monounsaturated, or polyunsaturated. By now you've most likely heard that saturated fats are responsible for raising blood cholesterol and for clogging of the arteries, while polyunsaturated and monounsaturated fats are not. In fact, when polyunsaturated and monounsaturated fats are used to replace saturated fats in the diet, cholesterol levels fall.

Just a few years ago authorities recommended polyunsaturated fats such as corn and soybean oil, viewing the monounsaturated fats as "neutral," neither raising nor lowering cholesterol levels. But today we know that both are efficient in reducing cholesterol counts, but that monounsaturated fats do a better job of protecting levels of the good cholesterol, the HDLs. Too much polyunsaturated fat can decrease the HDLs along with the LDLs.

All *fats* contain saturated, polyunsaturated, and monounsaturated fatty acids. But different foods have different fatty-acid profiles, with one kind of fatty acids predominant. That's why we use a kind of shorthand to describe foods as being saturated, polyunsaturated, or monounsaturated. We can simplify things further by generalizing that animal fats are principally sources of saturated fats. Vegetable oils, on the other hand, are mainly unsaturated or monounsaturated. But, of course, there are exceptions: the tropical oils, including coconut oil, palm oil, and palm kernel oil, are mainly saturated fats.

Saturated fats are solid to semisolid at room temperature, while the polyunsaturated and monounsaturated fats are liquid at that temperature. But some polyunsaturated fats can be hardened through the process of hydrogenation. By hydrogenating such oils as corn and soybean, food manufacturers extend shelf life and make products more appealing in taste and texture. In the past we have been told to avoid or at least limit hydrogenated or partially hydrogenated fats, since they have been made more saturated, but fortunately we've learned some facts that have changed that.

Working at the University of Texas Health Sciences Center in Dallas, Dr. Scott Grundy compared the effects of isolated specific fatty acids on cholesterol levels in the blood. He fed volunteers diets that contained one of three fatty acids. When effects of the saturated fats stearic acid and palmitic acid were compared with those of the polyunsaturated fat oleic acid, only the palmitic acid raised cholesterol levels. The process of hydrogenating polyunsaturated fats for such products as margarine creates stearic acid. So, while the products' fats are more saturated, we now know that the specific fatty acid, stearic, isn't a concern. So we can choose products containing hydrogenated fats, watching only that we limit the total amount of fat in the diet. We'll look at that limitation in just a little while.*

Dr. Grundy was the man who also brought the monounsaturated fats to the public attention. He and others had long noted that Italians, Greeks, and others of Mediterranean descent were largely protected from heart disease even though their diets were high in total fat. Dr. Grundy wondered whether it might have to do with the olive oil they were consuming. He was right. Olive oil, rich in monounsaturated fatty acids, was able to lower cholesterol as efficiently as polyunsaturated fats when used to replace saturated fats in the diet. Moreover, the monounsaturated fats did not lower HDL levels, thus making them superior to the polyunsaturated fats.

The recommendation today is strictly to limit saturated fats, replacing them with monounsaturated and some polyunsaturated fats. Here are the sources of those fats in the diet:

SATURATED FATS: Animal fats in meat, dairy products, and animal shortenings. Tropical oils, including coconut, palm, and palm kernel oils

MONOUNSATURATED FATS: Olives and olive oil, Peanuts and peanut oil, Avocados, Cashews, Canola oil (Puritan and others)

POLYUNSATURATED FATS: Vegetable oils, including corn oil, soybean oil, safflower oil, and others

For a complete breakdown of the percentages of saturated, monounsaturated, and polyunsaturated fatty acids in commonly consumed fats and oils, see the table on page 16. But as you limit total fat intake and replace saturates with unsaturates, how much is enough and how much is too much?

The average American consumes 40 percent of his or her calories as

---

*Early reports of Dr. Grundy's work misinterpreted the data. Since beef and chocolate contain stearic acid, some said this made these foods OK! They overlooked the fact that those foods also contain palmitic acid.

Comparison of Dietary Fats and Oils

Type	Saturated Fatty Acids (% of Total)*	Monounsaturated Fatty Acids (% of Total)*	Polyunsaturated Fatty Acids (% of Total)*
Canola oil	6	62	32
Walnut oil	9	23	64
Safflower oil	10	13	77
Sunflower oil	11	20	69
Corn oil	13	25	62
Olive oil	14	77	9
Soybean oil	15	24	61
Peanut oil	18	49	33
Margarine (tub)	18	47	31
Cottonseed Oil	27	19	54
Tuna fat	27	26	21
Chicken fat	30	45	11
Margarine (stick)	31	47	22
Shortening (can)	31	51	14
Lard	40	45	11
Mutton fat	47	41	8
Palm oil	49	37	9
Beef fat	50	42	4
Butterfat	62	29	4
Palm kernel oil	81	11	2
Coconut oil	86	6	2

*Percentages are averaged and thus may not total exactly 100 percent.

fat. The American Heart Association says that number should be reduced to no more than 30 percent for the entire population. Nathan Pritikin felt that one needed to go down to 7 to 10 percent in order to achieve significant cholesterol lowering. I believe that one can succeed with a compromise level of fat intake and still reduce cholesterol significantly because of the other foods that can bring the counts down. From my own experience and from that of thousands of others who have had success with my program, I find that a 20 percent fat intake allows one to see a dramatic cholesterol drop and still fully enjoy foods at home and away, and to live without a feeling of deprivation.

But most people's eyes just glaze over at the thought of calculating percentages. What do those percentages really mean in terms of what we eat? How can we really know what percentage of fat is being consumed? Not all foods have fat percentages printed on their labels, and even if we do know the specific percentage of fat for a specific food, how does that relate to the day's total? Fortunately, there is a practical, usable approach to monitoring fat intake.

If you look at the labels on foods, you'll see fat listed in grams per serving. That's pretty straightforward. But now how can one determine how many grams of fat should be in the daily diet? And will that number be the same for everyone? Here is a way to determine your personal prescription for daily fat intake.

As you know, you need a certain number of calories each day in order to maintain bodily functions and for energy. The more active you are physically, the more calories you need. Men typically burn more calories than women do, because they have greater muscle mass, and it is muscle that burns the calories. And, to a lesser degree, the need for calories diminishes as we get older.

A moderately active male needs about 15 calories per pound to maintain weight. More than that and he will gain weight, less and he'll lose. If he's a bit more active, he may need 16 calories per pound; a bit less active, and the calorie requirement drops. Women, on average, need a calorie or two less than men in each category of age and activity.

For a specific example, let's look at a moderately active male of middle age. Our sample specimen weighs 150 pounds to match his 5-foot-10-inch frame. Or he *wants* to weigh 150 pounds in which case he should feed only the pounds he wants, and the excess weight will gradually disappear. So he'll need 15 calories to maintain each of those 150 pounds. Let's do the mathematics:

$$150 \text{ pounds} \times 15 \text{ calories} = 2250 \text{ calories per day}$$

Of those 2250 calories we want our man to have 20 percent as fat. That bit of math is just as simple:

$$2250 \text{ calories} \times .20 = 450 \text{ calories as fat}$$

But how do we get from calories to grams of fat? One gram of protein or carbohydrate yields 4 calories. One gram of fat yields 9 calories. Therefore, 450 calories will come from 50 grams of fat, as determined in this simple calculation:

$$450 \text{ calories} \div 9 \text{ calories per gram} = 50 \text{ grams}$$

Now we know our male example will be allowed a total of 50 grams of fat daily. He can count those grams easily by just looking at food nutrition labels, by learning a bit about the amount of fat contained in some commonly consumed foods, and by looking at the grams of fat found in the recipes in this book.

Now it's time to plug your own numbers into the equations to determine your optimal fat intake as measured in grams.

$$\underset{\text{ideal weight}}{\underline{}} \times \underset{\text{calories per pound}}{\underline{}} = \text{daily calories}$$

$$\underset{\text{daily calories}}{\underline{}} \times .20 = \text{daily calories as fat}$$

$$\underset{\text{daily calories as fat}}{\underline{}} \div 9 = \text{daily grams of fat}$$

The American Heart Association and others recommend that, of the total amount of fat you eat, no more than one-third should come from saturated fats. Similarly, less than one-third should come from polyunsaturated fats. The balance of fat calories should be provided by monounsaturated fats.

It's impractical to calculate fat intake to such an extent. Moreover, you don't always know the fatty-acid profile of a given food. But by adhering to a few practical guidelines you will come very close to achieving the AHA recommendation.

First, limit your consumption of meat to two servings daily, with a serving being no more than 5 ounces, and usually about 3½ ounces. (The reason for that discrepancy is that servings in restaurants tend to be larger, and you'll want slightly larger servings at dinner, while you can feel very satisfied with a 3½-ounce serving at lunch or breakfast.) Of course there are some foods in this category that have very few grams of fat per serving, and you'll be able to enjoy larger servings of these more often.

You'll want to avoid completely many of the prime sources of saturated fat. Butter, lard, whole milk, high-fat cheeses, and premium ice creams have no place in a cholesterol-fighting program. The same applies to tropical oils; read labels carefully in order to keep them out of your shopping cart.

Second, use cooking oils known to be high in monounsaturated fats rather than polyunsaturated fats. Those include olive oil and canola oil. (The principal brand of canola oil is Puritan.) If there are certain recipes you have which you feel simply work better with corn or safflower oil, that's fine.

Polyunsaturated fats will come from a variety of foods, including breads and rolls made with corn or soybean oil, and filled cheeses. You'll also get polyunsaturated fats in margarine. I prefer the calorie-reduced tub margarines, such as the one made by Weight Watchers.

To further limit your fat intake for the day, try using Pam or other cooking oil spray, rather than oil or butter, when sautéing; this will save a lot of fat calories. Butter-flavored Pam or Baker's Joy can be used on hot-air popcorn and on toast.

But What About Dietary Cholesterol?

By now you've probably noticed that I haven't even mentioned cholesterol in the diet. Many years ago nutritionists and dietitians saw that limiting dieters' cholesterol had little impact on reducing cholesterol levels in the blood. In fact, that kind of research fueled the fires of controversy for years. It was only later that we realized that fat, especially saturated fat, had more influence than dietary cholesterol itself on blood cholesterol levels. So merely limiting cholesterol in the diet isn't enough; you must also cut back on total fat and saturated fat. However, that doesn't mean you can completely ignore the cholesterol in foods.

Actually, when you're watching out for saturated fats, the cholesterol pretty much watches out for itself. Only animal foods supply cholesterol. As you cut back on those animal foods, especially as you proceed from whole-milk dairy foods to the low-fat and nonfat varieties, you automatically cut back on cholesterol.

The American Heart Association calls for no more than 100 milligrams of cholesterol daily for each 1000 calories consumed. For a person consuming 2250 calories, as in our earlier example, total cholesterol intake should not exceed 225 milligrams. And, the AHA says, no one should eat more than 300 milligrams, regardless of the calories consumed.

Looking at the numbers in the table on page 16 you'll see that it won't be difficult at all to stay within those limits just by limiting your total fat consumption. You'll also notice that all meats—beef, chicken, turkey, fish, shellfish—have cholesterol. And most of those meats have equivalent amounts. Therefore, there's little point in choosing your meat on the basis of cholesterol content; choose rather by the amount of fat. That principle even applies to shellfish, which, as you'll observe, have more cholesterol than most meats.

There has been a great deal of confusion about shellfish. In the past, dietitians recommended not eating them because the cholesterol content was thought to be astronomically high. But those early testing methods were in error. Cholesterol is a sterol, and chemically related to the neutral sterols in plants. Testing devices at the time of those early tests couldn't tell the difference between sterols from animals—cholesterol—and sterols from plants, which do not affect cholesterol levels in the blood. We now know that shellfish have perhaps half the cholesterol listed in early charts; the plants they eat affect the readings.

Moreover, the fat content of shellfish is infinitesimal. Even if a portion of shellfish contains 100 milligrams of cholesterol, you can easily work that into the day's total. Dr. William Castelli, of Framingham Heart Study fame, says if you can't be a vegetarian, eat a vegetarian of the sea. He believes even shrimp, one of the highest in cholesterol of all shellfish, is as acceptable as chicken breast.

At first, keeping track of the grams of fat in foods will be demanding. But as with any new skill, you'll get better and better at it, until one day you realize you pay little or no attention to individual numbers and yet you're well within your limits. The quicker you learn where the fat is, and how to get rid of it, the easier it will be.

If you are not already used to keeping track of the fat in the food you eat, here's the best way to start. On your next three trips to the supermarket, allow yourself an extra twenty minutes. Use that time to read labels. You'll quickly see that what the manufacturer wants you to see may not be what you need to know about the food you're thinking about buying. For example, does the box of crackers proudly proclaim on the front of the package that the food is "cholesterol free . . . made only with vegetable oil"? Read the nutrition label and you just might see that the vegetable oil in question is coconut, palm, or palm kernel oil, which we've learned are responsible for raising blood cholesterol.

How about those peanut butters that boast "no cholesterol" when we know that *no* peanut butter has any cholesterol, which comes only from animal foods. The same goes for corn oil and other cooking oils. After a while you just might start to chuckle at what advertisers will say to make a sale. Actually, I get angry when I see television ads for Mazola corn oil in which they sing the jingle that "Mazola has no cholesterol at all" while showing the viewer how to use the product to deep-fry foods and otherwise drown them in the oil.

Pick up two packages of sandwich buns and read their labels. One might be made with corn or soybean oil, while another will list animal shortening. You know which one to buy. And you'll remember that brand when you come into the store the next time.

After three such shopping-reading trips, you'll have a pretty good idea as to what products are best for you and your family. By the third or fourth grocery run, you'll be repeating foods you frequently use and won't need to read those labels any longer.

Happily, a number of food manufacturers have begun to recognize that consumers want healthful foods and have started to remove some of the offending ingredients, such as animal shortening and tropical oils. You'll want to keep an eye out for such changes. An example is the old standby Bisquick. My wife used to make an absolutely wonderful strawberry shortcake with Bisquick, but we abandoned that dessert when we began eating heart-healthy, since Bisquick was made with animal shortening. Then one day I noticed that the product had been reformulated, completely removing the animal shortening and using vegetable oils instead. Now Bisquick is back on the shopping list.

Nutrition labels are required by federal law on all processed foods and on any food that makes a nutritional claim, such as "low-fat" or "reduced calorie." So you can expect to see labels on almost all foods, with the exceptions of fresh meats, fruits and vegetables, and fresh bakery goods.

Labeling is in two parts, the first giving the nutrition content of the food per serving. The serving size will be stated, along with the number of servings in the package. As an example, you'll see a breakdown of calories, protein, carbohydrates, fat, cholesterol, sodium, and potassium per serving, in grams and milligrams. Next you'll read the percentage of the U.S. Recommended Daily Allowances (percent USRDA) for some or all of the following nutrients: protein, vitamin A, vitamin C, thiamine, riboflavin, niacin, calcium, iron, vitamin D, vitamin B_6, folic acid, vitamin B_{12}, phosphorus, magnesium, zinc, and pantothenic acid. The double asterisk (**) used shows that the food contains less than 2 percent of the USRDA for that particular nutrient.

Finally, you'll come to an ingredients listing at the bottom of the panel. Ingredients are listed in descending order according to weight. Thus, even though reduced-calorie margarine provides 100 percent of its calories as fat, the first ingredient shown may be water if, in fact, there is more water in the product than oil. You'll also want to know just how much sugar might be lurking in a breakfast cereal. That's a bit more tricky, since sugars can be listed separately; you may well see four or five different kinds of sugar on one label. This allows the manufacturer to list flour or cereal as the principal ingredient, even though there's more sugar in the food than flour or cereal. As you can see by this last example, it's really up to you to learn what's in your food; food companies can't be entirely trusted.

Which brings us to the subject of claims made by food manufacturers and what they really mean. Here's how to decode those often cryptic messages.

Diet or *dietetic* are terms mandated by the U.S. Food and Drug Administration (FDA) to describe foods that contain no more than 40 calories per serving, or that have at least 33 percent fewer calories than the regular product sold by that company or others. That doesn't mean fewer than competitors' products, just fewer as compared with the company's own product.

Enriched or *fortified* foods have added vitamins, minerals, or protein beyond what the natural food contains. Often this is nonsensical, as when cereal makers spray the products with a penny's worth of vitamins in order to advertise its "nutritional superiority" and to sell it for a lot more than its actual worth.

Good, choice, and *prime* refer to grades of beef based on their fat content. The more fat or "marbling" the higher the grade. For health-conscious shoppers, then, "good" is best. Look also for *select,* which is a nicer-sounding term frequently used for *good* meats.

High in polyunsaturates is a nebulous phrase that does not specify a ratio of polyunsaturated to saturated fats. Generally speaking, products labeled as such contain vegetable oils other than coconut, palm, or palm kernel.

Imitation means not only a substitute for the "real" food but also implies nutritional inferiority. If the word *substitute* is used, nutrient content will be as good as that in the naturally occurring food it replaces.

Lean meat and poultry must contain no more than 10 percent fat by weight, according to new U.S. Department of Agriculture regulations. *Extra lean* means no more than 5 percent fat. *Leaner* means the product has at least 25 percent less fat than the regular product. In all cases, the actual fat content will be listed.

Light or *lite* have almost no specific meaning. As frightening as this may sound, those words can mean that the product weighs less, or simply that it has a lighter color or flavor. Don't be lulled into thinking you're buying less fat or fewer calories. Read those labels carefully.

Low-calorie means that the food contains either no more than 40 calories per serving or fewer calories than the regular product. The label will be more exact.

Low-fat can mean different things on different products. On milk and other dairy products it means no more than 2 percent fat and no less than .5 percent fat. On meat, it means no more than 10 percent fat. A lot of people think that low-fat milk is *really* low in fat; a look at the label shows that each eight-ounce glass contains about five grams of fat. Nonfat, or skim, milk is the best bet.

Natural may or may not mean anything at all. It has no significance on baked goods and is simply an advertising word. On meats and poultry, it means no artificial coloring or additive has been used. Let the buyer beware.

Naturally flavored means that the flavor is from the designated product itself, and does not have any artificial colors, preservatives, or other additives.

Naturally sweetened has no specific meaning. Sucrose is a "natural" sweetener because it comes from a vegetable source rather than a chemical factory. Manufacturers will often use the term to refer to other naturally-occurring sweeteners.

New is an advertising term that can be used within six months of the introduction of the product. It has no nutritional implications.

No preservatives means exactly what it says. But that's not necessarily good. Many of the preservatives used in food technology today are completely safe. In many instances I'd rather consume some preservatives than risk bacterial contamination resulting from spoilage.

Organic has no legal meaning whatever, and manufacturers can use the term to their hearts' content. Suffice it to say that *all* food is organic because all food is composed of naturally-occurring organic compounds consisting of carbon, hydrogen, and oxygen. The term is hype.

Reduced-calorie means that the food must have at least one-third fewer calories than the regular product. A comparison must be shown on the label.

Low-salt vs. *low-sodium* provides an insight into the minds of advertisers. Salt is not the only source of sodium in the diet. Thus a product could be low in salt yet still very high in sodium. Read the descriptive label on the back.

Sugar-free and *sugarless* both mean that sucrose is not used. But the product can contain any number of other sugars. On the one hand, this shows that advertisers may try to deceive the buyer. On the other hand, it shows the misunderstanding consumers have about sugar. The body handles sucrose and all other sugars in much the same way. All sugars supply a lot of calories without any nutrient contribution. Sucrose is no better and no worse than any other sugar. Other than for diabetics, ultimately it comes down to your ability to consume the sugar without gaining weight. The only other adverse reaction to sugar might be dental caries, but that can be avoided by simply rinsing the mouth out with water after eating sugary foods. Especially for anyone following a low-fat diet, sugar can be enjoyed in moderation with no guilt whatever.

The terms referring to cholesterol that have been regulated by the government were in the past rather misleading but are finally specific:

No cholesterol means just that. The food contains no cholesterol at all. But it could be loaded with fat. Ads for peanut butter and vegetable oils exemplify this.

Cholesterol-free means the product has less than 2 milligrams of cholesterol per serving.

Low-cholesterol means the food contains less than 20 milligrams of cholesterol per serving.

Cholesterol-reduced implies that the food contains 75 percent less cholesterol than a comparable product.

Ultimately, as you've seen, the responsibility for ensuring the quality of what gets from the supermarket shelf to your home resides with you. You have decisions to make with every purchase. Make those heart-healthy choices on the basis of the information you can glean from the nutrition labels on foods and on your increasing knowledge about foods in general. Obviously it's worth the effort, and that effort gets easier with each and every shopping trip.

Thus far we've discussed the role of the four basic food groups in nutrition, and fats and oils as two of the "other" foods that don't quite fit into the food groups. I also mentioned sucrose and other sugars as I explained the meanings of food claims, pointing out that, in moderation, sugar poses no health problems.

Next we come to alcohol. I'm happy to report that virtually every study done has shown that those who enjoy a drink on a fairly regular basis live longer than those who abstain from alcohol. Of course the watchword here is moderation. There are obvious health risks involved with heavy alcohol use and abuse, not the least of which is accidental death owing to drinking and driving. By moderation we mean one or two drinks daily—a cocktail before dinner or a glass of wine or beer with dinner.

Authorities have long wondered just why it is that those who imbibe moderately enjoy a longer life. Today we believe it may be owing to alcohol's effect in increasing levels of the protective cholesterol, the HDLs. Those who have a drink or two daily tend to have significantly higher HDL levels, affording them an added margin of protection against heart disease.

All this is not to suggest that you start to drink if you don't already do so. Rather, if you now enjoy a drink or two, by all means continue to do so with the knowledge that not only will this practice do no harm, but it will also very likely provide some health benefits.

The same can't always be said for coffee. Studies comparing coffee drinkers with those who don't indulge show that heart-disease rates tend to be higher for caffeine lovers. This has been an area of some controversy, however, since the coffee drinkers often tend to be the same ones who smoke cigarettes and who may be under greater tensions and stress levels. Efforts to equate coffee drinking with cholesterol levels have been contradictory in their results, with no final conclusion reached. The fact remains, though, that caffeine is a drug everyone can and should do without. In a stressful world, the last thing one needs is "coffee nerves." I keep a hot thermos of decaffeinated coffee near my typewriter at all times. I buy the kind made with the water process of decaffeination, since coffees decaffeinated through other processes can contain harmful chemicals, and use a bit more when I brew a cup in order to provide full, rich coffee flavor.

Finally our discussion of categories of foods brings us to salt. There's no question that most Americans eat way too much. Between salt used in home food preparation and added at the table and that found in processed foods and fast foods, the average American consumes an excessive amount of salt and other forms of sodium. The Surgeon General has suggested we all cut down.

The major health concern involving sodium is high blood pressure. That affects about 10 percent of the population, whose blood pressure will rise or fall depending on the amount of salt in the diet. There's no question but that if your doctor has diagnosed hypertension you'd do well to greatly limit the amount of salt consumed.

For the rest of the population as well, cutting back on salt and sodium can have benefits. First, we don't know whether we are prone to develop high blood pressure later in life. Second, salt leads to fluid retention in the body and no one needs that extra burden.

After a while it may grow boring to hear the same nutritional advice over and over. Virtually every health authority has called for generalized reductions in the consumption of fat, saturated fat, cholesterol, salt, and sugar, along with moderation in alcohol use. The latest call for such dietary change came in the form of the Surgeon General's Report on Nutrition and Health in 1988. But that universality of advice indicates that these recommendations have the weight of years of research and experience.

So many of our health ills can be at least partially linked to diet. Heart disease, high blood pressure, obesity, diabetes, some forms of cancer, and osteoporosis are in part caused by and strongly affected by what we eat. All of us would benefit from some modification away from the average American diet. And long before you realize the future benefits of a longer, healthier life, you'll simply start feeling better. With a good diet you'll experience more vitality, more energy, less tiredness, and far less digestive upset. After a while you'll wonder how you could have ever enjoyed eating the way you did, and, therefore, feeling the way you did. Good health and vitality are a joy in themselves, an absolute pleasure from day to day and year to year.

SPECIAL FOODS
THAT LOWER
CHOLESTEROL

As I stated earlier, what you do eat is as important as what you avoid, especially when it comes to lowering your cholesterol level to reduce your risk of heart disease. The first food shown to have potent cholesterol-lowering potential was oat bran, which is an essential component of my 8-week cholesterol cure. For those of you who haven't read my book, here's some background on this marvelous food.

The Wonders of Oat Bran

When *The 8-Week Cholesterol Cure* was first published, in 1987, one of the questions most asked by interviewers was "What *is* oat bran?" No one asks that anymore. Oat bran has quickly become the food of choice for those concerned about cholesterol. For many months demand outstripped supply, and oat bran was actually hard to find. Happily, today oat bran is in ample supply.

The oat-bran phenomenon began in the research laboratories of Dr. James Anderson at the University of Kentucky in Lexington. At the time he was working with diabetic patients, trying to determine whether one cereal would be more effective than another in controlling blood-sugar levels. When Dr. Anderson came to oatmeal, he found that not only were blood-sugar levels improved when participants ate oatmeal, but cholesterol counts fell as well.

Looking a bit more closely, Dr. Anderson determined that it was the bran fraction of the whole oat flake that was responsible for this effect. Specifically, he found that the soluble fiber of oat bran does the job. It works by binding onto the bile acids, which are made of cholesterol and shunting them out of the body before they can be recycled. Thus the body must make more of those bile acids for the digestive process, and to do so it must turn to the cholesterol in the blood. Little by little, as more bile acids are eliminated and more cholesterol is used to manufacture more bile acids, the cholesterol level in the blood drops.

One of the special things about the way oat bran works is that it lowers only the bad cholesterol, while levels of the good cholesterol, the HDLs, remain unchanged. This means an even better ratio between total cholesterol and HDLs, ensuring increased protection against heart disease.

How much effect can oat bran have in cutting into cholesterol? In one study, men were fed 100 grams, a little more than 3 ounces, daily. Their total cholesterol fell by 13 percent. In a controlled study in which six men ate all their meals under close supervision in a metabolic ward, and consumed 100 grams of oat bran daily, an amazing drop of more than 23 percent was seen after just twenty-one days.

It appears that the cholesterol-lowering effects increase over time. Administering an oat-bran diet in his laboratories, Dr. Anderson observed a 19 percent drop. After the subjects returned home, but continued to eat 50 grams of oat bran daily, cholesterol levels fell by a total of 24 percent.

Impressive results have been shown by researchers all over the country. Dr. Dennis Davidson, then of the University of California at Irvine and now at Stanford University, fed medical students muffins daily. The students didn't know whether they were getting oat-bran muffins or muffins made with wheat flour. The wheat muffins produced no cholesterol lowering, while the oat-bran muffins provided a significant reduction.

Since oat bran is part of the whole oat flake, one can expect lowering of cholesterol levels with oatmeal as well. Remember that was how Dr. Anderson first determined this benefit. But, since the "secret ingredient" is soluble fiber, and there is more soluble fiber in the oat bran than in the oatmeal, one would need more oatmeal—almost double the amount—to achieve the same effects as with oat bran.

At Northwestern University in Chicago, Dr. Linda Van Horn studied the effects of oat bran and oatmeal as part of a low-fat diet, and compared those results with low-fat diet alone. She found that both oat bran and oatmeal provided an additional 3 percent reduction over the lowering achieved by diet alone. But that low percentage of reduction was owing to the fact that the subjects in the study had normal cholesterol levels to begin with. Individuals with elevated cholesterol counts can expect a greater percentage of improvement. And, at those higher cholesterol levels, it's generally recognized that oat bran will provide more significant reduction than oatmeal.

While skeptical at first, the medical community has come to see the value of oat bran as part of a total cholesterol-reducing program. Dr. Bruce Kinosian at the University of Maryland's department of medicine compared the cost-effectiveness of treating patients with significantly elevated cholesterol levels with oat bran and the cholesterol-reducing prescription drugs colestipol and cholestyramine. He found that, in terms of lives saved by way of cholesterol reduction and thus lessened heart-disease mortality, oat bran was more cost effective. He concluded in his report in the *Journal of the American Medical Association* in 1988 that cholesterol reduction by way of diet and oat bran "may be preferred to a medically oriented campaign that focuses on drug therapy."

Those consuming oat bran regularly report a very favorable side effect: weight control. There are a number of reasons why oat bran can help you to lose weight and to maintain ideal weight. For one thing, oat bran, either as cereal or muffins, satisfies the appetite more efficiently than other, higher-calorie foods. And, of course, those higher-calorie foods are replaced in the process. You'll find you just don't get as hungry when eating oat bran. A hearty bowlful in the morning for breakfast will satisfy you until lunch.

Hunger satisfaction depends largely on how quickly foods move through the digestive tract. As it happens, oat bran slows down the rate of the so-called "gastric emptying," the time it takes to move out of the stomach. This adds to the feeling of fullness. Additionally, high-fiber foods provide more food mass in the small intestine.

Dr. Anderson reports three reasons why oat bran may help in weight reduction. First, there is a certain amount of calorie loss directly through the feces. Second, carbohydrates are not fully metabolized. And third, fiber-rich foods such as oat bran require more energy to digest, thus actually increasing the rate at which calories are burned. Compare that with fat calories, which authorities now feel provide more food energy than previously calculated, therefore requiring more activity to burn. While protein and carbohydrates yield 4 calories per gram, fat was long thought to supply 9. But that number may have been underestimated; it is now believed that the real figure may be closer to 10 or 11, possibly even 12 calories per gram.

On the down side, you might notice a bit of gassiness and flatulence when you first start eating oat bran regularly, particularly if your diet has been low in fiber. For most people, that flatulence gradually diminishes. But, if it poses a particular problem for you, back off from the oat bran for a while and then gradually begin to increase the amount you eat daily.

You can find oat bran in the hot-cereal sections of practically every supermarket and health-food store. For the most part it comes packaged in one-pound boxes. Though Quaker first put oat bran on the market, other companies now sell it as well. The package should list just one ingredient: oat bran. I advocate one-half cup daily, measured uncooked as it comes out of the box. That weighs a little less than 2 ounces, about 50 grams. (There are 28 grams per ounce.)

Unfortunately there is no standard of identity for oat bran. The bran is the outer layer of the whole oat flake, just under the hull. First a manufacturer makes oatmeal by treating the whole grain with steam and then passing the grain between rolls to produce flakes. Grinding the oat flakes and sifting result in two milling fractions. There's a fine fraction, flour, and a coarse fraction, the oat bran. Some brands of oat bran contain only that coarse fraction, while others include varying amounts of the fine fraction along with it. This means that one brand will have more soluble fiber than another. In some instances, a company's oat bran will be no more than ground-up oatmeal. While that would still be a nutritious product, it won't deliver the cholesterol-lowering effect you're after. As so often is the case, you get what you pay for, and you may well be better off sticking with the name brands of oat bran.

You'll also find a number of ready-to-eat cold oat-bran cereals on the market, some of which are better than others. I've listed a few of the available cereals in the table on page 31, but more enter the marketplace almost daily. Read the nutrition label carefully to see how much oat bran you're getting; is oat bran listed first, or third or fourth? Did the manufacturer add some fat that you don't want? Finally, check the actual fat content of the product. Oat bran itself has about 2 grams per 1-ounce serving. Does the product in question have more?

Don't be fooled by advertising claims that a certain oatmeal is nutritionally superior to another because of its vitamins and minerals. Some

Actual Oat Bran in Oat-Bran Products

Brand	Serving Size	Oat Bran (Grams)
HOT CEREALS		
General Nutrition		
Stone Ground Oat Bran Hot Cereal	1 ounce	28.0
Golden Temple Oat Bran	1 ounce	28.0
Health Valley	1 ounce	20.0
100% Natural Hot Cereal		
Quaker Oat Bran	1 ounce	28.0
Quaker Oat Meal	1 ounce	9.0
READY-TO-EAT CEREALS		
Cheerios	1 ounce	8.0
Common Sense Oat Bran	1 ounce	13.0
Cracklin' Oat Bran	1 ounce	9.0
Health Valley		
Oat Bran Flakes	1 ounce	15.0
Oat Bran O's	1 ounce	15.0
Kölln Oat Bran Krunch	1 ounce	19.6
Oatios	1 ounce	8.4
Quaker Oat Bran		
High Fiber Oat Cereal*	1 ounce	19.0
BAKED GOODS		
Oat Meal Goodness Bread	1 slice	2.3
Health Valley		
Fancy Fruit Muffins	1 muffin	17.0
Oat Bran Jumbo Fruit Bars	1 bar	12.5
Oat Bran Graham Crackers	7 crackers	4.1
Oat Bran Fruit Jumbo Cookies	2 cookies	4.6

*Contains a concentrated source of soluble fiber; soluble-fiber content greater than even pure oat bran.

companies simply spray some vitamins on the cereal, which costs them about a penny or two, but they charge you 50 or 60 cents more.

You should also know about a very special oat-bran cereal. A study at the University of Wisconsin revealed that an oat cereal with a concentrated form of oat bran provides more soluble fiber than oat bran alone. Researchers found that this cereal lowered cholesterol even more than the original oat bran. You can now buy this ready-to-eat cereal, available as Quaker Oat Bran High Fiber Oat Cereal. Each 1-ounce serving supplies 19 grams of oat bran, but you'll soon see that a 2-ounce serving or even more is more appropriate as a meal. This special cereal also delivers 40 percent of its oat bran as soluble fiber, for a total of 7.6 grams per 1-ounce serving. That's significantly higher than even the highest-quality pure oat bran. And it tastes good, too.

Is it best to eat your daily requirement of oat bran all at once, in the morning for example, or would you be better off with some oat bran throughout the day? Probably the latter, since bile acids are made throughout the day, and you'd do well to remove them throughout the day. With the recipes you'll find in this book, that's deliciously easy to do, with both oat bran and other foods rich in soluble fibers.

Oat bran's versatility makes it a natural in the kitchen. You may even want to put an oat bran canister next to your flour and sugar. It works beautifully in baking, can be substituted for bread crumbs in a number of recipes, and lends itself well to a variety of cooking situations.

I started experimenting with different ways to incorporate oat bran into my diet from the very start of my program, since I've never been much of a hot-cereal eater. So I played around with muffin recipes until I got them just right. A number of those recipes went into *The 8-Week Cholesterol Cure.* I didn't stop baking and cooking when the book came out, and over the years I've developed many more muffin varieties as well as other delicious baked goods. Then Michele Urvater contributed her expertise, and we now have found many new ways to cook and bake with oat bran. I hope you enjoy those recipes.

But oat bran is just one of the foods that provide a rich source of soluble fiber. Dried beans and peas, including garbanzos (chickpeas), pinto beans, kidney beans, black beans, red beans, white beans, black-eyed peas, split yellow and green peas, and on and on, provide soluble fiber as well.

Dried Beans and Peas

Although dried beans and peas are a regular part of the daily menu in Middle Eastern countries, Africa, Latin America, and Europe, most Americans aren't really familiar with cooking them. When I spoke to

Michele about developing some new recipes for these, she was delighted, for she loves to cook dried beans and peas and felt that people were really missing out by not knowing how to work with them. So I came up with a wish list of all the recipes I wanted. I'd enjoyed Cuban black beans, Cajun red beans, and many other ethnic specialties in restaurants but I didn't know how to cook them. I especially wanted recipes that were low in fat. And I didn't want recipes that called for hours and hours of cooking time. With that in mind, Michele went back to her kitchen and came up with several mouth-watering recipes.

We know that dried beans and peas work as well as oat bran in lowering cholesterol. Dr. Anderson proved it in his University of Kentucky laboratories, where he fed subjects a daily diet rich in beans for three weeks. His volunteers ate a bit more than 100 grams of pinto and navy beans daily as cooked beans or bean soup, and their cholesterol levels fell by an average of 19 percent. Other studies have shown similar reductions, especially when beans are included in a low-fat diet.

At first blush, 100 grams seems like a lot of beans; after all, that's double the 50 grams of oat bran needed to supply the soluble fiber we want to lower cholesterol. But that 100 grams, a bit less than 2 ounces, measures out to one-half cup of dried beans, the same as oat bran. The difference is that beans are heavier than oat bran.

Ultimately, we need to have the desired amount of soluble fiber provided by either oat bran or beans, or from other food sources as described in coming pages. One day you may want three oat bran muffins, and another day it'll be a bowl of oatmeal for breakfast and some beans as a side dish for dinner. Another day you'll have fruit for breakfast, with all your soluble fiber coming from an entrée featuring beans or peas. And we haven't even considered all those other food sources of soluble fiber yet. With so much potential variety, there's no reason to get tired of the foods that are not only good for you but that will actually drop your cholesterol level.

Barley

What could be more welcome on a cool evening in autumn than a steaming bowl of barley soup accompanied by some crusty bread and perhaps a glass of good white wine? Filled with vegetables, a bit of beef, and the barley, this soup is a meal unto itself. And barley also ranks as a cholesterol fighter.

Barley contains some soluble fiber, but as you'll see in the table on page 41, each 3½-ounce serving contains just 2.8 grams, which doesn't compare well with the 7.2 grams in the same amount of oat bran. Of course, every little bit helps. However, barley seems to have a capacity for cholesterol reduction far beyond what its soluble-fiber content would predict. Scientists are now at work trying to figure out just what it is about barley that makes it effective.

At the University of Wisconsin's Cereal Institute in Madison, Dr. David Peterson reports isolating two compounds in barley's protein-rich outer portion that appear to have a potent cholesterol-lowering effect. Interestingly, that's the portion that is normally discarded in processing. The effect is different from that achieved by the soluble fiber. Those barley-derived substances work on the activity of the enzyme HMG Co-A reductase, which determines the amount of cholesterol made by the liver.

Working at the Miller Brewing Company in Milwaukee, Dr. Frank Weber has found that barley-bran flour made from brewers' grain decreased total serum cholesterol by 44 percent, but only when the lipid, or fat, portion of the barley grain was left intact. Defatted barley lacked cholesterol-lowering capability.

At this time, studies have focused entirely on laboratory animals. No human studies have been performed. Therefore no one can say exactly how much barley, as the whole grain or flour, would be needed to lower cholesterol levels. As time goes on, perhaps research will result in a drug or a food supplement derived from barley, or reveal the benefits of barley as part of the diet.

In the meantime, there's no reason not to include barley as part of a total program of cholesterol reduction and good nutrition. You may not want to eat barley every day, but a look at the numerous recipes we've developed will show you some inventive ways to eat it more often than you likely do now. Today half of the barley harvested is used in brewing, and the other half goes to feed livestock; little barley finds its way into our diet. I think that will rapidly change, and you can be among the first to get on the bandwagon.

A *Is for Apple*

Leave it to American industry to come up with a way to improve on as basic a food as the apple. Now we all know that apples make a wonderful snack, that they're low in fat and high in fiber, and versatile in dozens of recipes. But did you know that the soluble fiber in apples, namely pectin, can lower cholesterol levels? Unfortunately, there's just a little bit of pectin in a medium-size apple, but now the apple industry has found a way to make this substance available in larger doses.

It all started when apple growers realized that, after squeezing apples to make juice and cider, they had to do something with the leftover pulp. In the past, that pulp was fed to livestock or disposed of as waste. In fact, it is a very concentrated source of both soluble and insoluble fiber. Then the Tastee Apple Fiber company of Newcomerstown, Ohio, came up with a way to dry the pulp and make it into a flourlike substance that can be used in a number of recipes. As you'll see, you can use it in baking muffins and cookies and as an added ingredient in tomato sauce for a thicker, slightly sweet sauce.

Apple fiber contains nearly 43 percent total dietary fiber. Of that amount, about 32 percent is insoluble and 11 percent is soluble. That means that you'll get a little more than 3 grams of soluble fiber per ounce. Compare that to a bit more than 1 gram of the soluble fiber, pectin, in a medium-size apple. It's also more soluble fiber than you get from oat bran! The bottom line is that apple fiber offers a wonderful alternative to oat bran.

But don't confuse apple fiber with pectin itself. You can find pectin, typically used for making jelly, in supermarkets and health-food stores, but pure pectin does not lend itself to most recipes and simply won't work in the recipes we've developed for this book. You can find Tastee Apple Fiber and Hearty Life Apple Fiber in supermarkets. Both brands contain the same benefits in terms of fiber content. And in health-food stores look for Sovex Apple Fiber.

Do we have any proof that pectin can lower cholesterol levels as well as oat bran? Indeed we do.

Dr. James Anderson of oat-bran research fame compared the effects of oat bran, guar gum, and pectin in terms of counteracting the blood-cholesterol increase expected when laboratory animals were fed dietary cholesterol. He found pectin to be the most efficient. None of the soluble fibers tested lowered the levels of protective HDL in the blood.

That study was done in 1979, before pectin was readily available in a form that could easily be worked into the diet. Using plain pectin was impractical in the dosages needed to get the desired effects. In a study that directly compared the effects of wheat bran, increased consumption of fruits and vegetables, and supplementation with citrus pectin, researchers found that citrus pectin reduced total serum-cholesterol levels significantly during the test period, while increased consumption of fruits and vegetables brought on a small but insignificant reduction.

Work in this area has been done all around the world. At the Institute of Human Nutrition in Czechoslovakia, Dr. Emil Ginter gave a group of twenty-one healthy persons with mildly elevated cholesterol levels a dose of 15 grams of citrus pectin for six weeks. He found a significant reduction in two-thirds of the patients.

We know that whether pectin is derived from citrus fruit or apples the effect is the same. Pectin is a soluble fiber that works exactly the same way as the soluble fiber in oat bran or dried beans and peas.

It shouldn't come as any surprise that the concentrated form of pectin provides more cholesterol-lowering capability than the smaller amounts found in apples. But that doesn't mean we can't derive additional benefits from eating fresh fruits and vegetables. As you'll see in the table on page 41, you do get some soluble fiber in a variety of foods. It all adds up. And you can't forget the nutrition provided in a balanced diet beyond the cholesterol-lowering effects of some foods. After all, man can't live by soluble fiber alone.

Today the availability of apple fiber, with the benefits of both soluble and insoluble fiber in a concentrated form, makes it possible and deliciously practical, to include apple pectin in the diet regularly. The same can now be said for another type of soluble fiber that has had much attention in the laboratory but until recently was impractical in real-life eating.

Go for Some Guar Gum

If you've been reading food labels, you may have noticed an ingredient called guar gum at the end of the listing for certain foods. And you may well have wondered what it is and what it's doing in food. The food industry uses guar gum as a natural thickening agent in foods such as yogurt, especially the nonfat variety, to give it extra body when the fat is removed.

Guar gum comes from the cluster bean, a plant in the legume family that grows well in arid regions such as Pakistan and certain areas of Texas. The plant bears pods containing six to nine beans that aren't very palatable. Guar gum is prepared by first removing the husk and the first layer of the beans, the endosperm, and then purifying the gum from the endosperm. The result is a powder that makes a gel in water.

The small amount found in various foods when used as a thickening agent has no effect on the body. But, when larger dosages are consumed, cholesterol levels fall. When research first began, guar gum wasn't available to the general public. It was difficult to work with, since large amounts cooked into foods such as soups or stews became too thick to enjoy. Given as a powder to mix with water or juice, guar gum frequently caused gastric upset and nausea. Early studies used guar gum capsules to get the substance into the body, but even then it didn't disperse well in the digestive tract.

Even with those difficulties, guar gum was found effective in lowering cholesterol levels in study after study around the world. In one study, it was incorporated into a crispbread given to eleven patients over an eight-week period of time. About 12 grams of guar gum were actually consumed daily. Total cholesterol fell by 13 percent while levels of LDL cholesterol came down by 16 percent. Unfortunately, there were the gastric side effects I mentioned earlier.

In another study, guar gum was given in capsule form to 24 healthy volunteers. They took 9 grams daily for four weeks, while another group received placebo capsules. At the end of the month, those receiving guar gum experienced a 16.6 percent drop in total cholesterol, and a 25.6 percent fall in LDL cholesterol. Those getting the placebo capsules showed no change in cholesterol levels at all.

A study conducted in Italy showed that 16 grams daily given to 12 patients for two months resulted in an average cholesterol drop of 46 mg, a 15 percent decline. In Finland, a country with one of the highest heart-disease rates in the world, patients were given 5 grams of guar gum four times daily. After four weeks, cholesterol levels had fallen by 20 percent. A Swedish study using 10 grams of guar gum twice daily demonstrated an average decline of from 239 to 220. And in Australia 17 patients completing a study with 6 grams three times a day showed a drop of 15 percent. Two patients dropped out because of gastric upset.

More recently in America, a specially processed, palatable guar-gum preparation was tested in six healthy subjects and in seventeen diabetic patients. They received 10 grams twice a day. Total cholesterol levels fell by 14 percent. But diabetic patients whose initial cholesterol counts were higher than 270 experienced a 26 percent reduction. And levels of the protective HDL did not fall at all. Any gastric disturbances such as flatulence disappeared after about a week. In publishing that report, Dr. Robert Superko of Stanford University wrote that guar gum provides a step between normal dietary intervention and the use of drugs to control cholesterol levels. Today we have guar-gum formulations that are easily incorporated into the diet without gastric disturbances; in fact, guar gum can be used in a number of very enjoyable ways. You can find guar gum in virtually all health-food stores nationwide, marketed principally by two firms, BioResource and Twin Laboratories. It is available in capsules and powder, and plain and orange flavors allow you to consume it either as a beverage mixed with water or incorporated into a variety of shake recipes. Each teaspoonful of powder contains about 5 grams of soluble fiber. Based on the research to date, a total of 15 grams—one teaspoonful three times daily—would be expected to yield a considerable cholesterol benefit.

Rice Bran

Rice has been grown for thousands of years, since well before the time of Christ and going back millennia in the Far East. Today rice remains the staple in the diets of more than half the world's population. Rice has a lot going for it: it's easily digestible, causes almost no allergic reactions, and is extremely versatile. But, as is recently becoming increasingly clear, there's even more to rice than we ever knew.

Mankind has long relied on rice as a major source of nutrients. Most people prefer polished white rice. Yet the bran layers of the rice kernel contain most of the nutrients, and that layer is discarded in processing rice to the polished white form. The highest nutrition, then, is available as brown rice, which has the bran fraction left in.

Until fairly recently, though, brown rice was the only way one could get the nutrition of rice bran, because when the bran was removed a biochemical reaction caused the bran to become rancid. So rice bran has traditionally been used exclusively as animal feed. However, a stabilization process originally developed by the U.S. Department of Agriculture has led to the introduction of stabilized rice bran, which has a much-lengthened shelf life. The product has a slightly sweet taste and crunchy texture. It can be used as is, sprinkled on top of other cereals and yogurt, baked into a variety of recipes, and pulverized to increase its versatility as you'll see in the recipes in this book.

But, beyond the general nutritive benefit of rice bran, it has the ability to lower cholesterol levels dramatically. For one thing, rice bran has a high concentration of soluble fiber. While it takes half a cup of oat bran daily to get enough soluble fiber to reduce cholesterol significantly, it takes only two tablespoons of rice bran to match that amount of soluble fiber. The kind we've used in our recipes, and with which I have the most experience and good luck, is called Vita Fiber, marketed by Pacific Rice Products. The product has become increasingly well distributed nationally in both health-food stores and supermarkets. But, if you can't find it easily, you can call the company to learn where Vita Fiber is sold in your area; their number is (916) 662-5056.

Just as I was finishing the manuscript of this book, some exciting research data were being reported in New Orleans at the annual meeting of the Federation of American Societies for Experimental Biology. There, Dr. Robin Saunders of the U.S. Department of Agriculture (USDA) in Albany, California told how rice bran was just as effective in reducing cholesterol levels as oat bran.

We can expect to hear more and more about rice bran in the future, as a number of studies are in progress or are in planning stages. But one of the most interesting aspects of Dr. Saunders' work is that rice bran worked to cut cholesterol counts only when the oil fraction of the grain was left intact. When rice bran was defatted, it did not have a cholesterol-lowering effect at all.

Obviously, there's something about the oil in rice bran that does the job. And, as we saw just a bit earlier, the oil fraction in barley appears to have a cholesterol-cutting property. Oat bran, interestingly, has the highest fat content of any of the usual cereal grains. Look at the box and you'll see that each one-ounce serving of oat bran has a full two grams of fat. But, since all that fat lowers cholesterol rather than raising it, we needn't even include those grams of fat into our daily fat-gram count.

But the rice story doesn't end there.

The Japanese have experimented with rice-bran oil for cooking, and have found that it has a dramatic effect on cholesterol levels as well. Dr. Shinjiro Suzuki, of the National Institute of Nutrition in Japan, has fed various combinations of this oil to subjects over the years. His most recent findings indicate that a combination of 70 percent rice-bran oil and 30 percent safflower oil has the ability to drop cholesterol levels by 26 percent when subjects consumed about a half cup daily. For reasons yet to be determined, that combination is more effective than either oil alone or any other combination, or, for that matter, any other edible oil in the world!

One-half cup of oil daily may seem like quite a lot, and for those attempting to limit the fat in the diet, it certainly is a large quantity.

In Dr. Suzuki's research, subjects consumed 60 grams daily. That's more fat than I eat from *all* food sources combined for the day. But many people simply will not cut their fat consumption that far. They like their fried foods, cookies, and salad dressings too much to do so. Now they have an alternative. Imagine French-fried potatoes prepared in rice-bran oil, which can lower your cholesterol count. And cookies using rice-bran oil instead of butter, which also reduces those numbers. It's certainly worth considering.

Rice-bran oil is bland-tasting, making it useful as a replacement for regular cooking oil. In fact, it has a very high smoke point, making it a natural for high-temperature cooking such as stir-frying in a wok. Pacific Rice Products now offers rice-bran oil in the supermarkets. Again, call the company if you can't find it in your area.

Tomorrow's Bran News

When I first wrote *The 8-Week Cholesterol Cure,* oat bran was *the* source of soluble fiber. Then we learned more about dried beans and peas. Next it was pectin from apple fiber. Now we have rice bran. And work continues on bran of other cereals. Watch, especially, for corn bran to be available soon, and barley bran may also reach the market shortly. The table on page 41 tells you the soluble-fiber content of various foods.

Fish and Fish Oils

I remember having a talk with my father during the 1960s about the cholesterol controversy. Dad was a pharmacist and I had begun my career in medical writing, so both of us read about health issues regularly. The gist of the conversation was whether there was anything to this business of diet and heart disease. I recall very well bringing up the point that Eskimos ate a diet high in fat and yet they had one of the world's lowest heart disease rates. Not very long after we had that chat, Dad learned that his cholesterol level was high, and the doctor advised a low-cholesterol diet, specifically recommending against the oysters Dad loved. We knew very little back then, and Dad died in 1969 of a massive heart attack.

We've come a long way since those days. The Eskimos' high-fat diet

Fiber Content of Various Foods

Food	Total Dietary Fiber*	Soluble Fiber*
GRAINS		
Barley, pearled	10.8	2.8
Cornmeal, whole-grain	15.3	9.0
Oat bran, uncooked	18.6	7.2
Oatmeal, uncooked	12.1	4.9
Rice, brown, dry	7.2	0.7
Rice bran (Vita Fiber brand Rice Germ and Rice Bran)	35.0	33.0
FRUITS		
Apple, raw	2.0	0.6
Apple fiber (Tastee Apple brand)	42.9	11.1
Prunes, dried	16.1	4.6
Raisins	6.8	1.7
DRIED BEANS AND PEAS		
Beans, kidney, canned	6.2	2.7
Beans, kidney, raw	19.9	8.5
Beans, pinto, raw	18.7	7.0
Beans, white, raw	16.2	4.7
Lentils, raw	16.9	3.8
Peas, black-eyed, raw	25.0	11.0
Peas, chick, raw	15.0	7.6
Peas, split, raw	11.9	4.0

*Grams per 100-gram serving (3½ ounces). Taken from Plant Fiber in Foods by James W. Anderson, M.D., with permission from the Nutrition Research Foundation, Box 22124, Lexington, KY 40522, and others.

actually protects against heart disease. And oysters definitely are back on the menu for even the most cholesterol-conscious person. Piece by piece researchers have put together a mosaic of information that now shows us that just about all fish and shellfish have an important place in heart health.

It all began with research conducted in the 1970s by Danish investigators, who wondered why the Eskimos could eat a diet rich in whale blubber, seal meat, and fatty fish and yet have virtually no heart disease. Danes with such a high-fat diet had a very high rate of that killer. And, when Eskimos left their homeland and migrated to Denmark, heart-disease rates soared. Obviously their genes didn't change in the boats during the trip away from home. The research conducted to find the answers to this enigma led to landmark reports casting a whole new light on how diet can protect against heart disease.

A close inspection revealed that those marine fish and mammals eaten by Eskimos are rich not in saturated fat but rather in the polyunsaturated forms. Specifically, the flesh of those creatures contains a class of fatty acids called the omega-3 fatty acids.

In working with the Eskimos, researchers noted that they had a tendency to bruise easily. It turns out the reason is that their blood platelets, those cells involved with clotting, are less sticky than is typical in Danes or Americans. Those scientists felt that the Eskimos were somehow protected from heart disease by whatever it was that was causing this difference in their blood. Interestingly, in studying blood samples further, they quickly saw that cholesterol levels were not much lower, if at all, than in Americans and Europeans who routinely succumb to heart attacks.

How does the platelet stickiness or lack of that stickiness make a difference? Platelets help to initiate the process of hardening of the arteries. First there is a bit of microscopic damage to the lining of the artery, frequently where blood flows turbulently around the bends and forks in the vessel. As part of the "healing" process, platelets come to the site, stick to the injured surface, and release chemical signals that, in turn, cause muscle tissue of the artery to grow and attract white blood cells traveling in the blood. The growing mass of muscle cells and white blood cells then accumulates deposits of cholesterol, thus becoming bulky. We refer to that bulkiness of the arterial surface as plaque. As the plaque becomes larger and fills more of the interior of the artery, blood flow is reduced.

In an ideal scenario, the person perfectly protected against heart disease would have less cholesterol in the bloodstream to accumulate at those damage sites. And the person's platelets wouldn't be so sticky as to start the process in the first place.

We've learned, of course, that saturated fat in the diet is more responsible for the production of cholesterol than is dietary cholesterol itself. People consuming less saturated fat tend to have lower levels of cholesterol. That's one way of getting protection.

The Eskimos have another. Oil in the diet finds its way into the membranes of the body's cells. The fish oil they consume gets in the way of the cell's production of a certain kind of prostaglandin called thromboxane. The less thromboxane in the platelet, the less sticky it is, and the less clotting occurs. Moreover, fish oils stimulate the production of another prostaglandin, namely prostacyclin, which actually inhibits platelet clotting. This is the chemical scenario responsible for the Eskimos' abnormal bruising. The fish oil in the Eskimos' diet inhibits clotting in the same way that taking aspirin lessens clotting in many arthritis patients. In fact, arthritis sufferers often bruise quite easily. And, as an additional benefit, it appears that fish oil can act as an anti-inflammatory agent just as aspirin does.

You and I can't very easily find whale blubber and seal meat in the meat case of our supermarket. But we can buy the fish richest in the oils now known to give heart-disease protection to the Eskimos. We'll look at the best choices for fish selection a bit later.

If the Eskimo research were the only evidence that fish should be on the menu of every heart-healthy man and woman, there might be some doubt. Other factors may be playing a role in that particular population. But we now have proof from around the world.

Researchers from the University of Leiden in the Netherlands have been working with the population of the town of Zutphen since 1960 to examine the relations of diet and other risk factors to chronic diseases, including heart disease. Zutphen is an old industrial town in the eastern part of the country, with a population of 25,000 at the time the study began.

For the purposes of their study, investigators focused on 1088 men who had lived in the town for at least five years. They examined food intake in terms of quantity and types of food eaten. Risk factors, including serum cholesterol, smoking habits, blood pressure, physical fitness and activity, occupation, and height and weight were recorded. Just one of the many items listed as variables in the population was fish consumption.

The average Zutphen man consumed 20 grams of fish daily, about two-thirds of which was lean and one-third fatty. About 19 percent of the men did not eat fish. Men with a high fish consumption had a significantly higher intake of monounsaturated and polyunsaturated fat, dietary cholesterol, animal protein, and alcohol in the diet than those who did not eat fish. Otherwise the fish eaters and abstainers were similar in their characteristics, both good and bad, pertaining to heart disease risk.

During twenty years of follow-up, 78 men died from coronary heart disease. Mortality from this disease was more than 50 percent lower among those who consumed at least 30 grams of fish per day than among those who did not eat fish. Researchers studying the data found that the more fish the men ate, the more protection they had against heart disease and death. Conversely, the less fish consumed, the greater the risk.

It's particularly important to note that the protection apparently conveyed by fish was separate from any other considerations. In other words, after carefully looking at lifestyles, one could not come up with any other possibilities, such as that, perhaps, those who died were also heavy smokers. The fact remained after exhaustive statistical analysis of the data that fish was somehow involved in protecting those men who did not die by heart attack.

The conclusion reached by the researchers was that eating even a moderate amount of fish on a regular basis could be expected to convey that kind of protection. How much would be enough? Remember that the more fish eaten the greater the protection demonstrated. But it would appear that two fish meals weekly would put one into the category termed fish eaters in this study.

Further evidence of fish's health benefits comes from Japan, whose population also enjoys a low rate of heart disease. Is that owing entirely to the low-fat diet, heavy in rice and vegetables? Research has shown otherwise. While it certainly remains true that low-fat diets pose less risk than high-fat diets, in Japan it has been demonstrated that those areas in which fish is regularly consumed have the lowest incidence of death by heart disease.

Most authorities today agree that the protection afforded by fish in the diet comes from the polyunsaturated omega-3 fatty acids, which are found almost exclusively in marine animals. One can find a small amount in certain plant sources—canola oil, most widely known under the brand-name Puritan, contains about 6 percent omega-3 fatty acids—but in the American diet, fish are the principal source.

Of the total omega-3 fats in fish, two types predominate: EPA, which stands for eicosapentanoic acid, and DHA, or docosahexaenoic acid. While authorities lean toward believing that the EPA is probably responsible for most of the effect enjoyed from fish oil, the DHA may well play an important role as well.

Moreover, there may be constituents of fish other than the omega-3s that are involved. The protection of the Eskimos comes from a diet almost exclusively derived from fatty fish and other animal sources, but the men of Zutphen eat lean fish, such as cod, most of the time. In other words, we just don't have all the answers yet. But we do know that a diet that includes two or three fish meals a week is good for the heart.

The table below lists the oil content of commonly consumed fish. Taking a clue from the Eskimo, we'll want to select those types rich in oil, such as salmon, mackerel, anchovies, and sardines. Conversely, we needn't ignore such fish as cod and halibut just because they don't have a lot of oil. In fish, as in all foods, enjoy a wide variety.

That seafood variety can certainly also include shellfish. As explained on page 20, all shellfish, even shrimp, can be used as part of a low-cholesterol diet. Dr. William Conner of the University of Oregon's Health Sciences Center has speculated that the potential detrimental effects of the cholesterol in shrimp may well be offset by the presence of the omega-3 fatty acids, even though there's just a tiny bit of fat in those delicacies. He sees no reason why shrimp can't be enjoyed in the same quarter-pound servings designated for chicken breast and fin fish. Oysters, mussels, clams, and scallops have very little cholesterol and virtually no fat at all. Just don't dip them into butter!

There are, however, a few seafood dishes one must be careful about. Caviar is high in both fat and cholesterol. For most of us, the price of

Omega-3 Fatty-Acid Content of 3½-Ounce Servings of Fish (in Grams)

Sardines (Norwegian)	5.1	Bluefish	1.2
Sockeye salmon	2.7	Pacific mackerel	1.1
Atlantic mackerel	2.5	Striped bass	0.8
King salmon	1.9	Yellowfin tuna	0.6
Herring	1.7	Pollock	0.5
Lake trout	1.4	Brook trout	0.4
Albacore tuna	1.3	Yellow perch	0.3
Halibut	1.3	Catfish	0.2

caviar is enough to keep consumption down, and if I'm offered some Beluga caviar at a special celebration, I certainly don't turn it down! Squid contains about as much cholesterol in a 3½-ounce serving as you'd find in a large egg. That definitely makes it a once-in-a-while treat rather than a staple. The same applies to abalone, with more than 100 mg of cholesterol per 3½-ounce slice, especially if deep-fried or sautéed in butter. Yet, if you find yourself in northern California with fresh abalone on the menu, go for it. Just ask the server to have it sautéed in a bit of olive oil instead of butter.

The recipes included in this book should give you some new ideas for cooking fish. But what about taking a short cut to protection by way of fish oil capsules? Virtually every medical authority agrees, and I concur, that the way to get fish oil into the diet is to eat more fish.

For one thing, those taking fish oil capsules still must make food choices. It makes little sense to continue eating foods rich in saturated fats and then swallow a few fish-oil capsules hoping to cancel out the effect of the fats. Actually, when taken in this way, fish-oil capsules can raise cholesterol levels rather than lower them. The fact remains that fish oil, whether from fish or from capsules, does not have a cholesterol-lowering effect at all. The protection afforded, as explained earlier, is by way of the clotting process. The oils do, however, lower triglyceride levels in the blood in individuals with elevations of those blood fats.

Fish supplies a wonderful nutrient profile; it is a great source of high-quality protein and vitamins. Fish-oil capsules provide no such nutrition.

Far too many questions remain concerning fish-oil capsules to recommend them blindly. How many capsules should one take daily? How much EPA should be in each capsule? Should the capsule also provide the DHA? If you're taking aspirin on the advice of your physician, do you also take fish oil capsules, knowing that they both inhibit clotting? Should women take fish-oil capsules if they're pregnant, lactating, or considering having a child, even though there are no data to show that the capsules are safe in such cases? The bottom line is that we have more questions than answers when it comes to fish oil supplements.

The Eskimos eat fish, not capsules. So do the Japanese and the Dutch. Why not you?

I know a lot of people who say they really enjoy a wide variety of fish, but that they eat it only in restaurants. They don't know how to buy and properly cook seafood, and haven't the confidence to try. I hope the recipes in this book will get you started on a life of fish and seafood at home as well as away.

It all starts in the supermarket or fish store. The place to buy seafood is the place that sells the most, so you can be sure of getting the freshest fish and seafood possible. Once you know and trust the person selling fish, ask what the freshest fish is for the day, and ask for tips on preparation. But until you develop that confidence in your fish seller, here are some tips as to what to look for and what to avoid. To preserve freshness and moisture, fish should be displayed in cases filled with crushed ice. The fish should not be directly on the ice, nor near melting water. At home, keep fish and seafood on the top shelf of the refrigerator, where the temperature is coldest. Look for firm, elastic flesh with a nice, translucent color and a moist, fresh-cut appearance. Fresh fish should not have a fishy odor. Some stores have dated packages to guide you. Avoid soft, flabby flesh, a milky color, any signs of drying, and an unpleasant, fishy aroma.

The most important advice I can give about preparing fish is simply this: don't overcook. More than almost any other food, fish dries out quickly. I really believe that the reason some people say they don't like fish is that they never have had the opportunity to taste it properly prepared. All the reasons those people give for not liking fish—fishy flavor, dry, tasteless, poor texture—can be traced to poor fish selection and preparation.

People all over the world consume fish raw. While I'm not advocating that you eat raw fish, I'm pointing out that fish has a naturally delicate, flavorful nature. Just look at the popularity of sushi and sashimi. Most seafood cookbooks call for cooking fish about 10 minutes per inch of thickness, regardless of the method of preparation. I think that's too much cooking time. Also remember that the piece of fish will continue to cook internally until it is served.

When all is said and done, I personally think fish tastes best when grilled over charcoal. All those juices get sealed in and the taste is wonderful. And nothing could be simpler. Even the preparation of the coals is pleasant on a nice evening outdoors. During inclement weather, turn to the broiler in the kitchen. In either case, count on no more than eight minutes per inch of total cooking time. Depending on the heat of the charcoal or your broiler, you may even need less time.

Dry fish such as halibut or orange roughy will need a bit of oil brushed on each side. Salmon is as "well marbled" as a prime steak, and needs no additional oil.

Explore a variety of ways of preparing your fish. Each will give a slightly different texture to the fish, and I think each bestows a special flavor. If you've never tried poaching fish, give the method a try.

Of all the ways to prepare fish, I think this next one is the most unusual, and it's a terrific way to cook fish for a large group of people. Select a large salmon or other whole fish, counting on about six ounces per person. Get the freshest fish you can find. Wrap it in aluminum foil along with some thin-sliced lemon. Next put it into a large, Ziploc plastic storage bag, and close carefully. Then put it into your dish-washer! Set the timer, and that's all there is to it. At the end of the wash-dry cycle you'll have a beautifully prepared fish, done at exactly the right moment to serve your guests. Put it on a platter, set it on the table, and enjoy all the compliments you get. It's a no-fail approach.

What about leftovers? There are two ways to deal with leftover fish. First, if the steaks or fillets you've bought are too large for you, cut off the amount you don't want to eat for that meal. Wrap the extra fish in plastic wrap, putting it into a plastic storage bag, and then into the freezer. Accumulate a bit of fish here, an odd shrimp or scallop there, and you'll have a wonderful frozen assortment with which to make a fish soup such as bouillabaise. Or use leftover cooked fish for tomorrow's lunch. Flake the fish and prepare sandwiches or salads in the same way you'd use chicken. There's no need for fish ever to go to waste.

While each fish and all the variety of shellfish have their distinct flavors and characteristics, all seafood lends itself to an array of seasoning possibilities, so keep your kitchen stocked with all the ingredients to prepare your seafood entrée for the day. Count on lemon, of course, but don't forget lime and orange for a change. Daubing fresh fillets with a good Dijon mustard prior to grilling yields a wonderful flavor. Flavorings that go particularly well with seafood include black peppercorns, fresh garlic, fresh or crystallized ginger, parsley, dill, and hot peppers. I think olive oil is best for sautéing. Use a nice white wine for poaching. Fish prepared teriyaki style is a welcome alternative to chicken. Try unusual vinegars for something entirely different. Just remember that fish needs very little flavoring; its delicate flavor shouldn't be overwhelmed.

Let's look at some of the ways to cook fish and seafood in a bit more detail.

GRILLING/BARBECUING. This dry-heat method of cooking can be done on an open rack over charcoal, gas, artificial coals or what have you. Equipment can be anything from the most simple campfire to elaborate brick enclosures or imported barbecues. Grilling works well for fish because it cooks quickly and efficiently. Cooking outdoors can be a lot of fun. For something different, soak some hardwood chips in water and toss them on the coals to provide a deep smoky flavor.

BAKING/ROASTING. This is another dry-heat method of cooking; no liquid is added. It's best to bake or roast on a rack so that juices don't accumulate. Use a high heat, about 450 degrees Fahrenheit, so cooking is quick. Count on about 8 minutes per inch rather than the traditional 10 minutes.

BROILING. While grilling refers to cooking over the heat source, broiling is done under the heat source, typically in the oven. Salmon and other fatty fish may throw off quite a bit of smoke; count on plenty of drainage for fat. Brush on a bit of oil for lean fish.

POACHING. This is a virtually foolproof method of fish cookery in which seafood is cooked in simmering liquid just below the boiling point. You can poach in the oven or on the stovetop, with the dish covered or not. A variety of liquids—vinegar, wine, soy sauce—provide flavor and distinction.

STEAMING. Here we cook seafood over boiling water, not in it, so that the steam itself cooks the fish, which is held out of the water by a rack of some sort. Steamed fish needn't be plain: onions, lemon slices, and vegetables can be placed on top of the fish on the rack.

STIR-FRYING. With just a tiny bit of peanut or other oil, you can whisk small pieces of fish, shrimp, and other seafood in a wok to cook it wonderfully and quickly. Prepare your vegetables in the same wok or frying pan and you'll have little cleanup time. Cook fish and other seafood just till the flesh loses its translucent color and turns whitish.

OVEN-FRYING. If you love the crunchiness of fried food but hate the fat, this is the method for you. Coat pieces of seafood with breading, cornmeal, oat bran, or crumbs, and spray them with vegetable-oil cooking spray. Bake on a cookie sheet in a hot oven (450 degrees F.) just till the crust is crunchy. Serve with some seafood sauce.

MARINATING. Using vinegar, citrus juice, or other acidic liquid, you can "cook" seafood without the use of heat. The acid denatures the protein, much the same way heat would. While the risk remains quite small, this method of seafood preparation does not kill all microorganisms. Marinating before cooking gives fish a fine flavor.

MICROWAVING. Fish will cook at high power in just 3 to 5 minutes. depending on the size and power of your microwave oven. As you cook more fish, the time for cooking increases.

STEWING. Even if you've never cooked fish in your life but you've made stews and soups, you can succeed on your first try in preparing seafood soups, stews, and chowders. Just remember that all seafood is delicate and requires very little cooking. First cook the vegetables and other ingredients, then add fish and shellfish during the last few minutes. This is simple yet elegant cookery.

When you multiply all the different kinds of fish and seafood by the number of cooking and seasoning methods at your disposal, it's easy to see that you never have to get tired of this wonderful food. Delicious, nutritious, and heart-protecting, there's nothing to match fish and seafood.

THE SHOPPING LIST

A few years ago, after learning that my son Ross's cholesterol level was elevated at the age of seven, I told him that eating a heart-healthy diet was going to get easier and easier. More and more people, I explained, were changing their eating habits, and the demand for low-fat, low-cholesterol foods would grow steadily. The food industry, spotting an economic niche to be filled, would satisfy that demand. Happily, we're seeing that happen as new and improved foods fill the supermarket shelves. Today we have low-fat, low-cholesterol options we never had before.

The Dairy List

How low do you want to go? Today you have the choice to go all the way from whole-milk dairy products down to the completely fat-free foods. Lest you shock your tastebuds and get discouraged, gradually wean yourself from the high-fat milk. If you use whole milk now, go to 2 percent fat, down to 1 percent fat, and finally graduate to skim milk. As the old saying goes, yard by yard it's very hard, but inch by inch it's a cinch.

For other dairy foods, a gradual change isn't necessary. You can start making the switch during your next trip to the supermarket. Weight Watchers, for example, makes a wonderful 1 percent fat cottage cheese, with just one gram of fat per serving. There's no reason to eat more fat than that, since this product delivers all the flavor you want, with amazing creaminess.

Sour cream is almost by definition a high-fat food. But you can cut out a lot of that fat by reading the labels of some of the reduced-fat sour creams many local dairies now produce. You can cut the fat grams per serving in half by mixing equal portions of the sour cream with nonfat plain yogurt. With minced chives, the mixture tastes terrific on a steaming baked potato.

You'll also find a number of brands of delicious nonfat yogurt in a wide variety of flavors. The texture and creaminess of the nonfat yogurt is so good I see no reason to buy the low-fat brands. Don't be put off by the formidable ingredients listed on some labels; guar gum, carrageenan, and zanthan gum are natural, vegetable-derived thickeners.

For dessert, as suggested earlier, opt for frozen nonfat yogurt rather than ice cream, since even the lowest-fat ice creams can't compare once you know what that saturated fat does to your arteries. Even my children love going out to get some frozen nonfat yogurt, and they don't miss ice cream at all.

Cheese contributes much of the saturated fat and cholesterol to the American diet. The National Dairy Board and other industry promotion groups want to sell their products regardless of their effects on health. Their goal is to sell whole-milk dairy products, since that's where the money is.

Just in case you think I might be exaggerating, let me quote from a dairy industry leader in a column published in the *Southeastern Dairy Review*. William Boardman, executive vice president of the trade group Dairy Farmers, Inc., told his readers in the industry that "it is of no concern to the dairy farmer businessman as to whether or not the general public is in better physical condition, weighs less or has a lower cholesterol count. The responsibility of industry promoters, educators and farmer leaders is to see that everything in their power is done to provide a profit for the dairy farming industry—and that means promoting the Whole Product!"

He warns that groups such as the American Heart Association are "influencing consumers to reduce their intake of whole milk, high quality cheeses and other 'palate-pleasing' dairy products. . . . Dairy farmer promotion and education programs should be designed to sell only *whole* milk and hence, enhance the income and hopefully the profit of the dairy farmer investor." Boardman complains that even some within the industry have been guilty of advocating low-fat dairy foods in programs geared to the needs of those concerned about cholesterol and heart disease.

The dairy industry for many years has promoted the use of the "Real" seal on dairy foods in an attempt to make consumers believe that it is the mark of superiority. But that seal really means that the food just might be "real" dangerous, which is certainly true when it comes to cheese. "Real" cheddar cheese delivers 120 calories, 9 grams of fat, and 30 milligrams of cholesterol per one-ounce serving. Compare that with the label on Formagg cheddar and you'll see a cut to 70 calories, 5 grams of fat, and zero cholesterol. Moreover the fat you get is of the polyunsaturated and monounsaturated types rather than the artery-clogging saturated fat of "real" cheddar.

Formagg products are made with casein, the protein of milk, along with soybean oil to replace the saturated fats and cholesterol. But what about nutrition? Aren't "real" dairy foods higher in nutrients? Again, take a close look at the labels and you'll see the truth, in percentage of USRDA.

	Formagg	Natural Cheddar
Protein	20%	15%
Vitamin A	15%	6%
Vitamin C	10%	*
Thiamine	15%	*
Riboflavin	15%	6%
Niacin	10%	*
Calcium	30%	20%
Iron	10%	*

*Contains less than 2% of the USRDA of these nutrients.

Those numbers just can't be debated. Women, in particular, will be pleased to see that Formagg delivers 30 percent of the daily calcium requirement, as compared to the 20 percent found in natural cheddar cheese. Those who are lactose intolerant, who lack the enzyme lactase to digest milk sugar properly, will be delighted to learn that Formagg contains no lactose whatever.

Certainly there are other products on the market that use the principle of replacing butterfat in cheese with soybean oil. They are all superior to natural cheese in terms of heart health. I personally lean toward Formagg for two reasons. First, Formagg comes in the widest variety of cheese types, including cheddar, mozzarella, provolone, ricotta, American, Swiss, and others. That way you'll be able to enjoy all your favorite cheese recipes as well as those you'll find in this cookbook. Second, Formagg works very well in cooking, performing in recipes better than other brands.

Formagg is made by the Galaxy Cheese Company of New Castle, Pennsylvania. You'll find it in many supermarkets. But if your market doesn't stock Formagg yet, have the manager call the company toll-free at (800) 441-9419 so you can enjoy all the varieties available. Or call the number yourself to find out where it is sold.

When it comes to coffee creamers you'll have to be extra-careful. We know that half-and-half contains a lot of saturated fat and cholesterol. So manufacturers try to deceive us by advertising their nondairy creamers as being cholesterol-free, but failing to mention that they're made with tropical oils such as coconut oil. I have two suggestions for those who enjoy their coffee light. Nonfat dry milk powder can be spooned into coffee in the same way you'd use nondairy creamers. Or you can try evaporated skim milk in cans. You get a lot of richness, since the milk is concentrated, but it has no fat. Evaporated skim milk works very well in any recipe calling for cream. It's great for mashing potatoes, for example.

Last, and I do mean last, on the dairy food list is butter, which is nothing more than a concentrated mass of saturated fat and cholesterol. This is a passé product that doesn't belong in any heart-healthy person's diet. Here you have two alternatives.

Margarine is butter's logical successor. Today's margarines have wonderful flavor and texture. Just a few are made with unhealthful ingredients such as tropical oils or animal fats. Read the labels. And as for those using "partially hydrogenated" soybean or corn oil, today we know that the hydrogenation processes used by manufacturers to harden oils into stick or tub margarine actually are not harmful. However, since total fat is also a consideration, look for fat-reduced margarines. Again, Weight Watchers is a good choice.

Your second choice for butter replacement comes in the form of a powder you can add to recipes or sprinkle over hot vegetables. Butter Buds, Molly McButter, and O'Butter are three brands currently on the market. You'll be pleasantly surprised how much butter flavor these products deliver. Look for them in the dietetic or spices section of your supermarket.

The Meat List

The first thing many people think of when modifying the diet to cut back on fats and cholesterol is red meat. While it's true that beef has been a major source of saturated fat, there's no need to eliminate this nutritious food entirely. Many of your favorite recipes probably call for ground beef. If you buy prepackaged beef in the supermarket you'll get meat that's 30 percent, 22 percent, or 15 percent fat. Ground beef labeled as lean usually will still contain 10 to 15 percent fat. But you don't have to settle for that. Instead, select a London broil, top round steak, or other very lean cut of beef. Ask your butcher to trim off all the visible fat, even if that means cutting into the meat a bit. Then have him grind it. I like to get several pounds at one time, which I can ask the butcher to wrap in individual one-pound packages for the freezer, and I can prepare patties for hamburgers and meatballs for future use. The resulting ground beef can be as low as 5 percent fat.

The only way you can do better than that would be to have your butcher grind a skinned and boned turkey breast. Note that the ground turkey for sale in the supermarket contains both white and dark meat, bringing up the fat content significantly. Some butchers may balk at grinding turkey, since the equipment must be cleaned between different kinds of meat. I get around this by purchasing a large quantity at one time, again storing the ground turkey breast in one-pound packages in my freezer for future use. While he's at it, I have the butcher cut some of the turkey breast as cutlets, which I use in a number of recipes that would call for veal. Although veal is lower in fat than beef, turkey is even leaner.

But what about steaks and roasts? There are times when only a nice cut of red meat will fill the bill. I'm thinking especially about those evenings when I want to barbecue a steak over the charcoal in my backyard. For a long while after I began my quest for heart health and a low cholesterol level, I limited my steak splurges to just a few times a year. I did use some beef in certain recipes in limited quantities, but a slab of meat sizzling over the coals was a rare treat.

Today I enjoy those steaks and roasts on a regular basis, thanks to a welcome development in the beef industry. Producers in various parts of the country have concentrated on delivering ultra-low-fat beef, raised without hormones, pesticides, or antibiotics. Steaks are as low in fat as fish or chicken breast. The problem in the past was that if a steak was low in fat it was also low in flavor, juiciness, and tenderness. Employing special techniques, today's producers of low-fat beef deliver all the flavor and tenderness you crave.

One caution, however. This new beef dries out fairly easily, and doesn't work very well for those who want their steaks well done. But if you enjoy a rare to medium-rare piece of meat, this is for you.

It took a few tries for me to get it right, since this beef cooks a lot faster than regular beef, but I've perfected cooking the steaks to get them sizzling on the outside and rich and tender on the inside. Since the steaks are so lean, there's no fat to sizzle on the grill and no burning fat to char the outside. So I brush the steaks with a little oil before tossing them on the fire. The oil burns off, charring the meat on the outside just the way I like it.

Dakota Lean Meats in South Dakota offers New York strip sirloins, ribeyes, and tenderloin steaks as well as roasts. The meat comes frozen in individual plastic packets and is delivered to your door by next-day air shipment. You can order by phone toll-free: (800) 727-5326. Prices are about one-third higher than you'd pay for premium beef in a supermarket or butcher mart, but the meat has been completely trimmed and there's no waste whatever.

For me, those frozen steaks in my freezer are the ultimate fast food. When I don't have time to prepare a meal I can always take out a steak and enjoy it along with a baked potato and a salad. Leaving the meat only partially thawed helps keep the inside nice and rare and tender, so after a few moments in the microwave to partially thaw it, I put the steak right under the broiler.

Other brands are also available, but I find that Dakota lean beef tastes better. My family and friends and I have taste-tested a variety of types, and prefer that brand over all others. However, the other brands are equally excellent in terms of their fat content.

Pork offers fewer options, since most of it comes with a hefty dollop of fat. But the remarkable exception is ham. You can enjoy dinners of ham steaks, sandwiches of thin-sliced ham, and breakfasts of ham or Canadian bacon, all of which is extremely low in fat. Just look at the labels of ham products in your supermarket and select those with very low fat contents.

Our ancient ancestors, the cavemen, ate lots of meat, but the meat that they ate was different from that sold in today's supermarkets. It was much lower in fat, and probably lower in cholesterol as well, since it came from animals in the wild, which are leaner than our domesticated livestock. Can we enjoy the same kind of meat? Actually we can, whether or not we know any hunters. All wild game is low in fat, and whether the hunter's prize is deer, rabbit, wild boar, squirrel, or game birds, you can eat it to your heart's content. If you don't happen to have a hunter in the family, or if he's not a very good shot, you can find game meats in some markets. New Zealand now exports high-quality venison. Specialty stores and mail-order firms supply a wide variety of game meats. Even domestic rabbit packs little fat, with baked rabbit yielding only 5 grams of fat per 3½-ounce serving.

When it comes to sausage, the picture in the supermarket is a lot bleaker. But all is not lost for those who love salami, pepperoni, bologna, breakfast sausage, and jerky. Seagull Family Products in Phoenix, Arizona, makes a product called Spice 'n Slice with which you can make your own low-fat sausage. Each box comes with two packets, one with salt and the other with spices and seasonings. Mix the two packets with freshly ground turkey breast or ultra-low-fat ground beef, form into patties or rolls, and bake in the oven. Like all sausage, Spice 'n Slice contains a good bit of sodium. But, since you'll be cutting down on sodium by not eating as many processed and fast foods, you'll be able to afford a bit of sodium in these sausages. And, if you prefer, you can cut back on the salt. A few markets carry the product, but if yours doesn't, you can order by mail. Call or write: Seagull Family Products, Inc., Box 26051, Phoenix, AZ 85068; (602) 861-4094.

Of course, in addition to beef and poultry, you'll want to include a variety of seafood in your monthly menu.

Although eggs provide the same high-quality protein as meat, they also supply a huge portion of cholesterol per yolk. Some egg producers are now saying that early cholesterol measurements weren't accurate, and that a large egg contains "only" 200 milligrams of cholesterol instead of the previously listed 274 milligrams. But the reality remains that no one trying to control his or her cholesterol level should consume more than 300 milligrams of cholesterol daily. That means that even at the lower level one egg yolk just about shoots the cholesterol allowance for the day, leaving you with non-animal sources of food for the balance of that day.

Your options for eggs include egg substitutes or the use of only the egg whites. Many excellent substitutes make wonderful omelets and work very well in recipes. Egg whites contain absolutely no cholesterol at all, and two egg whites in place of an egg works well in most dishes.

When baking muffins or other goods, here's a trick for making them come out lighter and fluffier. Don't just add the white to the rest of the moist ingredients and stir into the recipe. Instead, beat the egg whites till fluffy, and fold them into the recipe batter. It takes a bit more effort but the results make the work worth it.

Last but certainly not least in selecting protein foods, don't forget the lowly dried beans and peas. As discussed earlier, these are excellent sources of soluble fiber as well. With the tremendous variety of dried beans and peas, one could realistically include them in practically every day's menu. One day it might be soup, another day stew, the next day salad, and some days an entrée featuring beans. I think you'll enjoy the recipes that follow.

The Bread and Cereal List

At first glance, you wouldn't think that this food group would cause much trouble in the fat and cholesterol departments. Unfortunately, foods in this category are frequently a source of hidden fats. The only way to know which are healthful and which are hurtful is to read the labels carefully.

One package of rolls will be made with soybean oil while another lists animal shortening. Certain brands of cereal—even those made with oat bran—contain significant amounts of coconut oil. Bakery-shop goods typically bear no ingredient or nutrition labels, but are most often made with butter.

Happily, however, with a little scrutiny you can find breads and cereals that are truly heart-healthy. Many manufacturers have responded to consumer concerns by removing the offending fats and oils from their products.

Certainly oat bran will be high on your list of foods in this category. But read the labels to make sure you're getting the genuine article, not a product that contains a number of other ingredients. For the recipes in this book you'll need pure oat bran and oatmeal. That doesn't mean, though, that you need to avoid completely cereals that contain a number of ingredients. Those will add variety and nutrition to the diet, but they won't supply all the oat bran you need for the day.

Similarly, you'll want to stock your kitchen with whole-grain cereals and flours from grains other than oats as well. Wheat, for example, contains little soluble fiber, but is an excellent source of insoluble fiber, and we do need both.

In general, pasta offers a terrific way to get complex carbohydrates with little fat and no cholesterol. The many types provide tremendous variety. But egg noodles, until now, have presented a problem because of the cholesterol content. In the past I used fettuccine as an egg-noodle replacement. But now you can have egg noodles made without the egg yolks. No Yolks is a cholesterol-free product made with durum flour, corn flour, and egg whites. Regular egg noodles contain 50 to 54 milligrams of cholesterol per 2-ounce serving. No Yolks has none. The best part is that they're delicious.

Only about a third of supermarkets currently stock No Yolks. If you'd like your store to do so, have them call or write to Foulds, Inc., at 520 East Church Street, Libertyville, IL 60048. Their phone is (312) 362-3062. You can also order No Yolks directly by mail. Three varieties are available: extra broad (½ inch); broad (¼ inch); and medium (⅛ inch).

The Fruit and Vegetable List

We have practically no limitations in this category of foods. Nutritionists have calculated that adults need two servings of fruit and two of vegetables daily as a minimum. The word to stress there is *minimum.* Depending on your caloric needs, you can have as many servings as you like.

Go for the variety. Seek supermarkets with the widest choices in the produce section. If you don't know how to use some of the more exotic varieties, ask the produce manager for suggestions. Whenever possible, fresh is best. You'll get all the nutrients and all the flavor the vegetables and fruits have to offer. Next best are frozen fruits and vegetables, and as a last choice, canned. Just be a bit cautious and avoid fruits canned in heavy syrup rather than in natural juices and water, and vegetables canned with a lot of sodium.

No fruits or vegetables contain any cholesterol at all, and only olives and avocados supply a large percentage of their calories as fat. Because I'm such a fan of guacamole, but I limit the amount of avocados I eat, we've included here a nice recipe for a type of "guacamole" that has no avocados.

Practically every restaurant offers a fruit platter on the menu, and when it arrives at the table the appearance is enough to set anyone's mouth watering. But you needn't wait till you're dining out. Slice two or three types of fruit, arrange the pieces attractively, garnish with a bit of lettuce, and place a little dish of yogurt or cottage cheese in the center. Even kids enjoy the festive look and taste.

The Dessert List

I must admit that I miss desserts in restaurants. While I love fresh fruits and berries, I still hanker after all the gooey, elaborate concoctions. Maybe someday restaurants will offer more healthful versions of those desserts. But in the meantime you can enjoy sweet treats at home.

We've included some wonderful dessert recipes in this book, and remember, too, that dessert recipes in magazines and other cookbooks can be easily modified. You can replace half the flour in cake recipes with oat bran; this works particularly well in heavy cakes, such as carrot and banana cakes. Use egg whites or egg substitutes in place of whole eggs. Use margarine or oil instead of butter; frequently you can get by with quite a bit less shortening than called for.

In the dessert category, too, manufacturers have begun to fill an important niche. Weight Watchers sells a wide variety of frozen confections that will amaze your taste buds. It's hard to believe that their double-Dutch-chocolate bars have so little fat.

Nonfat frozen yogurt makes an excellent replacement for ice cream. Try topping it with fresh berries, and perhaps just a touch of liqueur. Chocolate nonfat yogurt topped with raspberries and a splash of Chambord (raspberry liqueur) is simply elegant, as is vanilla yogurt with a drizzle of crème de menthe.

Do you miss whipped cream? Try some YoWhip, made with nonfat yogurt. It's an aerosol whipped topping that comes in vanilla, strawberry, and chocolate. Look for it in the dairy case.

Now and then there's just no substitute for rich, gooey cakes. Birthdays, parties, anniversaries, and the like call for sweet, elaborate confections. But those typically come packed with fat and cholesterol. Enter the world of Sweet Deceit, a California-based company that makes all sorts of sinful goodies without the sin. While expensive, these once-in-a-while special treats have just 4 to 5 grams of fat per 3½-ounce serving. You can get Black Forest cakes, chocolate cakes, lemon cakes, carrot cakes, and on and on. For more information on how to order, write to Sweet Deceit, 11444 West Olympic Boulevard, Los Angeles, CA 90064. Or call (213) 312-9542.

You'll also want to look for Health Valley products. Many of them are made with oat bran, and all contain a reasonable amount of fat in the form of soybean oil. You can find graham crackers, animal crackers, fruit bars, and cookies. Health Valley's line of products grows regularly, so check for new foods.

Be far more careful with snack bars touted as being healthful. Frequently they include such ingredients as tropical oils, which you certainly don't want in your diet at all. Don't let advertising phrases like "all natural" and "organic" fool you. Read the labels carefully.

Kitchen Equipment

One of the best investments you can make as you plan a healthful diet is sensible, useful kitchen equipment. You'll probably notice that as you buy fewer and fewer processed and prepared foods, you'll see savings in your food budget. Why not invest those savings in a piece of equipment that will make it easier for you to enjoy a wide variety of good food? Little by little your collection will grow, and with it your enjoyment of a low-fat diet.

For openers, you'll save a lot of fat by using nonstick Teflon pans or those with other coatings. You'll be able to use two or three of them in different sizes for sautéing and frying foods.

Sharp knives make short work of slicing, chopping, and mincing vegetables and fruits. A good set of knives lasts a lifetime. And a good sharpener, either manual or electric, keeps the edges ready for action at the cutting board.

When first introduced, food processors were expensive and considered a luxury. Today the prices have come down and you'll find a hundred uses for the equipment. Vegetables for Chinese stir-fry, for example, can be prepared in just a few minutes.

Air-popped popcorn is the ideal snack food for munching while watching TV. Prices of air-poppers are reasonable and you'll use the machine often. I like to spray the corn with just a bit of butter-flavored Pam or Baker's Joy as it comes out of the popper, collect it in a brown paper bag, and shake it up with a tiny bit of salt. Or, if you limit the salt strictly, use one of the vegetable seasonings such as Mrs. Dash.

If you don't already use a steamer for seafood and vegetables, just purchase a little folding steamer rack that can go inside a large covered pot. There's no need to use an expensive one. You'll find such racks in the housewares section of almost every supermarket.

Now on to a few luxuries I recommend. One is an inexpensive little gadget called the Really Creamy Yogurt Cheese Funnel, with which you can make yogurt cheese—yogurt with the fluid removed. The funnel is very efficient, and you can then use the yogurt cheese to make cheesecakes, pâtés, sandwich spreads, and a number of recipes the company supplies along with the funnel. It's fun to use, and the recipes are really good. To order one by mail, send a check for $9.95 plus $2 for handling and postage to Millhopper Marketing, Inc., 1110 NW 8th Avenue, Suite C, Gainesville, FL 32601.

While dry pasta remains an old standby, fresh pasta provides a special taste treat. The problem is that fresh pastas are usually made with whole eggs, bringing a lot of cholesterol to otherwise healthy food. The answer is to make your own fresh pasta with a pasta maker. These sell for less than $100 in department stores. That's a big investment if you don't think you'd use it more than a couple of times, but if you really enjoy pasta you'll find the varieties of pasta you make to be truly delicious. If you have children, they'll love helping with pasta making.

And now for an item of pure, unadulterated luxury: How would you like to wake up tomorrow morning with the air filled with the aroma of freshly made bread, baked while you slept? All you need for this is an Auto Bakery such as the one made by DAK Industries. This contraption, slightly smaller than a bread box, allows you to just dump in the ingredients for bread at night, set the timer, and awaken to the scent of steaming loaves. Sound wonderful? You can place your order with a credit card by calling (800) 325-0800. The President of DAK, Drew Kaplan, relies on oat bran to control his own cholesterol levels, and he includes some of his personal recipes for oat-bran breads along with each of his Auto Bakeries. If you can possibly afford it, this is a pure delight.

We eat food because it tastes good. Sure, we know that food contains the nutrients we need for health, growth, and maintenance. But the reason we eat it, without any special prompting, is because it pleases the palate. Those foods we find distasteful we conveniently omit from our diets. Very few people eat certain foods just because they're "good for you."

Today we know that a wide variety of foods are good for us. And some of those foods, as we've seen, can actually lower our cholesterol levels. But to eat them on a regular basis they have to taste good.

That's where the next section of this book comes in. The recipes we've included here are designed to make these healthful foods as palate pleasing as possible. Whether for breakfast, lunch, dinner, or snacks, the dishes you'll prepare will give you a delicious new perspective on cholesterol control. Enjoy!

THE DIET-HEART
NEWSLETTER

Reading this book has helped bring you up to date on the latest information about how the foods we eat affect our risk of heart disease. But reducing the risk of heart disease is an ever-expanding area of research and developments. To keep you abreast of current happenings in the field, I have developed *The Diet-Heart Newsletter.*

This quarterly publication summarizes current articles in the medical literature, ideas that often are not available to the public. You'll receive insights from medical meetings and seminars not typically reported to the public. You'll get newly developed recipes and dietary suggestions about new products. There is also a regular question-answer forum in which you can participate.

For a sample of *The Diet-Heart Newsletter* and subscription information send a stamped, self-addressed business-size (large) envelope to:

> The Diet-Heart Newsletter
> Post Office Box 2039
> Venice, CA 90294

Part Two

WHEN FAT DOESN'T "COUNT"

I always look at the fat content of recipes I find in books and magazines. If the fat isn't listed in grams as it is in this book, I try to estimate the amount by way of the ingredients. For example, if the recipe calls for 1 tablespoon of oil of any kind, I know that contributes 14 grams of fat. A cup of whole milk adds 8 grams of fat. If necessary, I substitute. By sautéing in Pam or Baker's Joy instead of oil, I save virtually all 14 grams of fat. I do the same by replacing whole milk with evaporated skim milk.

There are times, however, when I don't count the fat at all. Oat bran contains 2 grams of fat per ounce, but since I know that oat bran actually lowers cholesterol levels I disregard its fat content entirely; while salmon and mackerel are very high in fat, this type of fat appears to protect the Eskimos from heart disease; even cholesterol-lowering garbanzo beans have 2.4 grams of fat per 3½-ounce serving.

As you go through these and other recipes, you might want to follow the same principles. Of course you'll want to replace saturated fat whenever possible. But when it comes to the fat content of oat bran, rice bran, beans, or fish, just ignore it.

Do bear in mind, though, that while such fat needs not be considered in terms of its potential to raise blood cholesterol, all fat supplies calories and must be remembered when considering weight control. However, on this low-fat diet you'll be cutting back on the harmful fats, and therefore the amount of calories contributed by the good fats in oat bran and fish needn't be a concern.

If you wish, you can further reduce the fat content of virtually all the recipes here: Instead of sautéing with even 1 tablespoon of oil, you can sauté with a spray of Pam or Baker's Joy; if a muffin recipe calls for oil, you can replace half the oil with light corn syrup (Karo) and you'll never miss the fat; if a recipe calls for 2 tablespoons of oil, you can use just one tablespoon. You're the one who knows how much fat you're consuming altogether each day.

[**NOTE:** *Special cholesterol-lowering ingredients are indicated throughout the recipes by lightface type.*]

RECIPES LISTED BY SPECIAL INGREDIENTS

■ *Dried Beans and Peas*

RECIPES LISTED BY SPECIAL INGREDIENTS ◆ 71

SAUCES AND TOPPINGS

DESSERTS AND SWEETS

■ *Barley*

SOUPS

SALADS

■ *Omega-3–Rich Fish*

■ *Ultra Lean Meats*

DESSERTS AND SWEETS

■ *Rice Bran*

APPETIZERS AND HORS D'OEUVRES

CEREALS, PANCAKES, BREADS, AND MUFFINS

DESSERTS AND SWEETS

■ *Apple Fiber*

SOUPS

VEGETARIAN ENTRÉES

SIDE DISHES

SAUCES AND TOPPINGS

■ *Oatmeal*

DESSERTS AND SWEETS

■ *Guar Gum*

DESSERTS AND SWEETS

APPETIZERS AND
HORS D'OEUVRES

Three-Color Bean Pâté

Hummus

Green Hummus

Bean and Mushroom Dip

Herb and Yogurt Dip

Spicy Roasted Chickpeas

Master Recipe for Boiled Dry Beans

Fat-Free Guacamole

Cabbage Strudel

Sardine and Sour Cream Dip

Salmon Mold with Dill

Potted Mackerel

THREE-COLOR BEAN PÂTÉ

Makes 1 loaf, about 12 slices

In the old days, before I saw the light about changing my diet, I loved pâtés of all sorts, and indulged to my heart's content. Then I began to avoid the obvious offenders such as those made with liver, sticking with vegetable pâtés—until I learned that they are almost always made with eggs. Now I enjoy pâté made at home. It's fresher and, to be honest, a lot tastier. ■

2 **cups cooked** green split peas

2 **teaspoons dried mint**

¼ **cup evaporated skim milk**

3 **envelopes gelatin**

2 **cups freshly cooked or canned** chickpeas **or** white cannellini beans, **drained**

¼ **cup reduced-calorie mayonnaise**

1 **tablespoon lemon juice**

2 **cups freshly cooked or canned** red **or** pink beans, **drained**

¼ **cup chili sauce**

Spray a loaf pan, about 8 by 4 inches, with Pam or Baker's Joy.

Place peas, with mint and skim milk in a blender or food processor and blend until smooth.

Place 1 package of gelatin in a small skillet and pour over 2 tablespoons cold water. Over low heat, dissolve gelatin in water until mixture is translucent and warm. Remove from heat, add to peas, and process until smooth. Spoon mixture into bottom of loaf pan and place in refrigerator for 10 minutes to set lightly.

Meanwhile, purée chickpeas or white beans with mayonnaise and lemon juice. As before, dissolve 1 envelope of gelatin in 2 tablespoonfuls of water in a small skillet. Heat gently until gelatin is translucent and warm and add to chickpeas or beans; process until smooth. Spoon this mixture on top of the green-pea mixture in loaf pan, and smooth with a spatula. Return loaf pan to the refrigerator to let the second layer set for 10 minutes.

Gently warm last envelope of gelatin in 2 tablespoons of water over low heat until translucent and warm. Purée kidney beans with chili sauce and gelatin until smooth. Spoon this mixture over white layer of beans, and smooth it with a spatula. Cover with wax paper and chill overnight.

Gently unmold the pâté and cut into slices.

SERVING SIZE: 1/12 loaf
CALORIES: 127
FAT: 2 grams

CHOLESTEROL: 1.88 milligrams
SODIUM: 109 milligrams

■ ■

Hummus (Garbanzo Bean Dip)

Makes about 1 ¼ cups (20 tablespoons)

This is the only recipe repeated from *The 8-Week Cholesterol Cure.* Just in case you don't have that book, I want you to have this wonderful Middle Eastern bean dip. Serve it to company or keep it in the refrigerator for quick snacks with wedges of toasted pita bread. I haven't gotten tired of this in nearly five years, and you can almost always find a supply in my refrigerator. ∎

⅓ **cup sesame paste (tahini)**

¼ **cup lemon juice (fresh is best)**

5 **cloves finely minced garlic**

5 **drops Tabasco**

¼ **cup water**

½ **teaspoon ground cumin**

Two 15-ounce cans garbanzo beans **(chickpeas), drained**

Simply combine all ingredients and blend until smooth. A food processor makes this really easy; use the large metal blade. Otherwise use a large bowl and electric mixer.

SERVING SIZE: 1 tablespoon
CALORIES: 63
FAT: 2.56 grams

CHOLESTEROL: 0
SODIUM: 62.7 milligrams

∎∎

GREEN HUMMUS

Makes about 2½ cups (40 tablespoons)

Maybe one of the reasons there's so little heart disease among people of the Middle East is that they eat plenty of hummus made with chickpeas (also known as garbanzo beans). This variation is great for parties because of its wonderful emerald color. If you plan to serve it to guests, assemble it at the last moment, or at least hold off on the lemon juice until you're ready to serve, because the lemon's acid will dull the spinach green to a drab olive color. Serve as a dip with toasted pita-bread wedges. ■

½ pound fresh spinach, stemmed, or 2 bunches watercress, stemmed

¼ cup cilantro or parsley leaves

2 cups cooked or canned chickpeas, drained

2 tablespoons tahini

2 small cloves of garlic or 1 large

3 tablespoons lemon juice

Cayenne pepper or Tabasco, as desired

Whiz all ingredients together in a food processor or blender until smooth. Refrigerate until ready to serve.

SERVING SIZE: 1 tablespoon
CALORIES: 16.7
FAT: .047 grams

CHOLESTEROL: 0
SODIUM: 56 milligrams

■ ■

BEAN AND MUSHROOM DIP

Makes about 3 cups (48 tablespoons)

This is far more delicate than hummus, and I find it goes well with crackers, celery, and peppers. It can be made with any type of cooked bean except black—the color wouldn't be very appetizing. ■

2 cups cooked or drained canned pinto beans

¼ pound raw mushrooms, chopped fine

2 stalks celery, chopped fine

1 teaspoon cumin powder

One 4-ounce can chopped green chilies or taco sauce

¼ teaspoon garlic powder

Pepper to taste

Mix all ingredients together in a food processor or an electric mixer. Cover and chill until ready to use.

SERVING SIZE: 1 tablespoon
CALORIES: 11
FAT: .068 grams

CHOLESTEROL: 0
SODIUM: 25.5 milligrams

Herb and Yogurt Dip

Makes about 3 cups

Here's a dip that combines the soluble fiber of oat bran with chickpeas. You might try toasting the oat bran first for added flavor, but the recipe will work well if you omit this step. Serve with toasted pita triangles or baked corn tortillas, or as a sandwich spread. ∎

½ **cup** oat bran

1 **cup nonfat yogurt**

2 **green onions**

½ **green bell pepper**

⅓ **cup fresh dill, basil, or cilantro leaves**

½ **cup fresh parsley**

1–2 **teaspoons each dried tarragon and mint**

1½ **cups canned** chickpeas, **drained and rinsed**

2 **teaspoons Worcestershire sauce**

Pepper

Heat an iron skillet, over medium-high heat, without any fat in it. After about 3 minutes, add oat bran. With a wooden spoon, stir continuously for 3 to 4 minutes or until the oat bran has a lovely toasted, nutty aroma.

In a food processor or blender, mix until smooth all of the ingredients, including the toasted oat bran.

SERVING SIZE: 1 tablespoon
CALORIES: 14.6
FAT: .24 grams

CHOLESTEROL: .08 milligrams
SODIUM: 12.7 milligrams

SPICY ROASTED CHICKPEAS

Makes 4 cups

To make this recipe turn out as tasty and terrific as possible, use soaked and cooked dried chickpeas; the canned ones are too soft. You can serve them as appetizers, as a side dish, or just as something to munch on for an evening snack. ■

1 **cup dried** chickpeas, **soaked by quick or slow method (see Master Recipe for Boiled Dry Beans, opposite)**	2 **egg whites** 1 **package (about 1¼ ounces) taco seasoning**

Slowly cook soaked chickpeas for 45 minutes or until just tender but with still some bite to them. Drain through a sieve and cool for 10 minutes.

Preheat oven to 325 degrees.

Blend egg whites with taco seasoning and mix this into the chickpeas, trying to coat them as evenly as possible. Pour chickpeas into a baking pan coated with Pam or Baker's Joy, and bake for 1 hour, stirring on occasion.

Let cool to room temperature and serve. They may be stored, in a covered jar, in the refrigerator. Bring to room temperature before serving.

SERVING SIZE: ½ cup
CALORIES: 102
FAT: 1.73 grams

CHOLESTEROL: 0
SODIUM: 42 milligrams

■ ■

MASTER RECIPE FOR BOILED DRY BEANS

Beans cooked from scratch have a much better texture and flavor than canned beans, which are always mushy. They can be cooked in large batches, then frozen, in 1- to 2-cup portions, for up to 5 months. A pressure cooker is an invaluable aid for cooking beans; most beans will be done in 15 minutes.

STEP 1. *Soaking*

When using dried beans (not lentils or split peas), soak them first to soften them, to cut down on the cooking time, and to make them more easily digestible. There are two soaking methods:

LONG SOAK: Cover the beans by three times their volume in water and let them soak, overnight. Drain the beans and use fresh water to cook them. Much of the flatulence ascribed to beans is due to the soaking water, not the beans.

QUICK SOAK: Cover the beans by three times their volume in water and bring the water to a boil; boil for 1 minute. Turn the heat off and soak them for 1 hour only. Drain them and use fresh water to cook them.

STEP 2. *Cooking the beans*

Place the soaked beans in a saucepan with just enough water to cover them and bring the water to a simmer. Do not add acidic ingredients, such as lemon juice, vinegar, wine, or tomatoes until the beans are already tender or the cooking time will be lengthened and the beans will remain tough.

Keep the beans covered with liquid as they cook but do not add any more than necessary or they can become waterlogged and their flavor will diminish.

One cup of dried beans yields about 2 cups cooked, except for limas, which will yield about 1½ cups.

Cooking times, after soaking, are listed below.

ADZUKI: Small red oval beans from Japan; take 1 to 1½ hours to cook; available in jars in health-food stores.

BLACK BEANS, TURTLE BEANS: Can be used interchangeably with red kidney beans in various dishes; take 1½ hours to cook; available in cans.

BLACK-EYED PEAS: Need no soaking; take 1 to 1½ hours to cook; available canned.

CHICKPEAS, GARBANZOS: Nutty-flavored; take 1½ to 2 hours to cook; available in cans.

CRANBERRY BEANS: Similar to pinto beans; take 1½ hours to cook; not available in cans or jars.

FAVA, LARGE AND SMALL: Very earthy-flavored beans; take 1½ to 2 hours to cook; large ones are available in cans.

GREAT NORTHERN WHITE BEANS, CANNELLINI; KIDNEY-SHAPED; take 1 to 1½ hours to cook; available in cans.

KIDNEY BEANS, LARGE AND SMALL: take 1½ hours to cook; available in cans or in jars in health-food stores.

LIMAS, BUTTER BEANS, LARGE AND SMALL: Flat and kidney-shaped; take 45 minutes to 1 hour to cook; large ones are available in cans.

MUNG BEANS: Round and small, olive-colored; take 30 to 45 minutes; not available in cans or jars; often used for sprouting.

NAVY OR PEA BEANS: Hold shape well after long cooking; used in baked dishes; take 1½ hours to cook; sometimes available in cans.

PINK OR PINTO BEANS: Similar to kidney beans; mild; take 1 to 1½ hours to cook; available in cans.

RED BEANS: Can be used interchangeably with kidney beans; take 1 to 1½ hours to cook; sometimes available in cans.

WHITE BEANS: Small and kidney-shaped; can replace Great Northern whites; take 1 to 1½ hours to cook; not available canned.

FAT-FREE GUACAMOLE

Makes about 2½ cups (40 tablespoons)

Maybe it's because I live in California that I dearly love guacamole. Unfortunately, this delicious dip comes loaded with fat from the mashed avocados. When I see some at parties, I can't resist having a chip or two covered with it, but I'd like to really dig in! The answer was to develop a recipe that was not only free of fat but also a good source of soluble fiber. This is it! Enjoy it with wedges of corn tortillas baked with a bit of Pam or Baker's Joy sprayed on. Bake the tortillas for 8 to 10 minutes or until crisp. ■

2 **cups cooked** green split peas, **drained and chilled**	1 **small tomato with seeds removed**
1 **tablespoon chopped green onions**	**One 4-ounce can green chilies**
2 **tablespoons lime juice**	**Tabasco to taste**
1 **fine-minced large garlic clove**	**Green food coloring**

Preparation couldn't be more simple: Just place all ingredients except for Tabasco and green food coloring in a food processor or blender and blend until smooth and creamy. If the color isn't quite green enough, add one drop of food coloring at a time and blend until nice and green. Then add Tabasco to taste.

SERVING SIZE: 1 tablespoon
CALORIES: 13.3
FAT: .05 grams

CHOLESTEROL: 0
SODIUM: 42 milligrams

■■

CABBAGE STRUDEL

Makes 1 strudel: 8 appetizer portions, or 10 to 12 hors d'oeuvre portions

If you've been looking for something really different, this is it. If you serve this as an appetizer, you'll want to serve some tomato sauce alongside it or drizzled over portions. Or you might want to consider it as part of an hors d'oeuvre platter when company calls. This dish takes a bit of time, but it's well worth the effort. ■

1 pound white or Savoy cabbage, cut into thin shreds as for cole slaw

1 onion, sliced thin

1 cup white wine

2 teaspoons caraway seeds

1½ cups cooked or canned white beans, drained

Pepper

1 tablespoon olive oil

10 frozen filo leaves, defrosted

2 cups tomato sauce, optional

In a large pot, simmer cabbage, onion, white wine, and caraway seeds, covered, for 45 minutes to an hour or until tender. Stir in white beans and season to taste with pepper.

Preheat oven to 375 degrees.

Pour oil into a small dish and get a pastry brush ready.

Lay 2 filo leaves, slightly overlapping, on a work surface and very lightly brush with oil. Lay another 2 leaves on top of the first and brush again with oil; repeat until all 10 leaves have been used.

Form cabbage-and-bean mixture into a sausage shape down the center of the filo, leaving 2 inches of border on each end. Fold one side flap of leaves over the cabbage and beans, then fold the 2-inch flaps over, then roll up the strudel. Place it, seam side down, on a baking sheet. With a sharp knife, make 4 or 5 slashes on top, to let the steam escape. Brush top of strudel with remaining oil and bake for 45 minutes.

Cool for 10 minutes to let it set before slicing. Serve with tomato sauce if you wish.

SERVING SIZE: ⅛ recipe
CALORIES: 125
FAT: 2.06 grams

CHOLESTEROL: 0
SODIUM: 70 milligrams

SARDINE AND SOUR CREAM DIP

Makes about 1 cup

You won't believe this recipe is actually good for you! It's simple to prepare yet elegant. Try eating it on fresh bagels, as a dip for raw vegetables, or as a sandwich spread. ■

One 4½-ounce can smoked sardines	¼ cup Formagg sour-cream substitute
One 3¾-ounce can sardines, packed in water, drained	1 green onion, sliced thin
	1 tablespoon lemon juice

Drain smoked sardines and pat them well with paper towels to absorb excess oil. Blend smoked sardines with other sardines, sour-cream substitute, green onion, and lemon juice, in a food processor or an electric mixer. Mix until smooth and chill for 1 hour before serving.

SERVING SIZE: 1 tablespoon
CALORIES: 30
FAT: 1.639 grams

CHOLESTEROL: 6.158 milligrams
SODIUM: 52.4 milligrams

■ ■

SALMON MOLD WITH DILL

Makes about 3 cups, or about 8 servings

Here's a healthful version of a classic recipe for entertaining, but once you try it you won't want to wait to have company over to make it again. You can use a ring mold or a fancy fish-shaped mold for a festive touch. Serve on leaves of lettuce, with cherry tomatoes and parsley as garnish. Leftover salmon mold makes a terrific sandwich spread. ■

1 teaspoon canola oil

1 envelope unflavored gelatin

1 cup (one 7½-ounce can) skinless, boneless salmon, packed in water, drained

Juice of 1 lemon

1 green onion

2 tablespoons minced fresh dill or 1 teaspoon dill weed

1 teaspoon Worcestershire sauce

¼ cup nonfat yogurt

½ cup oat bran or rice bran

For garnish: tomato wedges, watercress, fresh dill (optional)

Spread oil in a 1-quart mold.

Sprinkle gelatin over 1½ cups water in a saucepan and let it sit for 1 minute.

In a food processor or blender, purée salmon, lemon juice, onion, dill, Worcestershire, yogurt, and bran until smooth. Blend in yogurt gently by hand.

Gently heat gelatin and water until the liquid is clear and feels hot to the touch; do not let it boil. Add gelatin and water to the salmon mixture and whirl together until smooth; pour into the prepared mold.

Cover and chill for 2 hours or until set. To unmold, dip bottom of mold in a bowl filled with hot water for a few moments; turn mold upside down onto platter. You can decorate or serve with tomato wedges, watercress sprigs, and fresh dill.

SERVING SIZE: ⅛ recipe
CALORIES: 81
FAT: 3.52 grams

CHOLESTEROL: 16.1 milligrams
SODIUM: 13.1 milligrams

■ ■

POTTED MACKEREL

Makes about 2 cups

This recipe provides a delicious way to get healthful fish oils into the diet. It can also be made with canned salmon. Serve with crackers or use it as a sandwich spread. ■

One 15-ounce can mackerel, packed in water

¼ cup Formagg cream-cheese substitute

2 tablespoons ketchup

1 tablespoon sliced jalapeño pepper

2 tablespoons chopped sweet pepper

1 teaspoon chili powder

In a food processor blend all ingredients together until smooth. Place in small ramekins and chill for 2 hours. Serve as an hors d'oeuvre.

SERVING SIZE: 1 tablespoon
CALORIES: 21
FAT: .082 grams

CHOLESTEROL: 5.4 milligrams
SODIUM: 15 milligrams

SOUPS

Curried Pea-Bean and Brussels-Sprouts Soup

One-Cup Navy-Bean and Ham Soup

Bean Vichyssoise

Black Bean Soup

Black Bean and Onion Soup

Garbure

Swedish Yellow Split Pea Soup

Split Pea, Carrot, and Chicken Soup

Split Pea and Potato Soup

Three-Bean Soup with Celery and Lemon

White Bean Minestrone

Hearty Chickpea Soup with Ham

Portuguese Chickpea and Greens Soup

Chicken and Bean Gumbo

Southern Navy-Bean and Sweet-Potato Soup

Pasta e Fagioli

Provençal Bean and Garlic Soup

Indian Lentil Mulligatawny Soup

Lentil, Potato, and Ham Soup

Turkey, Barley, and Lentil Soup

Barley, Ham, and Carrot Soup

Scotch Broth

Mushroom, Barley, and Navy-Bean Soup

Russian Beet and Barley Borscht

Scottish Cock-a-Leekie Soup

Greek-Style Chicken Lemon Soup

Corn and Chili Soup

Cream of Cauliflower Soup

Cream of Spinach Soup

Cream of Cabbage and Apple Soup

Salmon Chowder

CURRIED PEA–BEAN AND BRUSSELS–SPROUTS SOUP

Makes 6 servings

Want a different way to have your vegetables tonight? How about drinking them as soup? The mixture of the beans or peas with the Brussels sprouts is a delight, and the curry adds a real zing. ■

1 **cup dried** pea **or** navy beans, **soaked (see page 89)**

1 **tablespoon curry powder**

1 **teaspoon garlic powder**

One 8-ounce no-salt-added tomato sauce

One 10-ounce package frozen Brussels sprouts, thawed and roughly chopped, or 2 cups fresh, trimmed, and roughly chopped

Pepper

½ cup chopped fresh parsley

1 cup no-fat yogurt

In a medium saucepan, bring soaked beans, curry powder, garlic powder, and 1½ quarts water to a boil. Cut back to a simmer and cook gently, partially covered, for 1 hour and 15 minutes.

Add tomato sauce and Brussels sprouts, and simmer for 15 minutes more. Cool slightly, then purée in a food processor or blender. Reheat gently and season to taste with pepper.

Whisk in parsley and yogurt and heat for 30 seconds, without boiling, or yogurt will curdle. Serve immediately.

SERVING SIZE: 1 cup
CALORIES: 100
FAT: .59 grams

CHOLESTEROL: .67 milligrams
SODIUM: 55.9 milligrams

■■■

ONE-CUP NAVY-BEAN AND HAM SOUP

Makes 8 servings

Measuring the ingredients for this soup is really easy: one cup for everything. Here's where a food processor can really come in handy, reducing the preparation time to just a few minutes. ■

1 cup dried navy beans, soaked (see page 89)

1 cup fine-chopped onions

1 cup fine-chopped carrots

1 cup fine-chopped celery

1 cup fine-chopped white turnips

1 cup fine-diced boiling potatoes

1 bay leaf

1 cup diced lean ham

1 cup shredded lettuce

Pepper

Place beans and 2½ quarts water in a large saucepan and bring to a boil. Cut back to a simmer and cook gently, partially covered, for 1½ hours or until beans are tender.

Add onions, carrots, celery, turnips, potatoes, and bay leaf, and simmer for 20 minutes more. Add ham and lettuce and simmer 5 minutes; season to taste with pepper and serve.

SERVING SIZE: 1 cup
CALORIES: 101
FAT: 1.14 grams

CHOLESTEROL: 5.13 milligrams
SODIUM: 84 milligrams

BEAN VICHYSSOISE

Makes 4 to 6 servings

The leeks, more than anything, give the characteristic flavor to a vichyssoise. Here, beans instead of potatoes give body and creaminess to the soup. Note that this tastes best when served chilled. ■

4 or 5 leeks

2 tablespoons olive oil

2 cups fat-free chicken broth or water

One 16- or 19-ounce can white kidney beans in their liquid

1 cup evaporated skim milk

2 tablespoons minced green onion or fresh chives

Cut 2 inches of dark green off the tops of the leeks and discard. Cut leeks in half vertically and wash them thoroughly. Cut into cross pieces about 1 inch thick.

In a medium saucepan heat oil. When hot, stir in leeks and sauté for 2 to 3 minutes. Add chicken broth or water, cover, and simmer for 10 minutes.

Uncover pot, add beans and their liquid. Cover and simmer gently for 10 minutes more. Purée solids with liquids in a food processor or blender. Return to pot. Stir in milk, heat until simmering, and serve garnished with minced green onions or chives.

SERVING SIZE: 1 cup
CALORIES: 178
FAT: 1.148 grams

CHOLESTEROL: 2.03 milligrams
SODIUM: 225 milligrams

■■

BLACK BEAN SOUP

Makes 6 servings

The first time I tried black beans was in a Cuban restaurant. I was surprised that instead of the refried-beans dish I expected I got a bowl of soup. But I surely wasn't disappointed! Here, too, you can make this a meal in itself by adding some diced low-fat ham. Serve with soft flour tortillas made without lard. ■

1 tablespoon olive oil	1 teaspoon ground cumin
1 carrot, chopped fine	Tabasco
1 small onion, chopped fine	½ red bell pepper, chopped fine
1 stalk celery, chopped fine	1 green onion, sliced thin
Two 1-pound cans black beans	¼ cup chopped cilantro or
2 tablespoons lemon juice	parsley

In a medium saucepan heat olive oil. When hot, sauté the carrot, onion, and celery for about 5 minutes or until soft. If vegetables are sticking or begin to burn add a few tablespoons of water and continue to cook.

Add beans and their liquid, lemon juice, cumin, and 4 cups of water. Simmer for 30 minutes. Season to taste with Tabasco. Serve, garnished with some chopped pepper, green onion, and cilantro.

SERVING SIZE: 1 cup
CALORIES: 138
FAT: 2.34 grams
CHOLESTEROL: 0
SODIUM: 11.5 milligrams

■ ■

BLACK BEAN AND ONION SOUP

Makes 6 servings

If you like onions you're going to love this soup. The red wine gives it a depth of flavor. If you have any left over, fill plastic drinking glasses and freeze for individual servings with sandwiches another time. ■

1½ **pounds (about 6) onions, sliced thin**

1 **tablespoon sugar**

1 **cup red wine**

2 **cups freshly cooked or one 6-ounce can black beans**

Pepper

Spray a 6-quart pot with Pam or Baker's Joy. Add onions and sauté for 5 minutes, stirring frequently. Add sugar and red wine; cover the pot and simmer, very gently, for 20 minutes. Check the onions frequently to make sure they are not burning. If they begin to stick to the bottom of the pot, then simply add some water to loosen them.

Add beans and 4 cups water, then cover, and simmer for 30 minutes longer. Season to taste with pepper.

SERVING SIZE: 1 cup
CALORIES: 113
FAT: .798 grams

CHOLESTEROL: 0
SODIUM: 147 milligrams

■■■■■■■■■■■■■■■■■■■■■■■■■■■■■■■■■■■■■■

GARBURE: A FRENCH SOUP OF BEANS AND CABBAGE

Makes 6 servings

Using the standard cooking methods, this soup must simmer for 1½ hours. With a pressure cooker, however, you can cut the time down to a mere 10 minutes at high pressure and another 10 minutes steeping before you open the pot. This is a real timesaver you'll appreciate having in your cooking repertoire. ■

1 **cup dried** Great Northern white **or** navy beans, **soaked (see page 89)**

1 **pound new potatoes, peeled and cut into ¾-inch cubes**

Two 14½-ounce cans no-salt-added stewed tomatoes

6 **cloves garlic, cut into thin slivers**

3 **cups shredded cabbage**

½ **teaspoon rosemary**

Salt and pepper to taste

Place beans, potatoes, tomatoes, 3 cups water, garlic, cabbage, and rosemary in a medium-large pot. Bring liquid to a boil, cover, and simmer gently for 1½ hours, or until the beans are tender. Make sure the level of the liquid remains constant during the entire time the soup is simmering; replenish evaporated liquid with water.

Season to taste with salt and pepper.

SERVING SIZE: 1 cup
CALORIES: 165
FAT: .35 grams

CHOLESTEROL: 0
SODIUM: 60.9 milligrams

■■

S WEDISH YELLOW SPLIT PEA SOUP

Makes 6 servings

S weden's version of split pea soup has a distinctive taste you'll enjoy. ∎

½ **pound** yellow split peas, **soaked
(see page 89) and drained**

2 **small onions, chopped fine**

½ **teaspoon thyme**

½ **teaspoon powdered marjoram**

2 **whole cloves or** ¼ **teaspoon
ground cloves**

1 **cup diced 96 percent fat-free ham**

½ **cup evaporated skim milk,
optional**

Pepper

Place soaked split peas, onions, herbs, and cloves with 1½ quarts water
in a large saucepan. Bring to a simmer and cook for 1 hour. Remove
whole cloves and purée the mixture in a blender or food processor until
smooth; return soup to the pot. Simmer with the ham for 15 to 30
minutes more. Add milk, if you wish, and season to taste with pepper.

SERVING SIZE: ⅙ recipe
CALORIES: 96
FAT: 1.369 grams

CHOLESTEROL: 7.68 milligrams
SODIUM: 291 milligrams

∎∎∎∎∎∎∎∎∎∎∎∎∎∎∎∎∎∎∎∎∎∎∎∎∎∎∎∎∎∎∎∎∎∎∎∎∎∎∎

SPLIT PEA, CARROT, AND CHICKEN SOUP

Makes 8 servings

Why is it that chicken tastes so tender in soups in restaurants but tough when made at home? Because one tends to overcook the chicken. Like fish, chicken breast meat takes just a few minutes in a bubbling broth such as this one. All you need to complete the meal is some noodles; try the No Yolks brand I discuss on page 59. ■

½ **pound green** split peas

½ **teaspoon each garlic powder and ground cumin**

¼ **teaspoon each powdered ginger and curry powder**

6 **carrots, cut into ½-inch rounds**

1 **pound skinless, boneless chicken breasts, cut into 1-inch cubes**

Pepper

Place peas, garlic, cumin, ginger, and curry powder in a medium saucepan. Add 6 cups water and slowly bring to a boil. Cut back to a simmer, cover, and cook gently for 30 to 45 minutes.

Add carrots and cook for 15 minutes longer; add chicken and cook for 5 minutes or until chicken is just cooked through. Season to taste with pepper.

SERVING SIZE: 1 cup
CALORIES: 132
FAT: .635 grams

CHOLESTEROL: 48.1 milligrams
SODIUM: 48 milligrams

■■■■■■■■■■■■■■■■■■■■■■■■■■■■■■■■■■■■■

SPLIT PEA AND POTATO SOUP

Makes 8 servings

Who'd have thought that this traditional favorite had such cholesterol-lowering potential? Unfortunately most restaurants make it with a lot of pork fat. This healthful version can be made into a main course by adding diced low-fat ham and serving with a chunk of crusty French bread. Because it takes a while to make, and freezes so beautifully, this recipe will give you enough to freeze for another evening. ■

1 **pound (2 cups)** split peas, **picked over and rinsed**

1 **cup minced carrots**

1 **celery stalk, minced**

1 **small onion, minced**

2 **tablespoons tomato paste**

¾ **teaspoon garlic powder**

½ **teaspoon marjoram**

1 **bay leaf**

2 **medium potatoes**

Pepper

¼ **cup minced fresh herbs, such as parsley, dill, and basil, optional**

Place split peas in a 6-quart pot and cover with 2½ quarts water. Slowly bring to a simmer; skim off foam that rises to the top. After all foam has been skimmed off, add carrots, celery, onion, tomato paste, garlic powder, marjoram, and bay leaf. Simmer, partially covered, for 45 minutes.

While soup is simmering, peel potatoes and cut into ½-inch cubes. After 45 minutes, add potatoes to the soup and continue to simmer, uncovered, for 30 minutes more. Remove bay leaf and season with pepper. Stir in optional fresh herbs. Serve as is or, with a wooden spoon, stir the soup quite vigorously to mash some of the peas into a purée and thicken the soup.

SERVING SIZE: 1 cup
CALORIES: 101
FAT: .56 grams

CHOLESTEROL: 0
SODIUM: 12.3 milligrams

THREE-BEAN SOUP
WITH CELERY AND LEMON

Makes 4 to 6 servings

The Greeks like to add a squeeze of lemon to just about everything they eat. The citrus flavor with the beans is unusual and delicious. If you can't find one of the three beans, you can either substitute another type or use 1½ cups each of just two kinds. ■

1 cup soaked or one 8-ounce can white beans, such as Great Northern or white kidney, drained

1 cup soaked or 8-ounce can lima or butter beans, drained

1 cup soaked or one 8-ounce can chickpeas, drained

4 stalks celery, chopped fine

1 small onion, chopped

4 tablespoons lemon juice

Pepper

¼ cup chopped herb such as parsley or dill, for garnish

In a 6-quart saucepan, bring 4 cups water, along with the beans, and chickpeas, celery and onion, to a boil. Cut back to a simmer, and cook gently, partially covered, for 1½ hours if you are using dried and soaked beans or 45 minutes to 1 hour if you are using canned beans.

When beans are soft, purée in a blender or food processor with lemon juice. Season to taste with pepper. Garnish, if you wish, with a fresh herb to liven up the color.

SERVING SIZE: 1 cup
CALORIES: 119
FAT: 1.094 grams

CHOLESTEROL: 0
SODIUM: 126.97 milligrams

WHITE BEAN MINESTRONE

Makes 6 servings

This classic soup is an Italian tradition. Serve with a meal of spaghetti or linguini with marinara or red clam sauce. A glass of Chianti complements this meal perfectly. ■

1 tablespoon olive oil	½ teaspoon dried oregano
1 cup fine-chopped carrots	3 cups shredded white cabbage
½ cup each fine-chopped onions and celery	1 cup peeled and diced boiling potatoes
¾ cup dry navy beans, soaked (see page 89) and drained, or 1½ cups cooked white beans, drained and rinsed	2 cups diced zucchini
	Pepper
	¼ cup minced fresh parsley or basil, optional
2 cups (14½-ounce can) no-salt-added stewed tomatoes	4–6 tablespoons grated Parmesan, optional

In a large saucepan heat olive oil. When hot, sauté the carrots, onions, and celery for 2 minutes, stirring constantly. Add 6 cups water, soaked dry beans, tomatoes, and oregano, and simmer for 1 hour. If you are using canned beans, add them now along with the cabbage and potatoes, and simmer 45 minutes.

Add zucchini and simmer for 5 minutes only. Season to taste with pepper, and add parsley or basil and Parmesan, if you wish.

SERVING SIZE: 1 cup
CALORIES: 146
FAT: 2.65 grams

CHOLESTEROL: 0
SODIUM: 48.3 milligrams

HEARTY CHICKPEA SOUP WITH HAM

Makes 8 servings

This makes a hearty meal-in-a-bowl. As with any of the bean soups you can always substitute another kind of beans for the chickpeas. In fact, you can combine two, three, or more types for interesting flavor and appearance. ∎

1 tablespoon olive oil

1 large onion, chopped fine

2 carrots, chopped fine

1 stalk celery, chopped fine

2 cloves garlic, minced

One 16-ounce can no-salt-added stewed tomatoes

1 pound potatoes, cut into 1-inch cubes

½ teaspoon crumbled dried rosemary

3 cups cooked or canned chickpeas, drained and rinsed

¾ pound 96 percent fat-free smoked ham, cut into ½-inch cubes

Pepper

½ cup chopped fresh parsley or watercress leaves

In a 6- to 8-quart saucepan, heat olive oil. When hot, add onion, carrots, celery, and garlic. Sauté for 2 minutes, stirring continuously.

Add stewed tomatoes and 4 cups water, and bring to a boil. Add potatoes and rosemary. Simmer for 30 minutes. Add chickpeas and ham and simmer 30 minutes more. Season to taste with pepper and garnish with parsley or watercress.

SERVING SIZE: 1 cup
CALORIES: 253
FAT: 5.62 grams

CHOLESTEROL: 12.5 milligrams
SODIUM: 326.55 milligrams

PORTUGUESE CHICKPEA AND GREENS SOUP

Makes 8 servings

The red wine vinegar really perks up the flavor of this soup the way salt would. ∎

2 medium onions, chopped

½ cup each chopped green bell pepper and celery

1½ cups cooked or canned chickpeas

8 ounces turkey breast or lean smoked ham, cut into ½-inch cubes

One 35-ounce can tomatoes, preferably no-salt-added, chopped coarse

1 bay leaf

1 pound fresh kale or ten-ounce package frozen kale, thawed

½ pound boiling potatoes, unpeeled and cut into ½-inch cubes

1 tablespoon red wine vinegar

Pepper

In a large pot, combine onions, pepper, and celery, along with chickpeas, turkey or ham, tomatoes, and 6 cups water. Add the bay leaf and bring to a boil. Cut back heat and simmer, partially covered, for 1 hour.

Meanwhile, remove and discard the tough stems from the kale; wash the leaves and chop them coarse. Add kale and potatoes to the soup and cook for 20 minutes more. Remove the bay leaf. Add the vinegar and plenty of pepper before serving.

SERVING SIZE: 1 cup
CALORIES: 163
FAT: 1.77 grams

CHOLESTEROL: 23.6 milligrams
SODIUM: 165.3 milligrams

■ ■

CHICKEN AND BEAN GUMBO

Makes 8 servings

Depending on what part of the country you're from, you'll think this soup is either fiery or just right. If you have less than adventurous tastebuds, you may want to cut back on the cayenne and *fines herbes*. ■

1 tablespoon olive oil

¾ cup each fine-chopped onion, red bell pepper, and celery

½ cup oat bran

¼ to ½ teaspoon cayenne

½ teaspoon dried *fines herbes*

½ teaspoon garlic powder

6 cups fat-free chicken broth or water

1 bay leaf

4 cups cooked small red or pink beans, or two 1-pound cans, drained and rinsed

1½ pounds boneless, skinless chicken breasts or turkey breast meat, cut into 1-inch cubes

In a 6- to 8-quart saucepan, heat olive oil. When hot, add onion, pepper, and celery and sauté for 5 minutes, stirring continuously.

Add oat bran and flavorings and continue to sauté, stirring continuously, for 3 minutes or until oat bran begins to film the bottom of the pot and turn brown.

Add broth or water and bring to a simmer. Add bay leaf and beans and simmer, uncovered, for 25 minutes. Add cubed chicken and simmer for 5 minutes or until chicken is just cooked through. Remove bay leaf and serve immediately.

SERVING SIZE: 1 cup
CALORIES: 264
FAT: 3.364 grams

CHOLESTEROL: 70.9 milligrams
SODIUM: 155 milligrams

■ ■

SOUTHERN NAVY-BEAN AND SWEET-POTATO SOUP

Makes 4 main-course servings

This is rich enough to serve as a meal, with only one pot to clean up. The sweetness of the beans and yams contrasts well with the smoky ham. Try this with some cornbread on the side. ■

1 tablespoon canola or olive oil	1 pound sweet potatoes, peeled and cut into ¾-inch dice
1 small onion, chopped fine	8 ounces smoked 96 percent fat-free ham, diced
1 celery stalk, chopped fine	⅛ teaspoon mace
1 carrot, chopped fine	¼ teaspoon grated orange zest
2 cups navy beans, **soaked (see page 89), or 1 pound canned, drained and rinsed**	½ cup frozen peas, thawed
	Pepper

In a large saucepan heat the oil. When hot, add onion, celery, and carrot, and stir-fry for 1 minute. Add 1½ quarts water. Bring to a boil and add navy beans. If you are using soaked dried beans, simmer them for 45 minutes before adding remaining ingredients.

After 45 minutes, if you are using canned beans, add the beans. Add sweet potatoes, ham, mace, and orange zest. Simmer, partially covered, for 30 minutes longer, or until the potatoes and beans are tender. Add peas and simmer 1 minute longer, then season with pepper to taste.

SERVING SIZE: 1 cup
CALORIES: 477
FAT: 7.83 grams

CHOLESTEROL: 16.6 milligrams
SODIUM: 718 milligrams

■ ■

PASTA E FAGIOLI

Makes 6 servings

Nutritionists point to this classic dish, lovingly referred to by the old Italians as *"pasta fazool,"* as a wonderful example of how the amino acids of the beans and the pasta combine to form complete protein as high in quality as that from meat. And now we also know that the beans contribute to low cholesterol levels in those who enjoy them regularly. ■

1 tablespoon olive oil

1 small onion, minced

½ carrot, minced

½ celery stalk, minced

1 clove garlic, minced

One 8-ounce can no-salt-added tomato sauce or chopped tomatoes

½ teaspoon dried oregano

2 tablespoons chopped fresh basil, optional

One 16-ounce can cannellini or white kidney beans, drained and rinsed

1 cup dried tubular pasta like elbow macaroni, penne, or rigatoni

Pepper

In a medium saucepan heat olive oil. When hot, add onion, carrot, celery, and garlic. Cover and simmer gently for 5 minutes. Stir once or twice, adding a tablespoonful of water if vegetables are sticking, then cover pot and simmer for 5 minutes more or until vegetables are very tender.

Add tomato sauce and oregano (and basil if you have it) and simmer 5 minutes. Add beans and simmer for 10 minutes. If you wish you can mash half of the beans against the sides of the pot to make the soup thicker. Add dry pasta and simmer for 10 minutes or until pasta is cooked and soup is quite thick. Season with pepper.

SERVING SIZE: 1 cup
CALORIES: 142
FAT: 2.75 grams

CHOLESTEROL: 0
SODIUM: 95 milligrams

PROVENÇAL BEAN AND GARLIC SOUP

Makes 8 servings

Those who love it maintain that there may be too little garlic, enough garlic, but never too much garlic! This dish has enough, not too much, so don't cut back. And, to enjoy to its fullest, use fresh basil leaves if you can get them, or the kind that come in a jar; dried basil just doesn't work here. This soup comes from the countryside of France—and they say French food isn't healthy! ■

1 **tablespoon olive oil**	3 **cups soaked (see page 89) or drained canned** navy, white kidney, **or** pea beans
1 **onion, chopped fine**	
6 **cloves garlic, minced**	4 **tablespoons chopped black olives**
3 **carrots, chopped fine**	
1 **stalk celery, chopped fine**	**One 10-ounce package frozen French-cut green beans, thawed**
1 **can (about 14½ or 16 ounces) no-salt-added stewed tomatoes, chopped**	2 **tablespoons minced fresh or jarred basil leaves, optional**
½ **teaspoon dried thyme**	**Pepper**

In a 6-quart saucepan heat olive oil, add onion, garlic, carrots, and celery, and sauté for 3 minutes, or until somewhat tender. Add 2 quarts water, tomatoes, thyme, and white beans.

Bring liquid to a boil, cut back to a simmer, and cook over low heat, partially covered, for 2 hours if you are using soaked dried beans or 30 minutes if you are using canned beans.

Add black olives and green beans, and basil if desired, and simmer 30 minutes more. Season to taste with pepper and serve.

SERVING SIZE: 1 cup
CALORIES: 154
FAT: 3.63 grams

CHOLESTEROL: 0
SODIUM: 167.83 milligrams

■ ■

INDIAN LENTIL MULLIGATAWNY SOUP

Makes 6 servings

If you've tried traditional mulligatawny soup at Indian restaurants you'll be delighted to have this dish frequently at home. Why not make a double batch and freeze half for another time? ∎

1 tablespoon canola oil	1 tablespoon curry powder
1 carrot, chopped fine	1 cup dry lentils
1 onion, chopped fine	One 8-ounce can no-salt-added tomatoes
1 stalk celery, chopped fine	
1 red bell pepper, chopped fine	Pepper

In a medium saucepan heat oil. When hot, sauté carrot, onion, celery, and red bell pepper for 2 to 3 minutes, stirring continuously.

Stir curry powder into the vegetables and sauté for 30 seconds. Add lentils, tomatoes, and 1 quart water. Bring to a boil, cut back to a simmer, and cook gently, partially covered, for 45 minutes or until lentils are very soft.

Serve as is, seasoned with pepper, or purée first and then serve.

SERVING SIZE: 1 cup
CALORIES: 115
FAT: 2.52 grams

CHOLESTEROL: 0
SODIUM: 35.8 milligrams

■ ■

LENTIL, POTATO, AND HAM SOUP

Makes 6 servings

Another example of a meal-in-a-bowl recipe that takes very little time and makes very little mess. ∎

1 **cup dried** brown lentils

1 **small onion, chopped fine**

1 **pound new potatoes, peeled and cut into ½-inch cubes**

4 **green onions, sliced thin**

1 **cup diced 96 percent fat-free ham**

1 **tablespoon white wine vinegar or lemon juice**

Pepper

In a medium saucepan, bring 6 cups water, lentils, onion, and potatoes to a boil. Cut back to a simmer and cook gently, covered, for 25 minutes.

Add green onions and ham and simmer 5 minutes more. Add vinegar and season to taste with pepper.

SERVING SIZE: 1 cup
CALORIES: 173
FAT: 1.26 grams

CHOLESTEROL: 6.83 milligrams
SODIUM: 289 milligrams

■ ■

TURKEY, BARLEY, AND LENTIL SOUP

Makes 8 servings

This is a very hearty thick soup; one needs only a salad to round out the meal. Add some snipped fresh parsley at the end to provide color. Make a double batch to freeze for another time. ■

1 **cup** brown lentils

1 **cup** pearled barley

4 **parsnips or carrots, peeled and sliced thin**

2 **teaspoons minced fresh garlic or 1 teaspoon garlic powder**

1½ **teaspoons curry powder**

2 **tablespoons tomato paste**

1 **pound turkey breast meat, cut into 1-inch cubes**

Pepper

1 **cup chopped fresh parsley or fresh spinach leaves**

½ **cup nonfat yogurt or Formagg sour-cream substitute, optional**

In a 4- to 6-quart pot bring 3 quarts water to a boil, along with lentils, barley, parsnips, garlic, curry powder, and tomato paste. Cut back to a simmer and cook gently, uncovered, for 45 minutes. If soup is too thick at that point add a cup or so water and simmer 5 minutes more.

Stir in cubed turkey and simmer 5 minutes more, or just enough to cook the turkey without toughening it. Season to taste with pepper, and stir in parsley. If you wish, put a dollop of yogurt or sour cream on each portion before serving.

SERVING SIZE: 1 cup
CALORIES: 248
FAT: .83 grams

CHOLESTEROL: 47.5 milligrams
SODIUM: 74.7 milligrams

BARLEY, HAM, AND CARROT SOUP

Makes 6 to 8 servings

I don't understand when people tell me they have no time to cook meals from scratch. This recipe is an excellent example of just how easy it can be to make a satisfying meal, with little time spent. Start the meal when you get home from work, then spend the next 45 minutes smelling the aromas while you relax from the day's labors. That's all there is to it. Serve with a crusty chunk of bread and, if you like, a glass of white wine. ■

8 cups fat-free chicken broth or water

1 cup barley, pearled or whole

1 pound 96 percent fat-free ham, cut into ½-inch cubes

6 carrots, cut into ½-inch rounds

1 onion, chopped fine

1 clove garlic, minced

Pepper

3 quarts water

In a large saucepan bring all ingredients slowly to a boil. With a skimmer or slotted spoon, skim off any grayish matter that rises to the top. Cover and simmer gently for 45 minutes.

SERVING SIZE: 1 cup
CALORIES: 192
FAT: 3.15 grams

CHOLESTEROL: 16.6 milligrams
SODIUM: 663 milligrams

■ ■

SCOTCH BROTH

Makes 8 servings

This soup can be served before the main course or it can be the main course. Either way, it's hearty and comforting. ■

½ pound or 4 cups shredded white cabbage

2 white turnips, peeled and cut into 1-inch dice

2 carrots, peeled and cut into 1-inch rounds

1 tablespoon sugar

4 cloves garlic, minced

¾ cup pearled barley

2 quarts fat-free chicken broth or water

One 10-ounce package frozen peas, thawed

1 pound turkey breast, cut into 1-inch cubes

Pepper

½ cup minced fresh herb, such as parsley or dill

In a large saucepan, place the cabbage, turnips, carrots, sugar, garlic, barley, and broth. Bring to a boil. Cut back to a simmer, cover, and cook gently for 1½ hours, adding water as liquid evaporates.

Add peas and turkey and simmer for 10 minutes more. Season to taste with pepper and fresh herb.

SERVING SIZE: 1 cup
CALORIES: 199
FAT: .86 grams

CHOLESTEROL: 47.3 milligrams
SODIUM: 95 milligrams

■■

MUSHROOM, BARLEY, AND NAVY-BEAN SOUP

Makes 8 servings

This is a terrific soup recipe just as is. But you can make it into a main course by adding some shredded chicken breast meat and vegetables. ∎

1 **cup dry** navy **or** pea beans, **soaked (see page 89), or 2 cups canned beans, drained and rinsed**

½ **cup** pearled barley

1 **pound mushrooms, sliced thin**

1 **teaspoon garlic powder**

One 8-ounce can no-salt-added tomato sauce

2 **quarts fat-free chicken broth or water**

Tabasco

Place all ingredients, except Tabasco, in a large, 8-quart pot. Slowly bring to a boil, and simmer, covered, for 2 hours, if you are using soaked dried beans, or for 1 hour if you are using canned beans. If the level of liquid goes down, replace it with water or the soup will end up being too thick. Season to taste with Tabasco. This soup keeps on improving with each reheating.

SERVING SIZE: 1 cup
CALORIES: 126
FAT: .62 grams

CHOLESTEROL: 0
SODIUM: 13.4 milligrams

Russian beet and barley borscht

Makes 6 to 8 servings

Regardless of what you think about *glasnost,* you're going to think this soup is the right step in culinary diplomacy. Just tasting this evokes in the imagination a picture of Russians gathered round the table on a cold winter's night enjoying their borscht with a chunk of hearty bread. The vodka is optional. ∎

Two 14- to 16-ounce cans
no-salt-added stewed tomatoes

2 stalks celery, chopped fine

1 pound shredded cabbage
(6 cups)

1 onion, chopped fine

1 clove garlic, minced

One 16-ounce can sliced beets

¼ cup red wine vinegar

1 tablespoon sugar

1 cup pearled barley

1 pound boneless chicken or turkey
breast or sliced turkey sausage,
diced fine

¼ cup minced fresh parsley or dill

Pepper

In a large pot, bring tomatoes, celery, cabbage, onion, garlic, beets with their juice, vinegar, sugar, and 1 quart water to a simmer. Cover and cook gently for 30 minutes.

Add barley and simmer, covered, for 30 minutes more. Add chicken or turkey and parsley or dill, and simmer 5 minutes. Season to taste with pepper.

SERVING SIZE: 1 cup
CALORIES: 252
FAT: .864 grams

CHOLESTEROL: 47.3
SODIUM: 113 milligrams

■■

SCOTTISH COCK-A-LEEKIE SOUP

Makes 4 servings

Q. What does a Scotsman call soup that combines leeks with chicken broth?
A. Cock-a-leekie soup! Get it?

Another comfort soup, this has a very soothing quality to it. ∎

1 **pound (about 4 medium) fresh leeks or 1 pound green onions**	½ **cup** oat bran
1 **quart fat-free chicken broth or water**	6 **pitted prunes, cut in half**
	1 **cup evaporated skim milk**
Pinch allspice	1 **tablespoon chopped parsley**

Cut about 2 inches off the top of the dark green part of the leeks and discard. Cut leeks in half vertically and rinse them well under cold water to rid them of sand. Chop into 1-inch pieces.

Place leeks, chicken broth or water, allspice, oat bran and prunes in a medium saucepan and slowly bring to a simmer. Simmer, covered, for 30 minutes or until leeks are tender. Stir the bottom of the pot every now and then to make sure the oat bran is not sticking and burning.

Add milk and parsley and serve.

SERVING SIZE: 1 cup
CALORIES: 738
FAT: 2.65 grams

CHOLESTEROL: 2.55 milligrams
SODIUM: 106 milligrams

■ ■

GREEK-STYLE CHICKEN LEMON SOUP

Makes 8 servings

Avgolemono soup, the classic chicken rice soup of Greece, gets its thick creaminess from egg yolks. Thanks to Vita Fiber you can have the same rich consistency without the cholesterol, and get a soluble fiber boost to boot. To get all the fat out of the chicken broth, store the cans in your refrigerator overnight and scoop out the congealed fat when you open the can. In fact, I always keep two or three cans of soup in the refrigerator so I can have them virtually fat-free whenever I want them. ■

1 quart fat-free chicken broth	8 ounces chicken breast, cut into thin strips
¼ cup long-grain rice	¼ cup chopped fresh parsley
½ cup Vita Fiber	2 green onions, sliced thin
4 tablespoons lemon juice	Pepper

Place broth, 1 quart water, rice, Vita Fiber, and lemon juice in a medium-large pot. Bring to a boil and simmer 15 minutes or until rice is tender.

Stir soup well with a whisk, and add the chicken, parsley, and onions. Season to taste with pepper and simmer for 5 minutes more, or until the chicken is just tender.

SERVING SIZE: 1 cup
CALORIES: 74
FAT: 1.261 grams

CHOLESTEROL: 24.6 milligrams
SODIUM: 21.8 milligrams

■ ■

CORN AND CHILI SOUP

Makes 10 servings

Did you know that chilies are an excellent source of vitamin C? In fact they're the main source of that vitamin for many Hispanics. Count on the apple fiber to thicken the soup and to supply some soluble fiber. ■

2 tablespoons canola or olive oil

1 onion, chopped fine

2 stalks celery, chopped fine

½ cup apple fiber

Four 8-ounce cans tomato sauce

1 quart fat-free chicken broth or water

Two 4-ounce cans chopped green chilies

¼ teaspoon each cumin and chili powders

One 10-ounce package frozen corn kernels

In a medium saucepan heat oil. When hot, add onion and celery and sauté for 5 minutes, stirring frequently. Add apple fiber, tomato sauce, chicken broth or water, chilies, cumin, chili powder and corn. Bring to a simmer and cook gently for 10 minutes.

SERVING SIZE: 1 cup
CALORIES: 100
FAT: 2.82 grams

CHOLESTEROL: 0
SODIUM: 36.4 milligrams

CREAM OF CAULIFLOWER SOUP

Makes 4 to 6 servings

Combine the red of the tomato with the white of the cauliflower and you have a lovely pink soup, thickened by Vita Fiber and flavored with garlic. The recipe calls for garlic powder, but it tastes even better if you use two large garlic cloves minced fine. ∎

4 cups cauliflower florets, frozen or fresh	1 teaspoon garlic powder
½ cup Vita Fiber rice bran	1 cup evaporated skim milk
2 tablespoons tomato paste or no-salt-added tomato sauce	Pepper
	Minced fresh parsley for garnish, optional

In a medium saucepan, cover cauliflower with 3 cups water and bring to a boil. Simmer, covered, for 10 to 20 minutes or until cauliflower is tender.

Drain cauliflower florets, reserving cooking liquid. Purée the cauliflower in a blender or food processor with Vita Fiber, tomato paste, garlic powder, and milk. When nice and smooth, thin out with the reserved cooking liquid.

Return soup to the heat and simmer for 5 minutes or until Vita Fiber has completely dissolved. Season with pepper to taste and serve immediately, garnished, if you wish, with parsley.

SERVING SIZE: 1 cup
CALORIES: 59
FAT: .63 grams

CHOLESTEROL: 1.7 milligrams
SODIUM: 60.4 milligrams

■■

CREAM OF SPINACH SOUP

Makes 4 servings

This soup has an elegant, gentle flavor, and the rice bran comes through to provide creamy texture. Low in fat, it is a nice alternative to salad. ∎

1 tablespoon vegetable oil	1 garlic clove, minced
1 small onion, minced	⅛ teaspoon nutmeg
¼ cup rice bran	½ cup evaporated skim milk
One 10-ounce package frozen chopped spinach, thawed, or 1 pound fresh spinach, washed, cooked, and chopped	Pepper

In a medium saucepan, heat vegetable oil. When hot, add onion and stir-fry for 30 seconds. Add ¼ cup water, cover, and simmer gently for 4 minutes, stirring every now and then to make sure onions do not burn.

Uncover pot, add rice bran, and stir for 30 seconds. Add spinach, garlic, and 4 cups water. Slowly bring to a boil; cut back to a simmer. Add nutmeg and cook gently, partially covered, for 25 minutes. Cool for 5 minutes, then purée in a blender or food processor with milk. Season with pepper to taste and serve.

SERVING SIZE: 1 cup
CALORIES: 154
FAT: 4.39 grams

CHOLESTEROL: .5 milligrams
SODIUM: 112 milligrams

CREAM OF CABBAGE AND APPLE SOUP

Makes 6 servings

The combination of cabbage and apple along with the onion yields a flavor that's distinct from any of the three. The rice bran gives it a wonderful, creamy texture. It's also simple to prepare. ■

1 **pound white cabbage, shredded (6 cups)**

1 **onion, sliced thin**

1 **apple, peeled, cored, and chopped**

½ cup Vita Fiber, **pulverized, or** ¼ cup rice bran

Pepper

Simmer cabbage, onion, and apple in 6 cups water, over low heat, covered, for 1 hour. Cool for 10 minutes.

Pour into blender or food processor, add Vita Fiber, and blend for 1 minute or until smooth. Reheat and season to taste with pepper.

SERVING SIZE: 1 cup
CALORIES: 42.6
FAT: .724 grams

CHOLESTEROL: 0
SODIUM: 14.8 milligrams

Salmon Chowder

Makes 6 to 8 servings

Like most people my age, I grew up thinking that fish was something that came only one way: fried and overdone. How wrong I was! Here's a nice way to get salmon, rich in protective oils, into the diet right along with the soluble fiber of beans. ■

1 tablespoon olive oil	1 bay leaf
1 onion, chopped fine	2 cups cooked or drained canned beans or chickpeas
1 rib celery, chopped fine	
2 carrots, chopped fine	One 10-ounce package frozen corn kernels
2 cloves garlic, minced	4 tablespoons parsley
4 cups tomato juice	1 pound boneless salmon, fresh or canned, cut into 1-inch chunks
1 cup clam juice	
1 cup white wine	Pepper

In a medium-large saucepan heat olive oil. When hot, sauté onion, celery, carrots, and garlic for 5 minutes. Add tomato juice, clam juice, white wine, and bay leaf. Cover and simmer for 10 minutes.

Add beans, corn, parsley and salmon, and simmer for 5 minutes, or until salmon is just cooked through. Season to taste with pepper.

SERVING SIZE: 1 cup
CALORIES: 290
FAT: 7.22 grams

CHOLESTEROL: 27.2 milligrams
SODIUM: 368 milligrams

■■■

SALADS

Japanese Adzuki Salad

Lentil and Cauliflower Salad

Italian Lentil and Parsley Salad

Barley Salad and Cucumbers

Carrot and Barley Salad

Three-Bean Salad

Black Bean, Rice, and Green Pea Salad

Chickpea, Corn, and Pimiento Salad

Chickpea and Four-Vegetable Salad

Black and White Bean Salad with Roasted Peppers

Bean Waldorf Salad

Mackerel and Corn Salad

Mackerel and Bean Niçoise Salad

Pickled Sardine and Beet Salad

Spicy Rice, Ham, and Green Bean Salad

Rice Tabbouleh with Mint and Plum Tomatoes

Chickpea Russian Dressing

Creamy Cucumber Dressing

JAPANESE ADZUKI SALAD

Makes 6 to 8 appetizer portions

If you have never tried adzuki beans, you're in for a treat. This salad makes a terrific appetizer. How about serving it with teriyaki chicken or salmon? ∎

One 24-ounce jar adzuki beans, drained and rinsed, or 3 cups freshly cooked adzuki beans

2   teaspoons sesame oil

2   teaspoons canola oil

3   tablespoons rice or white wine vinegar

1   tablespoon soy sauce

⅛ teaspoon each grated lemon zest and powdered ginger

¼ teaspoon sugar

2   green onions, sliced thin

1   tablespoon Japanese sesame seeds, optional

Pepper to taste

Boston lettuce

Place beans in a mixing bowl.

In another small mixing bowl, combine all remaining ingredients except lettuce and mix them well. Toss beans with this dressing, then cover the bowl and marinate for 2 hours at least or, preferably, overnight.

Serve the beans on Boston lettuce leaves.

SERVING SIZE: ⅛ recipe
CALORIES: 161
FAT: 2.675 grams

CHOLESTEROL: 0
SODIUM: 129 milligrams

LENTIL AND CAULIFLOWER SALAD

Makes 6 servings

Here's just the dish to serve with chilled poached salmon—on a warm summer evening, perhaps, along with a glass of cold white wine. ∎

1 **cup dried** lentils

1 **head cauliflower, cut into florets**

4 **tablespoons lime or lemon juice**

2 **tablespoons olive oil**

½ **cup chopped parsley**

4 **green onions, sliced thin**

Pepper

Cook lentils in water to cover for 25 minutes or until just tender. Drain and cool under cold water; drain again.

Cook cauliflower for 5 minutes or until tender but still crisp. Break florets into even smaller pieces and combine them with lentils in a mixing bowl.

Combine lime or lemon juice, oil, parsley, and onions. Season to taste with pepper and combine with lentils and cauliflower. Cover and chill for 2 hours before serving.

SERVING SIZE: ⅙ recipe
CALORIES: 77.2
FAT: 4.631 grams

CHOLESTEROL: 0
SODIUM: 11.4 milligrams

ITALIAN LENTIL AND PARSLEY SALAD

Makes 6 servings

Here's a tasty way to add soluble fiber to the diet and have an alternative to the usual dinner salad at the same time. I like having this salad as an accompaniment to spaghetti and marinara sauce or red clam sauce. ■

1½ **cups dry** lentils	½ **teaspoon dried oregano**
3 **tomatoes**	½ **cup minced fresh parsley or**
2 **tablespoons olive oil**	**basil**
1 **teaspoon Dijon-style mustard**	**Pepper**
2 **tablespoons red wine vinegar**	**Boston lettuce leaves**

Cook lentils in 3 cups water, covered, for 20 minutes or until just cooked through; take care not to overcook or they will become mushy. Drain and cool under cold water.

Cut tomatoes in half and with a small spoon scoop out the seeds and discard. Dice remaining tomatoes.

Make a dressing of olive oil, mustard, vinegar, oregano, and parsley, and season to taste with pepper.

In a large mixing bowl toss lentils, tomatoes, and dressing, and chill half an hour before serving on lettuce leaves.

SERVING SIZE: ⅙ recipe
CALORIES: 163
FAT: 4.74 grams

CHOLESTEROL: 0
SODIUM: 50.1 milligrams

■ ■

BARLEY SALAD AND CUCUMBERS

Makes 6 servings

The very first time I had a cucumber salad as a child, it was served with fried chicken, and to this day I associate the two. But today I make an oven-fried chicken instead to cut down on fat, and I add barley to round out the salad. ■

2 cups cooked pearled barley	3 tablespoons white wine vinegar
3 medium cucumbers, peeled and halved	2 tablespoons minced fresh dill or 1 teaspoon dried dillweed
2 tablespoons olive oil	Freshly ground pepper

Place barley in a medium mixing bowl. With a small spoon, scrape out cucumber seeds and discard them. Chop cucumbers into dice and add to barley.

Mix together olive oil, vinegar, and dill. Add this to barley and cucumbers and toss well; season with pepper. Cover with plastic wrap and refrigerate for 1 hour, or overnight if you wish.

SERVING SIZE: ⅙ recipe
CALORIES: 294
FAT: 5.366 grams

CHOLESTEROL: 0
SODIUM: 5.598 milligrams

■■■■■■■■■■■■■■■■■■■■■■■■■■■■■■■■■■■

CARROT AND BARLEY SALAD

Makes 6 servings

A nice alternative to lettuce salads, this dish supplies soluble fiber by way of both the barley and carrots. The soft cooked barley and the crunchy uncooked vegetables provide a nice contrast I think you'll enjoy. ■

1 **cup** pearled barley

2 **carrots, peeled and grated**

1 **celery stalk, grated**

2 **radishes, sliced thin**

2 **green onions, sliced fine**

1 **tablespoon olive oil**

3 **tablespoons lemon juice**

Pepper

Shredded lettuce or cabbage

Cook barley in 4 cups water, partially covered, for 25 minutes, or until just tender. Drain and cool to room temperature. Blend with carrots, celery, radishes, onions, olive oil, and lemon juice; season to taste with pepper. Serve on shredded lettuce or cabbage.

SERVING SIZE: ⅙ recipe
CALORIES: 156
FAT: 2.907 grams

CHOLESTEROL: 0
SODIUM: 19.7 milligrams

■■■■■■■■■■■■■■■■■■■■■■■■■■■■■■■■■■■■■■■

THREE-BEAN SALAD

Makes 6 to 8 servings

What would a buffet be without three-bean salad? And no cookbook focusing on the foods that lower cholesterol would be complete without a good recipe for this soluble-fiber-packed dish. Not planning a buffet? Keep a container filled with the salad to enjoy with your sandwich at lunch. ■

2 cups cooked **red** kidney **or** pink beans **or canned beans, drained and rinsed**

2 cups cooked **white** navy, pea, **or** kidney beans **or canned beans, drained and rinsed**

One **10-ounce package thawed frozen French-cut green beans**

One **3½-ounce jar cocktail onions, chopped**

4 tablespoons **chopped sour pickles**

1 tablespoon + 1 teaspoon olive oil

2 teaspoons **prepared Dijon-style mustard**

¼ **cup red wine vinegar**

½ teaspoon sugar

Pepper

Place red, white, and green beans in a mixing bowl. Stir in the cocktail onions and pickles.

In another small mixing bowl make a dressing out of olive oil, mustard, vinegar, sugar, and pepper. Toss the dressing with beans. Cover and chill for 1 hour before serving to allow the flavors to meld and mellow.

SERVING SIZE: ⅛ recipe
CALORIES: 152
FAT: 2.912 grams

CHOLESTEROL: 0
SODIUM: 159.8 milligrams

■■■

BLACK BEAN, RICE, AND GREEN PEA SALAD

Makes 6 servings

This salad creates a rainbow of colors. Serve it on crisp lettuce leaves. ∎

2 cups cooked long-grain rice

One 10-ounce package frozen petite peas, thawed

2 cups freshly cooked or drained and rinsed canned black beans

1 tablespoon olive oil

¼ cup chopped pimientos

1 teaspoon Dijon-style mustard

2 tablespoons ketchup

¼ cup red wine vinegar

Pepper

Lettuce leaves

Place rice, peas, and black beans in a mixing bowl.

In a blender or food processor combine olive oil, pimientos, mustard, ketchup, and vinegar, and season to taste with pepper. Toss this dressing with the rice and beans. Chill, covered, for 2 hours. Serve on lettuce leaves.

SERVING SIZE: ⅙ recipe
CALORIES: 192
FAT: 3.545 grams

CHOLESTEROL: O
SODIUM: 184.62 milligrams

CHICKPEA, CORN, AND PIMIENTO SALAD

Makes 6 servings

An attractive and colorful dish, this has a kind of Tex-Mex taste and can be made as spicy as you like with Tabasco. Along with a turkey sandwich it makes a nice summer's evening meal. ■

3 cups cooked or canned chickpeas, drained and rinsed in water

One 10-ounce package frozen corn kernels, thawed

One 4-ounce jar pimiento pieces, drained

1 cup fresh parsley leaves

2 tablespoons olive oil

¼ cup wine vinegar

Drops of Tabasco, optional

Lettuce leaves

In a mixing bowl, toss together chickpeas and corn. In a blender or food processor blend pimiento, parsley, oil, vinegar, and Tabasco until smooth. Toss with chickpeas and corn. Let stand for 1 hour if you wish to let chickpeas absorb the flavors of the dressing. Serve on lettuce leaves.

SERVING SIZE: ⅙ recipe
CALORIES: 272
FAT: 7.16 grams

CHOLESTEROL: 0
SODIUM: 1604 milligrams

CHICKPEA AND FOUR-VEGETABLE SALAD

Makes 4 servings

It takes so little time, yet makes such a difference, to prepare a really worthwhile salad. When salad consists of nothing but lettuce and a chunk of tomato or two with bottled dressing, I can understand why people get sick of it. Here's an example of how a variety of vegetables can be combined to make a special salad. But don't stop here—create your own combinations. ■

2 tomatoes, cut in half horizontally

2 carrots, chopped fine

2 stalks celery, chopped fine

1 green pepper, seeds and membranes removed, chopped fine

2 cups cooked or drained and rinsed canned chickpeas

1 tablespoon olive oil

4 tablespoons lemon or lime juice

1 teaspoon prepared Dijon-style mustard

1 teaspoon dried mint

½ teaspoon honey

Pepper

Lettuce greens, such as Boston, romaine, or watercress

With a spoon, remove seeds from each of the tomato halves, then cut them into small dice.

In a large mixing bowl combine the tomatoes with other vegetables and chickpeas.

In a small bowl, combine oil, lemon juice, mustard, mint, and honey to make a dressing, and pour over chickpeas and vegetables. Toss well and season to taste with pepper. Cover and chill 1 hour before serving on greens.

SERVING SIZE: ¼ recipe

CALORIES: 199

FAT: 6.01 grams

CHOLESTEROL: 0

SODIUM: 198.85 milligrams

BLACK AND WHITE BEAN SALAD
WITH ROASTED PEPPERS

Makes 6 servings

Marinating the beans gives them a full flavor, but if you don't have the time you can skip that step. You can also mix the two beans together rather than keeping them separate, but they're more attractive in distinct mounds on the platter. ■

1½ **cups cooked** black beans **or one 12-ounce can**

1½ **cups cooked** white beans **or one 12-ounce can**

Two 7-ounce jars roasted peppers, cut into ½-inch slices

½ **cup thin-sliced green onions**

1 **clove garlic or** ¼ **teaspoon garlic powder**

6 **tablespoons white wine vinegar**

1 **teaspoon paprika**

1 **teaspoon chili powder**

1 **tablespoon vegetable oil**

If you are using canned beans, drain and rinse them in cold water. Place black and white beans in separate bowls.

In a blender or food processor, combine peppers, green onions, garlic, vinegar, paprika, chili powder, and oil. Purée the sauce until smooth. Toss each batch of beans with ½ cup of the sauce. Cover and marinate at room temperature for at least 30 minutes or up to 2 hours.

To serve, mound each batch of beans, separately, on the sides of a platter, leaving some room in the middle into which you can pour the remaining sauce.

SERVING SIZE: ⅙ recipe
CALORIES: 95.6
FAT: 2.942 grams

CHOLESTEROL: 0
SODIUM: 172 milligrams

■ ▫ ■

BEAN WALDORF SALAD

Makes 4 to 6 servings

Why not stage a revival of this wonderful classic in your house, updated with the soluble fiber of chickpeas or beans? ∎

2 cups cooked or drained and rinsed canned chickpeas or beans, such as white, kidney, navy, or pea

2 Red Delicious apples, cored, unpeeled, and diced into ½-inch cubes

1 cup diced celery

¼ cup chopped walnuts

¼ cup reduced-calorie mayonnaise

2 tablespoons lemon juice

Greens such as Boston or romaine

Place all ingredients, except greens, in a mixing bowl and toss well. Cover and chill for 2 hours before serving on greens.

SERVING SIZE: ⅙ recipe
CALORIES: 159
FAT: 4.9 grams

CHOLESTEROL: 1.33 milligrams
SODIUM: 55.8 milligrams

■■■■■■■■■■■■■■■■■■■■■■■■■■■■■■■■■■■■■■

MACKEREL AND CORN SALAD

Makes 6 main-course servings

Decisions, decisions. Should you stick with the mackerel in this recipe or substitute canned salmon? Should you eat the salad on lettuce, or in a sandwich? Whatever your decisions, the recipe is delicious and you'll really enjoy it. ∎

Two 15-ounce cans mackerel packed in water

One 10-ounce package frozen corn kernels, thawed

2 tablespoons minced pickled jalapeño peppers

½ cup chopped sweet red peppers

⅓ cup reduced-calorie mayonnaise

4 tablespoons lime or lemon juice

¼ cup minced fresh cilantro or parsley

Shredded iceberg lettuce

Tomato quarters

In a mixing bowl, toss together mackerel, corn, jalapeños, and sweet peppers. In another small bowl, mix mayonnaise with lime juice and cilantro. Add this to the mackerel and mix well.

Chill, covered, for 2 hours. Serve on iceberg lettuce and garnish with tomato quarters.

SERVING SIZE: ⅙ recipe
CALORIES: 283
FAT: 12 grams

CHOLESTEROL: 61 milligrams
SODIUM: 154 milligrams

Mackerel
AND BEAN NIÇOISE SALAD

Makes 6 to 8 servings

Summertime and the livin' is easy—just the time for a light main-course salad like this one. You can substitute canned salmon for the mackerel. I like this with sourdough bread on the side, and a glass of chardonnay wine to toast the sunset. It also makes a nice appetizer. ∎

One 15-ounce can mackerel **packed in water**

One 16-ounce can white **or** pink beans, **drained and rinsed**

1½ cups green beans, freshly cooked or frozen and thawed

2 tomatoes, cut into 1-inch dice

1 cucumber, peeled and cut into 1-inch dice

2 tablespoons capers

¼ teaspoon garlic powder

½ teaspoon Dijon-style mustard

2 tablespoons olive oil

¼ cup lemon juice

Pepper

Salad greens

In a bowl, combine mackerel, beans, green beans, tomatoes, and cucumbers, and toss.

In a small bowl, combine capers, garlic powder, mustard, olive oil, and lemon juice to make a dressing and mix well; season to taste with pepper. Stir the dressing into the mackerel-and-bean mixture and toss well. Cover and chill for 1 to 2 hours before serving. Serve on salad greens.

SERVING SIZE: ⅛ recipe
CALORIES: 219
FAT: 6.965 grams

CHOLESTEROL: 21.2 milligrams
SODIUM: 284 milligrams

■ ■

PICKLED SARDINE AND BEET SALAD

Makes 4 to 6 servings

This certainly isn't a dish for everyone, but if you happen to be a sardine lover, you'll find it a great lunch along with a piece of crusty sourdough bread. If you don't like sardines, try the same recipe with canned salmon. Both fish supply the EPA fish oils that protect against heart disease. ∎

Four 3¾-ounce cans skinless, boneless sardines, packed in water, drained

One 16-ounce can sliced beets, drained

24 cocktail onions, halved

¼ cup fine-chopped sour pickles

2 teaspoons prepared mustard

2 tablespoons low-fat mayonnaise or nonfat yogurt

Lettuce leaves

2 tablespoons minced dill or parsley, optional

Empty sardines into a mixing bowl and break up.

Cut beets into small cubes and add to sardines. Add cocktail onions and pickles.

In a small bowl make a dressing of the mustard and mayonnaise; if too thick, thin with some juice from the cocktail onions or pickles. Toss with sardines and beets; chill for 1 hour. Serve on lettuce leaves and garnish, if you wish, with minced herbs.

SERVING SIZE: ⅙ recipe
CALORIES: 122
FAT: 2.23 grams

CHOLESTEROL: 7.87 milligrams
SODIUM: 586 milligrams

■ ■

SPICY RICE, HAM, AND GREEN BEAN SALAD

Makes 6 servings

I like to prepare salads such as this one early in the morning before starting the day's work, so it's ready later in the day for lunch. You can add the Vita Fiber rice bran during preparation and it will sort of "disappear" into the salad, or you can sprinkle it on at the last minute to give the salad a little crunchiness. ■

2 cups cooked long-grain rice

One 10-ounce package frozen French-cut green beans, thawed, or 2 cups freshly cooked green beans, cut into 2-inch lengths

8 ounces or 1 cup diced smoked 96 percent fat-free ham

⅓ cup chili sauce

¼ cup red wine vinegar

Pepper

½ cup Vita Fiber

Lettuce leaves

Place rice in a mixing bowl and toss with green beans and ham.

In a blender or food processor combine chili sauce and vinegar, and season to taste with pepper. Toss this dressing with the rice. Chill, covered, for 2 hours.

Right before serving, in order not to lose its special crunch, toss the salad with Vita Fiber and serve on lettuce leaves.

SERVING SIZE: ⅙ recipe
CALORIES: 143
FAT: 1.3 grams

CHOLESTEROL: 6.83 milligrams
SODIUM: 436 milligrams

■ ■

RICE TABBOULEH
WITH MINT AND PLUM TOMATOES

Makes 6 servings

One taste of this slightly modified Middle Eastern dish and you can almost see the minarets on the skyline. We've replaced the usual bulgar wheat with rice, but you can switch back to make the dish more authentic if you wish. ■

2 cups cooked long-grain rice

2 cups finely chopped fresh parsley

¼ cup rice bran or pulverized Vita Fiber

½ cup thin-sliced scallions

½ cup chopped fresh mint or 2 tablespoons dried mint

½ teaspoon grated lemon zest

2 tablespoons olive oil

¼ cup lemon juice

Pepper to taste

2 plum tomatoes, cut into ½-inch dice

Lettuce leaves

Place rice in a mixing bowl.

In a blender or food processor combine all remaining ingredients, except plum tomatoes and lettuce. Blend until smooth; if too thick, thin with water. Toss this dressing with the rice. Chill, covered, for 2 hours. Just before serving, stir in the tomatoes and serve on lettuce leaves.

SERVING SIZE: ⅙ recipe
CALORIES: 125
FAT: 5.39 grams

CHOLESTEROL: 0
SODIUM: 12.6 milligrams

■■■

CHICKPEA RUSSIAN DRESSING

Makes about 2 cups

Now even your salad dressing can be a source of soluble fiber. Enjoy with cold meats and chilled poached salmon in addition to salads. The chickpeas add extra body to the dressing when blended smooth. ■

1 **cup canned or freshly cooked** chickpeas

⅓ **cup reduced-calorie mayonnaise**

¼ **cup ketchup**

One 4½-ounce jar cocktail onions **and their juice**

1 **tablespoon Dijon-style mustard**

¼ **cup lemon juice**

Pepper

Blend all ingredients until smooth and chill, covered, for 2 hours before serving.

SERVING SIZE: ¼ cup
CALORIES: 44
FAT: 3.08 grams

CHOLESTEROL: 3 milligrams
SODIUM: 216.75 milligrams

■ ■

CREAMY CUCUMBER DRESSING

Makes about 2 cups

This dressing is delicious served over falafel (see page 158 for falafel recipe). ■

1 cup plain nonfat yogurt

½ medium cucumber, chopped fine

1 teaspoon fresh-squeezed lemon juice

1 clove garlic, minced very fine

½ teaspoon salt

½ teaspoon ground white pepper

Blend ingredients together in a jar and store in the refrigerator. Use generously with falafel as well as with fresh green salads.

SERVING SIZE: ¼ cup
CALORIES: 19.4
FAT: .081 grams

CHOLESTEROL: 3.004 milligrams
SODIUM: 145 milligrams

■ ■

VEGETARIAN ENTRÉES

Lasagna with Chickpeas

Green Peppers Stuffed with Barley and Raisins

Black Bean Soufflés

Bean Mini Pizzas

Creole Red-Bean Patties

Lentil Patties

White Bean and Broccoli Stew

Black Bean Chili

Falafel

Barley, Split Pea, and Vegetable Stew

Vegetable, Bean, and Lentil Stew

Carrot and Kidney-Bean Loaf

Middle Eastern Barley, Lentil, and Rice Casserole

Greek Pastitsio with Lentils

Black-Eyed Peas and Macaroni

Bean and Eggplant Curry

Hoppin' John

Bean Enchiladas

Indian Chickpea and Rice Biriyani

Barley, Pepper, and Bean-Curd Sauté

Tortilla and Black Bean Torte

LASAGNA WITH CHICKPEAS

Makes 8 servings

Between the ground meat and cheeses normally found in lasagna, this Italian dish comes laden with saturated fat, and virtually devoid of fiber. But all is not lost. Instead of ground meat, you can use chickpeas, and in place of the regular cheeses, you can substitute Formagg cheeses with no cholesterol or butterfat. The result is a delight, made better only by a nice salad on the side and a glass of Chianti. ■

1 **pound lasagna made without egg yolks**

2 **onions, sliced thin**

Two 4½-ounce jars sliced **mushrooms**

4 **cups freshly cooked or two 19-ounce cans** chickpeas, **drained, rinsed, and chopped coarse**

1 **teaspoon oregano**

Four 8-ounce cans no-salt-added tomato sauce

Pepper

2 **cups Formagg ricotta-cheese substitute**

4 **tablespoons Formagg Parmesan-cheese substitute**

Preheat oven to 350 degrees.

Boil lasagna noodles for about 10 minutes or until done. Drain and keep in a bowlful of water so that the noodles do not stick together.

Meanwhile, spray a large skillet with Pam or Baker's Joy. When hot, add onions and sauté for 2 minutes. Add mushrooms and their juice and simmer for 5 minutes. Add chick peas, oregano, and 2 cans of the tomato sauce. Simmer for 10 minutes, stirring on occasion. Season to taste with pepper. Drain lasagna and pat them dry.

To assemble, pour one of the remaining cans of tomato sauce on the bottom of a 9-by-13-inch baking pan. Place a layer of noodles on top. Spoon on one-third of the chickpeas, mushroom, and tomato sauce, one-third of the ricotta substitute, and 1 tablespoon of Parmesan. Repeat with two more layers of each. Then cover the last layer of chickpea sauce with a fourth layer of noodles and top that with the last can of tomato sauce. Sprinkle a tablespoon of Parmesan over and bake, uncovered, for 30 to 40 minutes.

SERVING SIZE: ⅛ recipe
CALORIES: 214
FAT: 4.753 grams

CHOLESTEROL: 15.1 milligrams
SODIUM: 121 milligrams

■ ■

GREEN PEPPERS STUFFED WITH BARLEY AND RAISINS

Makes 6 stuffed peppers

Stuffed peppers are usually a high-fat dish, made with greasy ground beef. This is a delightful alternative. You can add meat to this recipe by browning some very lean ground beef along with the onions and chopped peppers. Both versions taste great. ∎

1 **cup** pearled barley

6 **medium green or red bell peppers**

¼ **cup chopped onions**

¾ **cup raisins**

2 **tablespoons chopped fresh mint or 2 teaspoons dried**

¾ **teaspoon ground cinnamon**

2 **tablespoons lemon juice**

Pepper

Cook barley in 6 to 8 cups boiling water for 30 minutes; it should be tender but still have some bite to it. Drain and reserve for later.

Preheat oven to 350 degrees.

Cut ½-inch slice off stem end of each bell pepper. Discard stem but chop up what pepper remains and reserve for later. Empty peppers of seeds and ribs.

Spray a large skillet with Pam or Baker's Joy, add onions and reserved chopped peppers. Stir-fry for a couple of minutes. Add ½ cup water to the skillet, cover, and simmer over low heat for 10 minutes, or until vegetables are tender.

Add to the skillet the cooked barley, raisins, mint, cinnamon, and lemon juice. Stir around for a minute or so and remove from heat. Season to taste with pepper.

Scoop the barley mixture into the hollowed-out pepper cases. Fit the peppers into a baking pan so that the peppers touch and help support each other. Add about an inch of water to the pan, cover, and bake for 45 minutes to 1 hour or until tender.

SERVING SIZE: ⅙ recipe
CALORIES: 193
FAT: .77 grams

CHOLESTEROL: 0
SODIUM: 5.84 milligrams

BLACK BEAN SOUFFLÉS

Makes 6 servings

You'll have a hard time deciding whether to serve this as a side dish or the entrée. Either way it's delicious and nutritious, supplying ingredients from all four food groups. I think this will become one of your favorites. ∎

One 16-ounce can black beans, drained and rinsed

½ cup oat bran

One 4-ounce can chopped green chilies, drained

One 8-ounce can tomato sauce

1 jalepeño pepper, minced, optional

½ teaspoon each ground cumin and garlic powder

2 tablespoons lemon juice

½ cup Formagg shredded cheddar-flavored cheese substitute

4 egg whites

1 green onion, sliced thin

Preheat oven to 400 degrees.

With an electric mixer, food processor, or blender purée all ingredients, except egg whites and green onions.

Beat egg whites until stiff, then fold these into the purée. Spoon the mixture into 6 one-cup ramekins or ovenproof glass custard cups, and bake for 20 minutes. Sprinkle green onion over the tops and serve immediately.

SERVING SIZE: 1 soufflé
CALORIES: 132
FAT: 1.99 grams

CHOLESTEROL: 3.29 milligrams
SODIUM: 113.83 milligrams

■ ■

BEAN MINI PIZZAS

Makes 4 servings

And now for something completely different!" Who needs pepperoni when you have toppings like this? Serve with a salad with Italian dressing or a simple olive-oil vinaigrette and you're all set. A nice Italian red wine complements the meal perfectly. ■

4 **English muffins, split in half**	**One 1¼-ounce package taco seasoning**
1 **cup no-salt-added tomato sauce**	
2 **tablespoons** apple fiber	8 **tablespoons Formagg shredded mozzarella-cheese substitute or "pizza topping" cheese substitute**
One 1-pound can black beans, **drained and rinsed**	

Lightly toast English muffins and set aside.

In a small saucepan simmer tomato sauce and apple fiber for 2 minutes; set aside.

With an electric mixer or in a food processor, purée black beans and taco seasoning.

Preheat the oven to broil. To assemble the mini pizzas, spoon 1 tablespoon of tomato sauce onto each muffin, top with ¼ cup of black bean mixture, then top that with 1 more tablespoon of tomato sauce and sprinkle a tablespoonful of cheese substitute on top. Broil for 1 minute or until cheese topping begins to brown.

SERVING SIZE: 1 pizza
CALORIES: 272
FAT: 4.89 grams

CHOLESTEROL: 8.1 milligrams
SODIUM: 995 milligrams

■ ■

CREOLE RED-BEAN PATTIES

Makes twelve 2½-inch patties

The recipe calls for blending the beans and seasonings till smooth and shaping into patties. If you want additional texture, try chopping the beans instead. In either case, treat the patties like burgers; serve them on buns with onion rings, lettuce, and tomato slices with ketchup or mustard. ■

4 **cups cooked** red or pink beans, **drained**	¼ **teaspoon cayenne**
	Tabasco to taste
4 **green onions, sliced thin**	½ **teaspoon thyme**
½ **red bell pepper, chopped**	¼ **teaspoon garlic powder**
½ **cup chopped fresh parsley**	**About** ½ **cup** apple fiber

In a food processor or blender, combine beans, onions, red pepper, parsley, cayenne, Tabasco, thyme, garlic powder, and ¼ cup of the apple fiber. Process until smooth.

Place remaining apple fiber in a shallow bowl. Dipping your hands in the apple fiber, shape the bean purée into patties about 2½ inches in diameter and ¾ inch thick.

Spray a skillet with Pam or Baker's Joy and heat. Cook patties for 5 minutes on each side.

SERVING SIZE: 1 patty
CALORIES: 83.6
FAT: .38 grams

CHOLESTEROL: 0
SODIUM: 101.79 milligrams

■ ■

LENTIL PATTIES

Makes eight 3-inch patties

This dish comes absolutely packed with soluble fiber, from both the lentils and the rice bran. In fact, it has as much soluble fiber as 2½ cups of oat bran. If you missed having oat-bran muffins or cereal for breakfast, you can get your day's supply of soluble fiber at lunch. Serve the patties on hamburger buns or English muffins. Or turn them into "cheeseburgers" by melting a slice of Formagg Swiss cheese over each patty. They're mighty tasty. ■

1 **cup** lentils, **picked over and rinsed**

1 **tablespoon olive oil**

½ **cup chopped onions**

1 **cup chopped carrots**

1 **egg white**

½ **teaspoon garlic powder**

½ **cup** rice bran **or** pulverized Vita Fiber

2 **tablespoons ketchup**

Pepper

Chopped parsley for garnish, optional

Bring 2 cups water to a boil, add lentils, cover, and simmer gently for 25 minutes or until lentils are just done; you don't want them too mushy. Drain through a sieve and keep them in the sieve for about 1 hour or until all the water drains away.

In a small skillet heat olive oil. Add onions and carrots and stir-fry for 1 minute. Add some water to the skillet, cover, and simmer for 10 minutes or until the vegetables are tender.

In a food processor or blender, mix the lentils, cooked vegetables, egg white, garlic powder, ¼ cup of the rice bran, ketchup, and pepper to taste.

Right before cooking, put remaining rice bran in shallow dish. Shape the mixture into 8 patties about 3 inches in diameter. Coat each patty with the rice bran. In a nonstick skillet or one sprayed with Pam or Baker's Joy, sauté over medium-high heat, for about 4 minutes, on one side. With a spatula, carefully turn patties over and cook for 3 minutes on the second side. Sprinkle parsley on top and serve.

SERVING SIZE: 1 patty
CALORIES: 122
FAT: 1.94 grams

CHOLESTEROL: 0
SODIUM: 66.2 milligrams

■ ■

WHITE BEAN AND BROCCOLI STEW

Makes 6 servings

Mint gives this Middle Eastern food its characteristic flavor. You can use all one type of bean, but for more pizzazz go for one cup each of all three. ■

1 tablespoon olive oil

1 onion, chopped fine

2 red or green bell peppers, seeds and membranes removed, sliced thin

½ pound fresh mushrooms, sliced thin

1 tablespoon fresh or 2 teaspoons dried mint

3 cups cooked or canned white, navy, kidney, or pea beans, drained and rinsed

4 cups fresh broccoli florets or one 10-ounce package frozen broccoli

Pepper or Tabasco

In a medium saucepan heat olive oil. Add onion and peppers and sauté for 5 minutes, stirring constantly. If vegetables begin to brown too quickly or stick to the saucepan, add a few tablespoons of water.

Add mushrooms and mint, cover, and simmer for 5 minutes; add beans and simmer for 10 minutes. Add broccoli, 1 cup water, cover, and simmer 5 minutes, or until broccoli is just tender; season to taste with pepper.

SERVING SIZE: ⅙ recipe
CALORIES: 169
FAT: 3.26 grams

CHOLESTEROL: 0
SODIUM: 24.7 milligrams

BLACK BEAN CHILI

Makes 6 servings

The word "chili" refers, of course, to chili peppers, from which the flavor of this dish originates. Original chili recipes used no beans at all—just meat and chili peppers. Today the emphasis is on the beans. This recipe calls for no meat at all, but you can add some browned very-lean beef or turkey breast, either ground or shredded. Or you can add cooked elbow macaroni to make what we term "chili mac" in our house. ■

2 red bell peppers, sliced thin

1 tablespoon olive oil

1 tablespoon each chili powder and ground cumin

½ teaspoon garlic powder

2 cans (15 or 16 ounces each) black beans

¼ cup ketchup

OPTIONAL ACCOMPANIMENTS

½ cup chopped cilantro

¼ cup chopped green onions

Nonfat yogurt

1 cup Formagg shredded cheddar-cheese substitute

In a medium saucepan, sauté red peppers in olive oil for 2 minutes. Cover and simmer for 5 to 10 minutes or until soft; if peppers stick to the saucepan, add a tablespoon or two of cold water.

Stir chili powder and cumin into the peppers and stir-fry for 30 seconds. Add garlic powder and black beans with their liquid. Simmer, covered, for 30 minutes. Uncover and add ketchup. If chili is too soupy, simmer for 15 minutes more uncovered.

Serve with optional accompaniments.

SERVING SIZE: ⅙ recipe
CALORIES: 129
FAT: 3.36 grams

CHOLESTEROL: .67 milligrams
SODIUM: 316.33 milligrams

FALAFEL

Makes eighteen 1-inch balls

Falafel is the original veggieburger, served throughout the Middle East. Instead of the traditional deep-frying, this recipe cuts the fat content by baking. Use the patties as appetizers or served in pita pockets with chopped tomatoes, lettuce, and Creamy Cucumber Dressing. ∎

2 **cups cooked** chickpeas **or** black-eyed peas, **drained**

¼ **cup pulverized** rice bran

2 **cloves fresh garlic, minced**

½ **teaspoon ground coriander**

1 **teaspoon ground cumin**

¼ **teaspoon cayenne**

1 **teaspoon dried or 2 tablespoons minced fresh cilantro**

Pepper

Flour

Creamy Cucumber Dressing (see page 145)

In a food processor or blender combine all ingredients, except flour. The purée will not be entirely smooth, which is good.

Preheat oven to 350 degrees.

Dipping your hands lightly in flour, if you need to, shape the purée into balls, about 1 inch in diameter. Spray a large skillet with Pam or Baker's Joy and heat until very hot. Sauté the balls on all sides, then transfer them to a baking pan and bake for 30 minutes. Serve with Creamy Cucumber Dressing.

SERVING SIZE: 1 ball (without dressing)
CALORIES: 21.7

FAT: .16 grams
CHOLESTEROL: 0
SODIUM: 1.01 milligrams

■■

BARLEY, SPLIT PEA, AND VEGETABLE STEW

Makes 6 servings

This stew is thick with ingredients and flavor, rich in soluble fiber, and bursting with color. You may also wish to add chicken, cubes of very lean beef, or fish. If you opt for the fish, add whatever amount you wish during the last 10 minutes of simmering. ■

½ **cup** pearled barley

½ **cup** green split peas

1 **small onion, minced**

1 **clove garlic, minced**

2 **cups (one 14½-ounce can) no-salt-added stewed tomatoes**

½ **teaspoon celery seed**

2 **carrots, chopped fine**

1 **cup green beans, fresh and cut into 1-inch lengths or half of a 10-ounce package frozen cut green beans**

1 **cup or half of a 10-ounce package frozen corn kernels**

1–2 **tablespoons lemon juice**

Pepper

Bring barley, peas, onion, garlic, 3 cups water, and stewed tomatoes to a boil. Add celery seed, cover, and simmer gently for 45 minutes.

Add carrots and green beans if you are using fresh ones, cover again, and simmer 15 minutes longer. Uncover, add corn and frozen green beans if you are using them. Simmer, uncovered, for 10 to 15 minutes or until the juices have been almost entirely absorbed by the barley and split peas. Season to taste with lemon juice and pepper.

SERVING SIZE: ⅙ recipe
CALORIES: 150
FAT: .62 grams

CHOLESTEROL: 0
SODIUM: 125 milligrams

■ ■

VEGETABLE, BEAN, AND LENTIL STEW

Makes 8 servings

This easy one-pot meal is positively bursting with color. ∎

½ **cup dried** lentils

½ **cup dried** split green peas

One 14½-ounce can no-salt-added stewed tomatoes

½ **cup fine-chopped onions**

½ **cup fine-chopped bell peppers**

1 **carrot, chopped fine**

1 **stalk celery, chopped fine**

One 1-pound can pink beans

One 10-ounce package frozen corn kernels

Pepper

In a 6-quart saucepan bring to a boil lentils, split peas, tomatoes, onions, peppers, carrot, celery, and 2 cups water. Simmer, covered, for 25 minutes.

Add beans and their liquid and corn. If needed, add some water to just cover mixture. Cover and simmer for 15 minutes more or until lentils and peas are cooked through and tender; season to taste with pepper and serve.

SERVING SIZE: ⅛ recipe
CALORIES: 196
FAT: .64 grams

CHOLESTEROL: 0
SODIUM: 101 milligrams

∎∎∎∎∎∎∎∎∎∎∎∎∎∎∎∎∎∎∎∎∎∎∎∎∎∎∎∎∎∎∎∎∎∎∎∎

CARROT AND KIDNEY-BEAN LOAF

Makes about 6 to 8 servings

The color and texture of this dish make it an attractive and satisfying main course. The tastes of carrot and bean play off each other very well. ∎

1 tablespoon canola oil	½ teaspoon thyme
1 onion, sliced thin	Pinch allspice
½ pound (about 3) carrots, grated	Pepper
4 cups freshly cooked or drained and rinsed canned red kidney or pink beans	2 egg whites
	Tomato sauce (see page 253), optional

Preheat oven to 350 degrees.

In a large skillet heat oil. When hot, add onion and stir-fry for 1 or 2 minutes. Add a tablespoon of water and cook for another 2 minutes or until the onion begins to soften.

Add the grated carrots and cook, stirring frequently, for about 2 minutes or until they just begin to wilt. Do not overcook because you want to preserve some of their crunch to give texture to the bean loaf.

Put half the beans with the onions and carrots in the bowl of a food processor or in a blender. Process with spices and egg whites. In a mixing bowl, toss this bean paste with the remaining whole beans.

Spoon the mixture into a loaf pan about 8 by 4 inches and bake for 45 minutes. Remove from oven and let sit for 15 minutes. Spoon the servings out of the loaf pan and serve, if you wish, with tomato sauce.

SERVING SIZE: ⅛ recipe
CALORIES: 149
FAT: 2.28 grams

CHOLESTEROL: 0
SODIUM: 160 milligrams

∎ ∎

MIDDLE EASTERN BARLEY, LENTIL, AND RICE CASSEROLE

Makes 6 to 8 servings

You'll find the combination of apricots and raisins along with the lentils and barley in this dish to be exciting, with just a touch of sweetness. Enjoy with toasted pita bread. ∎

1 tablespoon olive oil	½ cup pearled barley
1 small onion, chopped fine	½ cup long-grain rice
2 cloves garlic, minced	¼ cup chopped dried apricots
1 teaspoon ground cinnamon	½ cup raisins
1 teaspoon sugar	1½ teaspoons dried mint
½ cup dried lentils	Pepper

In a medium-large saucepan heat oil. When hot, add onion and garlic and sauté for 2 minutes. Stir in cinnamon and sugar, then add 4 cups water. Add lentils and barley. Cover and simmer gently for 20 minutes.

Add rice, apricots, raisins, and mint. Stir ingredients together, cover the pot again, and simmer for 20 minutes more or until all ingredients are tender and have absorbed the liquid. Season to taste with pepper.

SERVING SIZE: ⅛ recipe
CALORIES: 168
FAT: 1.95 grams

CHOLESTEROL: 0
SODIUM: 10 milligrams

GREEK PASTITSIO WITH LENTILS

Makes 8 servings

The traditional pastitsio comes with more than its share of saturated fat. Even the Greeks eat that dish just once in a while. Here's a way to make it positively healthful. ∎

½ **pound (about 2 cups) dry macaroni**

1 **cup dry** lentils

1 **tablespoon canola oil**

1 **small onion, chopped fine**

¼ **cup white wine**

½ **teaspoon ground cinnamon**

One 8-ounce can no-salt-added tomato sauce

1 **cup evaporated skim milk**

2 **tablespoons** oat bran

Pinch nutmeg

1 **cup Formagg grated Fontina-cheese substitute**

Cook macaroni in boiling water for about 10 minutes and drain; cool under cold running water and reserve for later. Cook lentils in 4 cups boiling water for about 25 minutes or until tender. Drain.

Preheat oven to 350 degrees.

In a large skillet, heat oil. When hot, add onion and sauté for 2 minutes. Add wine and simmer for 10 minutes or until wine has evaporated and onion is tender. Add cinnamon, tomato sauce, and lentils; simmer for 3 to 4 minutes.

In a medium saucepan, heat milk. Whisk in oat bran and nutmeg and simmer for 1 minute, stirring constantly; remove from heat. Stir macaroni into milk and mix well.

Spoon half of the macaroni in the bottom of a 9-inch-square baking pan. Spoon half of the lentil mixture on top and spread evenly. Repeat with remaining macaroni and lentils. Sprinkle on cheese. Cover with foil and bake for 15 minutes or until casserole is hot.

SERVING SIZE: ⅛ recipe
CALORIES: 214
FAT: 2.6 grams

CHOLESTEROL: 1.28 milligrams
SODIUM: 60.5 milligrams

■ ■

BLACK-EYED PEAS AND MACARONI

Makes 6 to 8 servings

Black-eyed peas have more soluble fiber than any of the other dried beans or peas. You can also use this southern favorite in a number of the recipes in this book. ■

1 **cup dried** black-eyed peas	¼ **cup** oat bran
½ **pound (about 2 cups) dried elbow macaroni**	**Pinch nutmeg**
	Pepper
One 12-ounce can evaporated skim milk	⅓ **cup Parmesan or Parmesan-cheese substitute**

Cook black-eyed peas in 4 cups water, covered, for 45 minutes or until tender; drain.

Cook macaroni in boiling water for about 10 minutes. Drain and refresh under cold water.

Bring milk, oat bran, nutmeg, and pepper slowly to a simmer, whisking constantly so that oat bran does not burn. Cook gently for 2 minutes. Add black-eyed peas, macaroni, and cheese to sauce, and simmer, mixing thoroughly, for 2 minutes or until everything is hot throughout.

SERVING SIZE: ⅛ recipe
CALORIES: 151
FAT: 2 grams

CHOLESTEROL: 4.88 milligrams
SODIUM: 127 milligrams

■ ■

BEAN AND EGGPLANT CURRY

Makes 4 servings

I find eggplant a bit on the mushy side when used as the main ingredient. Yet I love the way it absorbs flavors such as curry. In this dish, the combination of the eggplant and the beans works beautifully. Served over rice, this makes a very satisfying meal, with or without meat on the side. You might also consider including a half pound of very lean browned ground beef at the end of the recipe to satisfy any carnivorous cravings. ■

1 **cup dried** white beans, **such as navy, pea, Great Northern, or kidney, soaked (see page 89), or 2 cups canned white beans**

1–1½ **pounds eggplant, cut into 1-inch pieces**

2 **carrots, peeled and cut into ½-inch rounds**

1 **onion, sliced thin**

2 **teaspoons curry powder**

1 **teaspoon ground cumin**

1 **tablespoon lemon juice**

Pepper

Place all ingredients except lemon juice and pepper in a large pot. If you are using dried beans, add just enough water to cover the beans. Cover and cook slowly for 1½ to 2 hours or until beans are tender and vegetables are cooked. While beans are simmering, check them every now and then to make sure they are always just covered with liquid, or they will not soften.

If you are using canned beans, place all ingredients, including liquid from beans in a large pot. Add ½ cup water, cover and simmer gently for 45 minutes or until eggplant is tender.

Drain beans and eggplant, and place in a clean pot, reserving liquid. Place cooking liquid in a large skillet and boil it until you have only ½ cup left. Stir this liquid and lemon juice into the stew and season to taste with pepper.

SERVING SIZE: ¼ recipe
CALORIES: 124
FAT: .77 grams

CHOLESTEROL: 0
SODIUM: 21.3 milligrams

■ ■

Hoppin' John

Makes 6 servings

Instead of the usual sandwich for lunch, try this dish on lettuce leaves with some chopped tomatoes. Spoon a low-fat dressing over it and serve with fresh corn-bread. ▪

1 **cup dried** black-eyed peas	½ **cup chopped 96 percent fat-free ham**
1 **small onion, chopped fine**	1 **bay leaf**
½ **teaspoon cayenne**	1 **cup long-grain rice**

In a medium saucepan simmer black-eyed peas, onion, cayenne, ham, bay leaf, and water to cover (about 3 cups) for 45 minutes or until black-eyed peas are soft.

Add rice, cover, and simmer for 15 minutes, or until rice is soft and has absorbed liquid. Remove bay leaf and serve.

SERVING SIZE: ⅙ recipe
CALORIES: 131
FAT: 1.55 grams

CHOLESTEROL: 3.42 milligrams
SODIUM: 145 milligrams

BEAN ENCHILADAS

Makes 6 servings

While preparing these enchiladas, try making some tortilla chips to dip in salsa while waiting for the main course. Just take some corn tortillas, cut them into wedges, place on a cookie sheet, spray with a bit of Pam or Baker's Joy on both sides, sprinkle with a touch of salt if you wish, and bake at 350 degrees F. for about 10 minutes. Serve the enchiladas with rice. ■

½ cup chopped onion

8 ounces chicken breast, cut into ½-inch squares

One 1-pound can black beans, drained

One 4-ounce can chopped green chilies

½ cup chopped fresh cilantro or parsley

12 corn tortillas or 10 flour tortillas

One 10-ounce can mild or hot enchilada sauce

1 cup no-salt-added tomato sauce

½ cup shredded Formagg cheddar-cheese substitute

Nonfat yogurt

Chopped cilantro

Preheat oven to 350 degrees.

Spray a large skillet with Pam or Baker's Joy. When hot, sauté onion for 3 to 4 minutes or until softened. Add chicken, beans, and chilies, and simmer for 10 minutes or until chicken is cooked. Let mixture cool.

Heat tortillas gently. Spoon some filling along one edge and roll up the tortillas. Place each one, seam side down, in a large baking pan.

In a mixing bowl, combine enchilada sauce and tomato sauce; pour over tortillas. Top with cheese and bake 25 to 30 minutes. Serve with nonfat yogurt and chopped cilantro.

SERVING SIZE: ⅙ recipe
CALORIES: 293
FAT: 4.66 grams

CHOLESTEROL: 36.1 milligrams
SODIUM: 208.33 milligrams

■■

INDIAN CHICKPEA AND RICE BIRIYANI

Makes 6 servings

Biriyani is the Indian word for this rice dish, which is another example of how another culture uses the combined amino acids from rice and beans to form a complete protein. While it can be a meal itself, you may prefer it as a side dish, or to use as an appetizer course. ■

- 2 small onions, chopped fine
- 2 cloves garlic, minced
- 1 red bell pepper, chopped fine
- ¼ teaspoon each ground cardamom, cayenne, cloves, coriander, ginger, and mace
- ½ teaspoon ground cinnamon
- 1 teaspoon ground cumin

- 1 cup long-grain rice
- ½ cup raisins
- 2 cups cooked or one 19-ounce can chickpeas, **drained and rinsed**
- ¼ cup nonfat yogurt
- Chopped cilantro or parsley for garnish, optional

Preheat oven to 350 degrees.

Spray a flameproof, ovenproof casserole with Pam or Baker's Joy. When hot, add onions and garlic, and sauté for 2 minutes. Add red pepper, cover, and simmer gently for 10 minutes, adding ¼ cup water or so, if you need to prevent burning.

Add spices, rice, raisins, chickpeas, and 2 cups water. Bring liquid to a simmer, cover casserole, and set in the oven. Bake for 25 minutes. Remove cover, fluff up rice and chickpeas with a fork, and stir in yogurt. Garnish if you wish with chopped herb and serve immediately.

SERVING SIZE: ⅙ recipe
CALORIES: 181
FAT: 2.023 grams

CHOLESTEROL: 0
SODIUM: 131.7 milligrams

■■

BARLEY, PEPPER, AND BEAN CURD SAUTÉ

Makes 4 servings

Bean curd is another name for tofu, widely eaten around the world as a major source of protein. If you haven't eaten it before, try it this way to see how you like it as a meat alternative once in a while. If you don't like it at all, you can substitute turkey breast chunks. ■

1 **tablespoon minced garlic**	2 **bean-curd cakes, cut into ½-inch dice**
2 **red bell peppers, seeds and membranes removed, sliced thin**	½ **pound fresh spinach, chopped**
2 **cups cooked** pearled barley	**Pepper**
2 **tablespoons lemon or lime juice**	

Spray a large skillet with Pam or Baker's Joy, and sauté garlic for 30 seconds.

Add peppers, cover, and simmer for 5 minutes over medium heat. Remove the cover and add barley and lemon juice.

Stir for 5 minutes without a cover. Add bean curd and spinach. Cover and simmer over low heat for about another 5 minutes or until the spinach has wilted. Season to taste with pepper.

SERVING SIZE: ¼ recipe
CALORIES: 519
FAT: 9.655 grams

CHOLESTEROL: 0
SODIUM: 63.4 milligrams

TORTILLA AND BLACK BEAN TORTE

Makes 4 servings

Torte usually refers to a dessert cake with many layers. This dish, however, is a multi-layered main course. I like it served with rice and a wedge of lemon. A glass of Mexican beer washes it down very nicely. It can also be served as an appetizer. ∎

4 cups cooked or drained and rinsed canned black beans

2 tablespoons pimiento pieces

One 4-ounce can chopped green chilies

1 teaspoon chili or cumin powder

Tabasco to taste

8 corn tortillas or flour tortillas made without lard

Nonfat yogurt or salsa or chopped fresh tomatoes

Preheat oven to 350 degrees.

In a blender or food processor, coarsely purée the black beans with the pimientos, chilies, and chili or cumin powder. Season to taste with Tabasco.

Spray a large skillet with Pam or Baker's Joy; add the black bean purée and sauté for 5 minutes, stirring constantly with a wooden spoon; remove from heat.

Place a tortilla on a baking sheet and spread with black beans. Place another tortilla on top of the beans, press down, and layer with more beans. Continue until you have made a little "torte" or cake of 4 tortillas with 3 layers of black bean purée in between. Make another such torte. Cut each torte in 4 wedges and bake for 10 minutes or until hot throughout.

Serve with yogurt, salsa, or tomatoes on the side to moisten the wedges, which might otherwise taste too dry.

SERVING SIZE: ¼ recipe
CALORIES: 265
FAT: 3.969 grams

CHOLESTEROL: 0
SODIUM: 107 milligrams

MEAT
AND POULTRY
ENTRÉES

Pot Roast

Beef Stew and Wine

Chinese Stir-Fried Beef

Brazilian Black Bean and Beef
Casserole

Savory Pinto Beans and Beef

Meatloaf

Spectacular Meatloaf

Hamburger and Meatball
Preparation

Sloppy Joes

Moroccan "Tagine" (Stew) of
Chickpeas and Beef

Pot au Feu

Spanish Lentil, Barley, and Ham
Casserole

Black-Eyed Pea Casserole with Ham
and Carrots

Hungarian Bean and Sauerkraut Stew
with Ham

Cassoulet with Ham

Bean and Turkey Skillet Dinner

Jambalaya

POT ROAST

Makes 8 to 10 servings

This unique approach to preparing a beef roast is specially suited to the ultra-lean qualities of Dakota lean beef. Do not overcook. It may take you once or twice, as it did for me, to realize how easy it is to overcook. ∎

4 small onions, sliced thin	1 teaspoon Worcestershire or A-1 steak sauce
¼ cup red wine vinegar	
2 teaspoons sugar	Pepper
4 carrots, peeled and sliced thin	One 3-pound Dakota lean chuck roast, sliced frozen *(do not thaw)*
Four 8-ounce cans no-salt-added tomato sauce	

Preheat oven to 350 degrees.

Spray a large skillet with Pam or Baker's Joy; sauté onions for 4 to 5 minutes, stirring every now and then. Add vinegar and sugar and simmer 2 to 3 minutes. Add carrots, tomato sauce, and Worcestershire. Simmer gently, covered, over low heat, for 30 minutes.

Place this sauce in the bottom of a roasting pan. Set roast on top of the sauce and cook according to instructions, for 1 hour, then turn oven off and let roast sit in oven for 1½ hours more. Remove roast from oven and remove the string net that holds it together. Slice or cut into cubes. Toss meat with sauce and serve.

SERVING SIZE: ¹⁄₁₀ recipe
CALORIES: 203
FAT: 1.825 grams

CHOLESTEROL: 37.4 milligrams
SODIUM: 124 milligrams

BEEF STEW WITH WINE

Makes 8 servings

My mother long ago taught me a trick to make very lean roasts juicier and more tender. About halfway through the cooking time, take out the meat and slice it. Then return the slices loosely to the juices for the balance of the time. The meat will not only be more tender but will absorb the flavors of the vegetables and seasonings. Serve with boiled or mashed potatoes. ■

4 onions, sliced thin	1 bay leaf
4 carrots, sliced thin	2 pounds Dakota lean stew beef, frozen
3 cups red wine	
½ teaspoon thyme	Pepper

Spray a medium saucepan with Pam or Baker's Joy, and sauté onions for 2 minutes. Cover and simmer for 10 minutes, adding water if the onions stick to the pot.

Add carrots, red wine, thyme, bay leaf, and meat. Cover and simmer for 1½ hours or until the meat is somewhat tender; note that this type of meat will always remain somewhat chewy. Remove bay leaf and discard.

Drain meat and solids through a colander, reserving the juices. Place juices in a small saucepan and boil them down until only 1 cup remains. Return meat, solids, and boiled-down juices to the pot and simmer, covered, for 5 minutes or until heated through. Season to taste with pepper.

SERVING SIZE: ⅛ recipe
CALORIES: 226
FAT: 1.59 grams

CHOLESTEROL: 31.1 milligrams
SODIUM: 98 milligrams

■ ■

CHINESE STIR-FRIED BEEF

Makes 4 servings

For a long while after I started to cut back seriously on saturated fat in my diet, I relied entirely on chicken and seafood to do my stir-fry cooking. Dakota Lean Meats has changed all that, broadening the possibilities considerably. The trick to using this ultra-lean meat is to cook it very quickly, leaving it on the rare side for best flavor and juiciness. ■

1 pound Dakota lean steak, partially frozen

2 tablespoons soy sauce

½ teaspoon powdered ginger

½ tablespoon sugar

½ tablespoon chili paste

1 teaspoon sesame oil

1 teaspoon canola oil

1 small onion, chopped fine

1 garlic clove, minced

One 8-ounce can sliced water chestnuts

Slice flank steak, across the grain, into pieces about 1 inch square; set aside. (The meat is much easier to slice if it is partially frozen.)

Combine soy sauce, ginger, sugar, and chili paste in a small bowl and set aside for later.

In a large skillet heat sesame and canola oil. When oils are very hot and just about smoking, add onion and stir-fry for 1 minute. Add garlic, meat, and water chestnuts, and stir-fry for 2 minutes longer. Add soy-sauce mixture and sauté for 1 minute more. Serve immediately before meat toughens.

SERVING SIZE: ¼ recipe
CALORIES: 197
FAT: 3.775 grams

CHOLESTEROL: 31.1 milligrams
SODIUM: 599 milligrams

BRAZILIAN BLACK BEAN AND BEEF CASSEROLE

Makes 8 servings

Orange zest gives this dish a distinctive flair. Serve the casserole with a salad and a mound of rice or barley. ∎

1 stalk celery, chopped fine	One 14½-ounce can no-salt-added stewed tomatoes
2 carrots, chopped fine	
2 onions, chopped fine	1 pound Dakota lean stew beef, cut into ½-inch cubes
3 cloves garlic, minced	
1 small bell pepper, chopped fine	4 cups cooked or drained and rinsed canned black beans
½ teaspoon grated orange zest	Pepper

Spray a medium-large pot with Pam or Baker's Joy, and sauté celery, carrots, onions, garlic, and bell pepper. Cover and simmer gently for 5 minutes, stirring every now and then to make sure vegetables are not sticking.

Add orange zest and tomatoes, along with meat. Cover and simmer for 30 minutes, stirring every now and then. Add black beans and simmer, uncovered, for 15 to 30 minutes more until stew is nice and thick. Season to taste with pepper.

SERVING SIZE: ⅛ recipe
CALORIES: 172
FAT: 1.619 grams

CHOLESTEROL: 15.6 milligrams
SODIUM: 242 milligrams

■ ■

SAVORY PINTO BEANS AND BEEF

Makes 6 servings

The unusual taste and texture in this dish comes from the shredded Dakota lean beef. The easiest way I've found to prepare the beef is to shred partially frozen steaks with a kitchen grater in the same way you'd grate carrots. Since the meat is in such small pieces, it takes just a flash in a nonstick pan coated with Pam or Baker's Joy to cook the meat through. Then add the beef shreds to the rest of the ingredients just before serving. ■

½ **pound dried** pinto beans, **soaked**

1 **tablespoon olive oil**

½ **cup chopped onions**

1 **clove garlic, minced**

One 4-ounce can chopped green chilies

½ **teaspoon cumin seeds**

1 **jalapeño pepper, seeded and minced**

1 **tomato, chopped**

8 **ounces Dakota lean beef in shreds (fillet, not stew meat)**

Place pinto beans and all other ingredients except beef in a medium-large saucepan. Add enough water to cover the beans and bring to a boil.

Cut back to a simmer and cook gently, covered, for 1½ hours or until beans are tender. Be sure to keep the beans covered with liquid at all times or some will not cook properly.

Meanwhile, heat a nonstick skillet, coated with Pam or Baker's Joy, until hot. Add beef and quickly stir-fry on all sides, about 30 seconds. Add to the beans when they are done, and serve at once.

SERVING SIZE: ⅙ recipe
CALORIES: 137
FAT: 3.006 grams

CHOLESTEROL: 10.4 milligrams
SODIUM: 94.9 milligrams

■ ■

MEATLOAF

Makes 4 servings

Some meatloaf recipes call for a lot more ingredients and take a lot more time. This approach is straightforward and works nicely when you just don't have the time to do a lot of chopping and mincing. Serve it with potatoes mashed with evaporated skim milk and Butter Buds and a side dish of vegetables. ∎

1 **pound Dakota lean ground beef**	¼ **cup ketchup**
½ **cup** oat bran	2 **tablespoons chopped parsley**
1 **egg white**	¼ **cup evaporated skim milk**
2 **teaspoons lemon juice**	**Pepper**

Preheat oven to 350 degrees. Spray an 8½-by-4½-inch loaf pan with Pam or Baker's Joy; set aside.

Blend all of the above ingredients in a large mixing bowl and pat them into the prepared loaf pan. Cover loaf pan with foil, and bake for 45 minutes. Let meatloaf sit for 10 minutes before slicing and serving.

SERVING SIZE: ¼ recipe
CALORIES: 210
FAT: 2.413 grams

CHOLESTEROL: 31.8 milligrams
SODIUM: 268 milligrams

■ ■

SPECTACULAR MEATLOAF

Makes 4 servings

Once upon a time, meatloaf was a meal you'd serve to your family but never to company. Here's a recipe, based on a high-fat version at a trendy Los Angeles restaurant, that you'll be proud to put on your table regardless of who's coming to dinner. It does take some time to prepare, but it's well worth the effort for special occasions. I like to serve this wonderful meatloaf with spinach and mashed potatoes. ■

¾ **cup each minced onion and minced green onion**

½ **cup each minced celery and minced carrot**

¼ **cup each minced green pepper and minced red pepper**

2 **teaspoons minced garlic cloves**

1 **teaspoon salt and pepper**

½ **teaspoon each white pepper, ground cumin, ground nutmeg**

¼ **teaspoon cayenne pepper**

½ **cup tomato ketchup**

4 **ounces egg substitute**

½ **cup evaporated skim milk**

1 **pound each ultra-lean ground beef and ground turkey breast**

¾ **cup** oat bran

Spray a large skillet lightly with Pam or Baker's Joy. Sauté vegetables until soft and water has evaporated. Set aside to cool in large mixing bowl. Measure herbs and seasonings, blend together, and add to vegetables. Next add ketchup, egg substitute, and milk, followed by meat, and finally the oat bran. Mix well and form into one or two loaves. Place in a baking pan, and bake 50 to 55 minutes in a 350 degree oven.

SPECTACULAR MEATLOAF SAUCE

8 **medium-sized shallots, minced**

3 **tablespoons Butter Buds**

1 **tablespoon ground thyme**

3 **bay leaves**

½ **teaspoon crushed black pepper**

2 **cups each dry white wine, chicken broth, beef broth**

Spray skillet with Pam or Baker's Joy and sauté shallots along with herbs and pepper until tender. Add wine and reduce to a glaze over high heat. Add beef and chicken broth and Butter Buds and reduce over high heat until 2 cups of sauce remain.

SPINACH

Plan on one bunch of spinach per person. Wash thoroughly to get rid of all the sand and grit. Pick off stems. Shake off water and place in large pot. Cover and cook with no added water over medium heat for 2 minutes. The little bit of moisture clinging to the spinach will cook it and it'll turn out emerald green and delicious.

MASHED POTATOES

Plan on one medium-size potato per person. Place in cold water with optional salt. Heat to a boil uncovered, and simmer for 15 to 20 minutes until potatoes are tender to a fork. Drain and mash with one packet of Butter Buds per 4 potatoes and enough evaporated skim milk to whip the potatoes as creamy as you like.

SPECTACULAR MEATLOAF
SERVING SIZE: ¼ loaf
CALORIES: 456
FAT: 4.047 grams
CHOLESTEROL: 95.5 milligrams
SODIUM: 1037 milligrams

SPECTACULAR MEATLOAF SAUCE
SERVING SIZE: ⅛ recipe
CALORIES: 52
FAT: .035 grams
CHOLESTEROL: .25 milligrams
SODIUM: 197 milligrams

SPINACH
SERVING SIZE: 1 cup
CALORIES: 12
FAT: .2 grams
CHOLESTEROL: 0
SODIUM: 44 milligrams

POTATO
SERVING SIZE: 1 potato
CALORIES: 116
FAT: .14 grams
CHOLESTEROL: 0
SODIUM: 7 milligrams

■■

HAMBURGER AND MEATBALL PREPARATION

Makes 4 patties

Simply season the meat with garlic powder and pepper, then form it into patties and cook 3 minutes per side. Or add ingredients to make it a little more "cholesterol-fighting." ■

1 **pound Dakota lean ground beef**

½ **cup** oat bran

1 **egg white**

½ **teaspoon Worcestershire sauce**

¼ **teaspoon garlic powder**

TO MAKE AND COOK AS HAMBURGERS:

Mix all of the above ingredients and shape into 4 patties. Spray a skillet with Pam or Baker's Joy. Sauté patties 3 minutes per side—not longer as this type of meat must be eaten rare or medium rare. Serve immediately. *Do not broil* or meat will become dry and dusty-tasting.

SERVING SIZE: 1 burger
CALORIES: 226
FAT: 3.32 grams
CHOLESTEROL: 31.1 milligrams
SODIUM: 111 milligrams

TO MAKE AND COOK AS MEATBALLS:

Mix all of the above ingredients and shape into 24 one-inch meatballs.

Bring 2 cups no-salt-added tomato sauce to a simmer; add meatballs, cover, and simmer for 2 minutes. Turn meatballs over and cook, covered, for 2 minutes more. Do not overcook or meatballs will be dry; serve immediately as is or with spaghetti.

SERVING SIZE: 3 meatballs
CALORIES: 136
FAT: 1.663 grams

CHOLESTEROL: 15.5 milligrams
SODIUM: 72.3 milligrams

■ ■

SLOPPY JOES

Makes 4 servings

It may be years since your schoolroom days, but no one forgets childhood memories of Sloppy Joes. Taste the mix before ladling it onto the hamburger rolls or English muffins. The Sloppy Joes in your past might have been a bit sweeter than these, and you can add a bit of granulated or brown sugar to taste. ■

1 onion, chopped fine

1 bell pepper, chopped fine

2 teaspoons chili powder

½ teaspoon garlic powder

2 cups no-salt-added tomato sauce

1 pound Dakota lean ground beef

4 hamburger rolls or English muffins, split in half, toasted

Spray a large skillet with Pam or Baker's Joy, and sauté onion and pepper for 5 minutes, stirring constantly. If vegetables begin to stick, add a few tablespoons water and cook until soft.

Add chili powder, garlic powder, and tomato sauce and simmer 1 minute. Mash and stir ground meat into the sauce and simmer 2 minutes more, stirring constantly. What you are doing is getting rid of the red of the meat and heating it through; do not overcook.

Arrange 2 toasted rolls or muffin halves on each of 4 serving plates.

Spoon some of this mixture onto each of the bun halves and serve immediately.

SERVING SIZE: ¼ recipe
CALORIES: 330
FAT: 2.885 grams

CHOLESTEROL: 31.1 milligrams
SODIUM: 474 milligrams

Moroccan "Tagine" (Stew) OF CHICKPEAS AND BEEF

Makes 4 servings

If you've never heard of "tagine" don't feel too bad. I never did either until I met Michele Urvater, who came up with this recipe. I've got a feeling it's a lot better than what you'd find in Morocco, thanks to our superior beef. Like all stews, this one needs to simmer quite a while to make the meat nice and tender. ■

- 1 medium onion, chopped fine
- 1 teaspoon ground ginger
- 1 teaspoon ground coriander
- 1 teaspoon ground cinnamon
- 2 apples, peeled, cored, and chopped fine
- 1 pound Dakota lean beef stew meat

- 1 tablespoon honey
- 1 tablespoon tomato paste
- 1 cup pitted prunes
- 2 cups cooked or canned chickpeas, drained and rinsed
- Pepper

Spray a medium saucepan with Pam or Baker's Joy, and sauté onion for 2 minutes. Add spices and ½ cup water, and simmer 5 minutes or until onions are soft. Stir in apples and meat, cover, and simmer gently for 1½ hours or until meat is tender. (Its texture and flavor will be like veal.)

Add honey, tomato paste, prunes, and chickpeas, and simmer for 30 minutes more. Season to taste with pepper. This stew tastes better and the texture of the meat becomes more tender if you make it a day in advance and reheat it for 45 minutes, at very low heat.

SERVING SIZE: ¼ recipe
CALORIES: 422
FAT: 4.24 grams

CHOLESTEROL: 31.1 milligrams
SODIUM: 591 milligrams

■■

POT AU FEU

Makes 6 servings

This is basically a boiled dinner, made in the French manner. The French, however, use lots of pork or other fatty meats. This version includes lean meats only, along with white beans to add a cholesterol-lowering dimension. ■

3   carrots, peeled and cut into
    ½-inch rounds

2   white turnips, peeled and cut into
    1-inch pieces

2   cups shredded white cabbage

2   onions, cut into 8 wedges

1   leek, washed and cut into 1-inch
    lengths

½   teaspoon dried thyme

One 14½-ounce can no-salt-added
stewed tomatoes

½   pound 96 percent fat-free
    smoked ham, cut into 1-inch
    chunks

½   pound Dakota lean stew meat cut
    into ½-inch cubes

2   cups cooked or drained canned
    navy, pea, or white kidney beans

1   pound chicken breasts

Pepper

½   cup chopped fresh herb, such as
    dill or parsley, optional

In a large pot, place all ingredients, except beans, chicken, pepper and fresh herb, and cover with 1½ quarts water. Slowly bring to a boil and, with a slotted spoon or skimmer, remove any grayish foam that rises to the top. Cover and simmer very gently for 1 hour, adding water to keep the level of the liquid constant.

Add beans and chicken and simmer for 10 minutes more. Season to taste with pepper and stir in herb if you wish.

SERVING SIZE: ⅙ recipe
CALORIES: 352
FAT: 3.5 grams

CHOLESTEROL: 84.5 milligrams
SODIUM: 301 milligrams

■ ■

SPANISH LENTIL, BARLEY, AND HAM CASSEROLE

Makes 6 to 8 servings

Casseroles mean easy preparation and easy cleanup. You can alter this recipe by replacing the ham with either chicken or fish. ∎

1 onion, chopped fine	¼ teaspoon saffron
2 carrots, chopped fine	½ cup lentils
1 stalk celery, chopped fine	½ cup pearled barley
2 green onions, sliced thin	½ cup dry white wine
1 clove garlic, minced	1 pound boiling potatoes, peeled and cut into 1-inch dice
⅓ cup chopped pimientos	
8 ounces 96 percent fat-free ham, cut into ½-inch dice	Pepper

Preheat oven to 350 degrees.

Spray a 6-quart flameproof casserole with Pam or Baker's Joy; sauté onion, carrots, celery, green onions, and garlic for 2 to 3 minutes, stirring frequently. Add pimientos, ham, and saffron, and sauté for 1 minute. Add lentils, barley, and white wine, along with 3 cups water. Add potatoes and season to taste with pepper.

Bring liquid to a simmer, cover casserole, and place in oven. Bake for 45 minutes to an hour or until potatoes, lentils, and barley have absorbed all the liquid and are tender.

SERVING SIZE: ⅛ recipe
CALORIES: 168
FAT: 1.659 grams

CHOLESTEROL: 8.303 milligrams
SODIUM: 124.4 milligrams

BLACK-EYED PEA CASSEROLE WITH HAM AND CARROTS

Makes 4 to 6 servings

With the beans, ham, and carrots, this dish is truly a meal in a pot. In my house we have a wonderful alternative to the ham—sausages specially made with turkey breast, with virtually no fat at all. Our local sausage shop makes up batches for us and we keep plenty in our freezer. You can do the same. Call your various meat markets and ask a butcher who makes his own sausage to prepare some for you with turkey breast, using all their usual herbs, spices, and smoking methods. We now enjoy hot dogs, bratwursts, and Italian sausage regularly. So can you. ■

4 cups cooked or two 1-pound cans black-eyed peas, **drained and rinsed**

1 teaspoon dried sage

One 8-ounce can no-salt-added tomato sauce

½ teaspoon garlic powder

4 carrots, peeled and grated

8 ounces lean smoked ham or home-made turkey sausage, diced

2 tablespoons olive oil

Pepper

Preheat oven to 350 degrees.

Combine all ingredients in a mixing bowl, then transfer to a 9-by-13-inch baking pan. Cover and bake for 30 minutes.

SERVING SIZE: ⅙ recipe
CALORIES: 246
FAT: 7.32 grams

CHOLESTEROL: 11.1 milligrams
SODIUM: 461 milligrams

■■■

HUNGARIAN BEAN AND SAUERKRAUT STEW WITH HAM

Makes 8 servings

Paprika gives Hungarian stews their distinctive flavor. The recipe calls for ham, but you can also use salmon in this dish. If you choose to do so, add the fish during the last 10 minutes of simmering. Serve with wide No Yolks noodles. ∎

1 tablespoon olive oil

2 onions, chopped fine

2 tablespoons paprika

1 tablespoon caraway seeds

2 pounds sauerkraut, drained

1 pound 96 percent fat-free ham, cut into ½-inch cubes

4 cups cooked or drained and rinsed canned navy or white kidney beans

2 tablespoons minced fresh or 2 teaspoon dried dill

Pepper

In a medium-large pot heat oil. When very hot, add onions, cover, and simmer gently for 5 minutes, stirring every now and then to make sure onions are not sticking.

Remove pot from heat and stir paprika and caraway into the onions. Return pot to the heat and add sauerkraut, ham, and beans. Cover and simmer for 30 minutes, stirring every now and then. Stir in dill and season to taste with pepper.

SERVING SIZE: ⅛ recipe
CALORIES: 233
FAT: 5.168 grams

CHOLESTEROL: 16.6 milligrams
SODIUM: 277 milligrams

CASSOULET WITH HAM

Makes 8 servings

Traditional cassoulet is laden with fat from goose, duck, and lamb. We can preserve all the flavor with practically none of the fat by long simmering of the soaked dried beans and by using ham. ■

2 tablespoons olive oil

4 cloves garlic, minced

1 large onion, chopped fine

2 carrots, chopped fine

One 14½-ounce can no-salt-added stewed tomatoes

1 teaspoon thyme

8 ounces 96 percent fat-free smoked ham, cut into ½-inch dice

Pepper

1 pound dried Great Northern white or navy beans, soaked and drained

½ cup seasoned oat-bran crumbs (see page 256)

Preheat oven to 350 degrees.

In a flameproof casserole, heat olive oil. When hot, add garlic, onion, and carrots, and sauté for 3 to 4 minutes. Add tomatoes, thyme, and ham, and sauté for a minute more; season to taste with pepper. Stir in beans and add just enough water to cover the beans. Bring liquid to a boil, cut back to a simmer, cover, and place in oven.

Bake for 1½ hours. Uncover casserole, sprinkle with crumbs, and bake for 30 minutes to an hour more or until beans have absorbed liquid and top is somewhat crusty.

SERVING SIZE: ⅛ recipe
CALORIES: 205
FAT: 5.335 grams

CHOLESTEROL: 8.3 milligrams
SODIUM: 344 milligrams

■■■

BEAN AND TURKEY SKILLET DINNER

Makes 6 servings

Instead of the usual meat sauce with your next meal of spaghetti, try this dish as an alternative. Then sprinkle some Formagg grated Parmesan cheese substitute on top so it melts in and provides just the right touch. ∎

- 1 tablespoon olive or canola oil
- 1 onion, chopped fine
- 4 carrots, chopped fine
- 1 pound ground turkey breast
- ½ cup no-salt-added tomato sauce

- ½ teaspoon oregano
- 2 cups freshly cooked or drained and rinsed canned beans, such as red beans, navy or pea beans, or chickpeas

Pepper
- ½ cup chopped parsley

In a 12-inch skillet heat olive oil. When hot, add onion and carrots and stir-fry for 5 minutes. Add turkey and stir-fry, breaking up turkey, until there is no more pink. Add tomato sauce, oregano, and beans, and season to taste with pepper. Stir-fry for another minute or so, or until all ingredients are very hot. Stir in parsley and serve immediately.

SERVING SIZE: ⅙ recipe
CALORIES: 233
FAT: 3.285 grams

CHOLESTEROL: 63 milligrams
SODIUM: 341 milligrams

■ ■

JAMBALAYA

Makes 8 servings

Louisiana cuisine didn't get famous for nothing. But one of its star dishes, jambalaya, almost always comes loaded with fat in the form of sausage. This recipe substitutes chicken breast, losing the fat and keeping all the flavor. Make it as hot and spicy as you like. Good jambalaya is meant to be a bit soupy; don't be ashamed to sop it up with a chunk of bread. ■

1   tablespoon olive oil

2   onions, chopped fine

2   bell peppers, preferably red, chopped fine

4   stalks celery, chopped fine

2   teaspoons dried thyme

½   teaspoon sage

½–1   teaspoon cayenne pepper

1   bay leaf

Four 8-ounce cans or 4 cups no-salt-added tomato sauce

1½   pounds skinless, boneless chicken breasts, cut into ½-inch cubes

2   cups converted long-grain rice

½   cup rice bran **or pulverized** Vita Fiber

2   green onions, sliced thin, optional

In an 8-quart saucepan, heat olive oil. When hot, stir in onions, peppers, and celery, and stir-fry for a minute or so. Add a few tablespoons of water, cover, and simmer gently, stirring on occasion, for 8 to 10 minutes or until vegetables are soft.

Add thyme, sage, cayenne, bay leaf, and tomato sauce and simmer for 2 minutes. Add chicken, rice, and rice bran, along with 4 cups water. Bring liquid to a simmer, stir, cover, and cook gently for 20 minutes, or until rice is tender.

Remove pan from heat, stir ingredients together and leave, off heat, covered, for 10 minutes. Remove bay leaf, spoon into a serving bowl, garnish with scallions if you wish, and serve.

VARIATION.   You can turn this into a vegetarian main course by substituting 3 cups cooked or canned red or pink beans for the diced chicken; don't use black beans because they will muddy up the gorgeous color of this dish.

SERVING SIZE: ⅛ recipe
CALORIES: 256
FAT: 3.154 grams

CHOLESTEROL: 70.9 milligrams
SODIUM: 95.5 milligrams

■ ■

FISH ENTRÉES

Poached Salmon with Green Sauce

Poached Salmon Steaks

Teriyaki Salmon

Salmon Bouillabaisse

Blackened Cajun Salmon

Skewered Salmon

Salmon Barley Pilaf

Salmon and Vegetable Packages

Warm "Seviche" of Salmon

Fish and Fiber Stew

Scandinavian Salmon-Rice Stew

Soused Mackerel

Baked Sardines and Chickpeas

Sardine and Potato Pie

Bluefish Parmigiana

Broiled Bluefish with Spicy
   Dressing

Fish Paella

POACHED SALMON WITH GREEN SAUCE

Makes 2 servings

For poaching, you can use plain water, a combination of water and some dry white wine, or, better still, a court bouillon such as the one I've described here. Most preparations can be done ahead so you can just pop the salmon into the court bouillon and to your guests it'll look as though you're one of those people who can entertain effortlessly. This recipe is for just two people, for a nice candlelit dinner, but you can double or triple the amounts for groups. ∎

2 salmon **steaks, 1 inch thick**

COURT BOUILLON

1 **quart water**	2 **bay leaves**
Juice of ½ **lemon**	6 **peppercorns**
2 **small carrots, sliced thin**	1 **teaspoon salt, optional**
1 **small onion, sliced**	

GREEN SAUCE

¼ **cup plain nonfat yogurt**	1 **green onion, chopped fine**
1½ **tablespoons fat-reduced mayonnaise**	5 **tablespoons chopped fresh dill or 2 tablespoons dried**
¼ **teaspoon salt, optional**	**Parsley and lemon for garnish**
½ **teaspoon white vinegar**	

Preheat oven to 350 degrees. Place all court bouillon ingredients in a shallow flameproof casserole and heat on stovetop to boiling; simmer for 10 minutes. Slice remaining lemon half into thin circular slices (you may do this in advance). Place salmon in casserole, spoon ingredients over the salmon pieces and top with sliced lemon. Cover with a piece of wax paper and bake 20 minutes.

You can prepare the green sauce in advance or while salmon is poaching in the oven. Simply place all ingredients in a blender and blend at high until well mixed, stopping the blender occasionally to scrape down the sides. By the way, using fresh rather than dried dill makes all the difference in the world. The recipe yields 4 servings of sauce.

SERVING SIZE: 5 ounces salmon with 2
  tablespoons green sauce
CALORIES: 341
FAT: 14.4 grams

CHOLESTEROL: 83.7 milligrams
SODIUM: 214 milligrams

■ ■

POACHED SALMON STEAKS

Makes 6 servings

Many diners enjoy a fine luncheon of chilled salmon when eating out in restaurants but don't think of preparing the dish at home. Yet poaching is one of the easiest and most foolproof methods of cooking fish. This can be prepared well in advance. Serve with a crisp green salad and bread. ■

6 salmon **steaks, fresh or frozen, each weighing about 6 ounces**

½ **cup dry white wine**

½ **teaspoon dill seed**

DRESSING (OR USE 2 CUPS CHICKPEA RUSSIAN DRESSING, PAGE 144)

⅓ **cup reduced-calorie mayonnaise**

½ **cup diced tofu**

¼ **cup white wine vinegar**

¼ **cup minced fresh dill or 2 tablespoons dill weed**

Place salmon steaks in a single layer in a large nonreactive skillet. Cover with white wine and dill seed. Add enough water to just cover the salmon steaks. Slowly bring liquid to a simmer and simmer 2 minutes. Remove salmon from heat and let the steaks cool to room temperature in this cooking liquid; this will keep them moist. When cool, remove salmon from the cooking liquid and place on a platter; chill, covered, for 1 hour.

Meanwhile, in a blender or food processor, combine mayonnaise, tofu, vinegar, and dill, and blend until smooth; if the dressing is too thick, thin with water to the desired consistency. Serve with chilled salmon.

SERVING SIZE: 1 steak
CALORIES: 389
FAT: 17.6 grams

CHOLESTEROL: 85.6 milligrams
SODIUM: 205 milligrams

TERIYAKI SALMON

Makes 4 servings

Of all the fish that swim the seas, my all-around favorite remains salmon. How happy I was to discover it's one of the richest fish in omega-3 fish oils. You can substitute mackerel, bluefish, or other fish in this or any of my recipes with no problem. This is a truly simple yet delicious meal that you can serve to company with pride. Just marinate the fish for a while before you broil or grill. ■

1 **pound** salmon **steaks or fillets**

MARINADE

⅔ **cup low-sodium soy sauce**

¼ **cup sweet sherry**

1 **tablespoon brown sugar**

½ **teaspoon freshly grated ginger root**

1 **large garlic clove, minced fine**

Juice of 1 lemon

Mix together marinade ingredients in a large plastic storage bag, place fish in the bag and cover with the marinade. Marinate in the refrigerator 2 to 3 hours. Drain and broil or grill 3 minutes on each side.

Serve with mounds of steamed rice and a pile of stir-fried bamboo shoots and bean sprouts.

SERVING SIZE: 4 ounces salmon with ¼ marinade recipe
CALORIES: 281
FAT: 8.502 grams
CHOLESTEROL: 54.4 milligrams
SODIUM: 147.3 milligrams

■ ■

SALMON BOUILLABAISSE

Makes 4 hearty servings

I just love bouillabaisse, and find that every restaurant's version is a bit different. One thing I've never seen, though, in this marvelously aromatic soup, is salmon. So here's the way I make it at home. I've also included a classic recipe for rouille, which is a condiment you add to the bouillabaisse just before serving or at the table. It is optional but adds a nice touch. Serve this meal with some crusty French bread and a bottle of red wine. ∎

1 **pound** salmon **steaks or fillets cut into pieces**	2 **garlic cloves, chopped coarse**
½ **pound shrimp, lobster, crab, or a combination of all**	1 **large tomato cut into wedges**
	Water or fish broth to cover
8 **clams or mussels**	**Bouquet garni (thyme, bay leaf, parsley, celery, rosemary)**
1 **tablespoon olive oil**	
2 **leeks (chopped white portion only)**	**Pinch of saffron**
1 **medium onion, chopped**	**Salt, pepper, cayenne pepper to taste**

Heat olive oil in a large soup pot and add vegetables, sautéing them until onion becomes transparent. Add water or fish broth along with the bouquet garni and simmer for 5 minutes. Add salmon and shrimp and simmer 5 more minutes. Add clams or mussels and simmer a final 5 minutes, or until the shells open.

Add a healthy pinch of saffron, and season with salt, pepper, and cayenne pepper to taste. That's all there is to it! You never want to prepare this dish in advance; it should be served immediately, so the fish and vegetables remain firm, not mushy. You may add the rouille as you serve the bouillabaisse, or each person can add it to his or her own bowl.

SERVING SIZE: ¼ recipe
CALORIES: 391
FAT: 13.5 grams
CHOLESTEROL: 82.4 milligrams
SODIUM: 219 milligrams

ROUILLE

2 garlic cloves

1 small red pepper

1 tablespoon oat bran or apple fiber

2 tablespoons bouillon

1 tablespoon olive oil

½ teaspoon paprika

1 tablespoon tomato paste

Put all ingredients into a blender or food processor and blend until smooth.

SERVING SIZE: 2 tablespoons
CALORIES: 67
FAT: 5.018 grams

CHOLESTEROL: 0
SODIUM: 2.691 milligrams

■■■■■■■■■■■■■■■■■■■■■■■■■■■■■■■■■■■■■

BLACKENED CAJUN SALMON

Makes 6 servings

When Chef Paul Prudhomme hit the scene with his Cajun cooking in New Orleans, he caused an actual shortage of redfish, which he specialized in blackening. As he later pointed out, blackening works well with many fish, not only redfish. I think one of the best for this approach is salmon. You can make your own blackening seasoning to keep on hand for this and other dishes as well. ∎

6 salmon **fillets, 4 ounces each**

2 **tablespoons margarine**

CAJUN BLACKENING SEASONING

1 **tablespoon paprika**

1 **teaspoon garlic powder**

1 **teaspoon cayenne**

¾ **teaspoon black pepper**

½ **teaspoon ground thyme**

½ **teaspoon oregano**

½ **teaspoon dried basil**

1 **teaspoon onion powder**

2 **teaspoons salt (optional)**

Mix all seasoning ingredients together. Sprinkle seasonings liberally over salmon fillets (you can use steaks, but the fillets work a lot better). Place seasoned salmon along with a small pat of margarine in a *very* hot (smoking) cast-iron skillet. Sear for 2 minutes, then turn, using another pat of margarine to blacken the other side for another 2 minutes. This is a spicy dish, and a glass of cold beer fits the bill perfectly.

There's only one drawback to making blackened fish: expect an enormous amount of smoke when the margarine and fish hit the searing-hot cast-iron skillet. I put the skillet directly on charcoal on the barbecue grill outside. It's just too smoky to make inside.

SERVING SIZE: 4 ounces
CALORIES: 243
FAT: 8.56 grams
CHOLESTEROL: 54.39 milligrams

SODIUM *(with optional salt in seasonings):*
505 milligrams
SODIUM *(without optional salt):*
138.64 milligrams

■ ■

SKEWERED SALMON

Makes 4 servings

There's something really festive about skewering foods to broil or grill. This recipe provides a particularly colorful dish. Serve it with lots of steamed rice and a nice bottle of crisp white wine. ∎

2½ tablespoons lemon juice (juice of 1 large lemon)

1½ tablespoons lime juice (juice of 1 lime)

¼ cup olive oil

2 tablespoons fine-minced onion

1 fine-minced garlic clove

1 teaspoon crushed red pepper flakes

1 teaspoon rosemary

1 pound salmon steaks, cut into chunks

1 green bell pepper, cut into 1½-inch pieces

1 red bell pepper, cut into 1½-inch pieces

8 large mushrooms

Mix juice, oil, onion, garlic, pepper flakes, and rosemary in a large plastic storage bag. Add pieces of salmon, peppers, and mushrooms. Marinate in refrigerator 2 hours. Skewer salmon, peppers, and mushrooms alternately and broil or grill 3 minutes per side. Do not overcook; serve immediately.

SERVING SIZE: ¼ pound with ¼ marinade recipe
CALORIES: 334

FAT: 22.06 grams
CHOLESTEROL: 54.4 milligrams
SODIUM: 134.6 milligrams

SALMON BARLEY PILAF

Makes 6 servings

Barley brings additional soluble fiber to this pilaf. Salmon delivers its protective oils. And vinegar gives the dish zip. While the recipe calls for either rice or white wine vinegar, you might want to experiment with other vinegars, such as balsamic, as well. ∎

1 tablespoon olive oil	1 cup pearled barley
1 onion, chopped fine	¼ cup white wine or rice vinegar
1 carrot, chopped fine	1 tablespoon dried parsley or cilantro or 3 tablespoons minced fresh herb
1 celery stalk, chopped fine	
Two 6½-ounce cans salmon, drained	
	Pepper

Preheat oven to 350 degrees.

In a 6-quart flameproof casserole heat olive oil. When hot, add onion, carrot, and celery, and sauté for 2 to 3 minutes, stirring constantly.

Add salmon and stir around to break up the fish, then stir in barley, vinegar, herb and 2 cups water. Season to taste with pepper. Bring liquid to a simmer, cover, and bake for 45 minutes or until barley has absorbed all of the liquid and is just tender to the bite. Stir ingredients around with a fork just before serving.

SERVING SIZE: ⅙ recipe
CALORIES: 248
FAT: 6.29 grams

CHOLESTEROL: 24.5 milligrams
SODIUM: 332 milligrams

■ ■

SALMON AND VEGETABLE PACKAGES

Makes 6 servings

Where do I begin listing the advantages of this cooking approach? First, I guess, would be that the recipe is absolutely foolproof; it just can't fail. Second, it takes little preparation time. Third, you can make up the packages ahead of time in case you're on a tight schedule after work or when entertaining. Fourth, you have no pots and pans to clean up; just toss out the aluminum foil. Fifth, and probably the most important, the dish is delish! ■

6 salmon **steaks, each about 6 ounces**

4 **celery stalks**

1 **parsnip, peeled**

2 **carrots, peeled (or 4 carrots if you don't have the parsnip)**

½ **cup white wine**

2 **teaspoons sugar**

Pepper

Preheat oven to 375 degrees.

Place each salmon steak on a piece of aluminum foil, about 10 inches square, sprayed with Pam or Baker's Joy; set aside.

Cut celery, parsnip, and carrots into thin strips, about 2 inches long and ¼ inch thick. Simmer these in the white wine and sugar, in a covered skillet over medium heat, for about 10 to 15 minutes or until tender.

Spoon some of this vegetable mixture on top of each salmon steak, and season to taste with pepper. Bring all four corners of each piece of foil to the center; crimp them together to enclose the fish. Set the packages on a baking sheet and bake for 30 minutes.

Open packages and serve salmon with the vegetables and natural juices.

SERVING SIZE: 1 steak
CALORIES: 418
FAT: 15 grams

CHOLESTEROL: 94 milligrams
SODIUM: 267 milligrams

WARM "SEVICHE" OF SALMON

Makes 6 servings

Here's a dish with two compromises. First, seviche normally is made with scallops; we've substituted salmon. Second, seviche is "cooked" during the marinade process; here we cook the salmon in the oven after marinating, and serve it warm, along with the marinating mixture and pan juices. If fresh cilantro is unavailable, substitute another fresh herb such as parsley, although the flavor will be less than authentic. I like to serve this with baked herbed cherry tomatoes. ∎

6 **fresh** salmon **steaks, 6 ounces each**	½ **cup minced fresh cilantro leaves**
½ **onion, minced**	¼ **cup each lemon and lime juice**
1 **clove garlic, minced**	1 **tablespoon olive oil**
	Cayenne pepper to taste

Set salmon steaks in an ovenproof enamel or glass dish. Mix onion, garlic, cilantro, lemon and lime juices, and olive oil. Season to taste with cayenne and pour over the salmon steaks. Cover dish and refrigerate for 6 hours at least or, preferably, overnight.

Preheat oven to 350 degrees. Place the dish with the salmon, covered, in the oven, and bake for 15 to 20 minutes or until just done through. Serve with pan juices.

SERVING SIZE: ⅙ recipe
CALORIES: 328
FAT: 18.1 grams

CHOLESTEROL: 102 milligrams
SODIUM: 244 milligrams

FISH AND FIBER STEW

Makes 8 servings

Here's the ultimate healthy stew. You get the protective oils of the salmon in the same dish with soluble fiber from the lentils and peas. At the same time we balance the meal with vegetables. If you wish, you can even add some chunked potatoes when you cook the vegetables. Serve with some crusty bread and you have all four food groups represented. ■

½ **cup dried** lentils

½ **cup dried** split green peas

One 14½-ounce can no-salt-added stewed tomatoes

½ **cup fine-chopped onions**

½ **cup fine-chopped bell peppers**

1 **carrot, chopped fine**

1 **stalk celery, chopped fine**

1 **pound** salmon, **cut into chunks**

One 1-pound can pink beans

One 10-ounce package frozen corn kernels

Pepper

In a 6-quart saucepan bring to a boil lentils, split peas, tomatoes, onions, peppers, carrot, celery, and 2 cups water. Simmer, covered, for 25 minutes.

Add salmon, beans, liquid from the can, and the corn. If needed, add some water to just cover mixture. Cover and simmer for 15 minutes more or until lentils and peas are cooked through and tender; season to taste with pepper and serve.

SERVING SIZE: ⅛ recipe
CALORIES: 243
FAT: 3.85 grams

CHOLESTEROL: 22.9 milligrams
SODIUM: 342 milligrams

■ ■

SCANDINAVIAN SALMON-RICE STEW

Makes 6 servings

There's no question about it, salmon is my favorite fish. One of the reasons is its versatility, which this Scandinavian dish demonstrates beautifully. ■

One 8-ounce bottle clam juice

½ cup white wine

¼ cup fine-chopped parsnips

½ cup fine-chopped carrots

1 onion, chopped fine

¼ cup long-grain white rice

One 10-ounce package frozen spinach, thawed

¼ cup rice bran or Vita Fiber

Two 7½-ounce cans salmon packed in water, drained

¼ cup fine-chopped fresh dill or parsley

In a medium-large saucepan bring to a boil clam juice, white wine, 2 cups water, parsnips, carrots, onion, rice, and spinach. Simmer, covered, for 10 minutes.

Add rice bran or Vita Fiber, salmon, and dill, and simmer 5 minutes more.

SERVING SIZE: ⅙ recipe
CALORIES: 182
FAT: 5.78 grams

CHOLESTEROL: 34 milligrams
SODIUM: 131 milligrams

■ ■

SOUSED MACKEREL

Makes 6 servings

Mackerel is very rich in omega-3 fish oils, and mackerel lovers will enjoy this dish served hot with potatoes or rice, or chilled with fresh greens. Those who aren't so fond of mackerel might want to substitute canned salmon. ■

Two 1-pound cans mackerel packed in water, drained

One 8-ounce can no-salt-added tomato sauce

One 10-ounce jar cocktail onions, drained

2 tablespoons rice or white wine vinegar

1 teaspoon prepared mustard

Pinch ground nutmeg and/or mace

Preheat oven to 350 degrees.

Break up mackerel and place in a 9-inch-square baking pan.

In a small bowl, mix the tomato sauce with the cocktail onions, vinegar, mustard, and spices. Pour over fish and mix. Bake for 15 minutes to heat through. Serve hot or cool to room temperature and chill overnight before serving.

SERVING SIZE: ⅙ recipe
CALORIES: 246
FAT: 9 grams

CHOLESTEROL: 60.4 milligrams
SODIUM: 809 milligrams

■■

BAKED SARDINES AND CHICKPEAS

Makes 6 servings

Here's your chance to get the benefits of both soluble fiber and fish oil in one dish. As always, you can substitute canned salmon for the sardines. This is great served with rice. ■

Two 16-ounce cans chickpeas, drained and rinsed

Three 3¾-ounce cans smoked sardines, drained and patted dry

1 cup no-salt-added tomato sauce

1 teaspoon garlic powder

1 tablespoon dried parsley flakes

Pepper

2 tablespoons Formagg grated Parmesan-cheese substitute

Preheat oven to 350 degrees.

Mix all ingredients in a 9-by-13-inch baking pan and bake for 20 to 25 minutes.

SERVING SIZE: ⅙ recipe
CALORIES: 169
FAT: 4.81 grams

CHOLESTEROL: 22 milligrams
SODIUM: 221.47 milligrams

■■

Sardine and Potato Pie

Makes 6 servings

This was inspired by shepherds pie. You can adapt the idea of using mashed potatoes as a topping for the pie to other recipes that normally use a traditional pie crust, for example, chicken pot pie. In this dish you can substitute canned salmon for the sardines if you prefer. ■

1½ pounds boiling potatoes

¼ cup evaporated skim milk

Pepper

½ cup chopped fresh parsley or dill

1 tablespoon olive oil

1 onion, sliced thin

3 small red or green bell peppers, sliced thin

Red pepper flakes, optional

Three 3¾-ounce cans sardines, packed in water, drained

Peel potatoes and cut into 1-inch cubes. Boil them in water to cover for about 20 to 25 minutes, or until tender. Drain, and with a ricer or food mill mash them with the milk. Do not mash them in the food processor or they will become gummy. Season to taste with pepper and blend in parsley or dill.

Preheat oven to 350 degrees.

In a large skillet, heat olive oil. When hot, add onion and bell peppers, and sauté, stirring constantly, for 3 to 4 minutes. Add ½ cup of water, cover, and simmer 10 minutes more, or until tender. Remove cover and cook, over medium-high heat, for about 5 minutes, or until all the liquid has evaporated. Season to taste with red pepper flakes if you wish. Stir in sardines and break them up a bit.

Scoop onion, pepper, and sardines into a 10- or 11-inch ovenproof glass pie plate. By spoonfuls, pat mashed potatoes on top and bake for 30 minutes.

SERVING SIZE: ⅙ recipe
CALORIES: 209
FAT: 5.478 grams

CHOLESTEROL: 20.2 milligrams
SODIUM: 278 milligrams

■ ■

BLUEFISH PARMIGIANA

Makes 4 servings

Here, too, you can substitute salmon or any other fish for the bluefish if you can't find or don't like bluefish. The oatmeal gives the fish a lovely crunchy coating. I like this with a bit of pasta on the side and a small salad. ∎

2 cups no-salt-added tomato sauce, seasoned with ½ teaspoon oregano

1½ pounds bluefish fillets, preferably fresh and about ¾ inch thick

¼ cup oat bran

1 egg white mixed with 2 tablespoons water

1 cup oatmeal

1 tablespoon canola oil

¼ cup Formagg grated Parmesan-flavored cheese substitute

Preheat oven to 350 degrees.

Pour seasoned tomato sauce into an ovenproof baking pan and set aside.

Cut bluefish fillets into 4 portions. Dip fillets first into oat bran, then into egg-white mixture, and then pat on the oatmeal to cover all sides.

Heat oil in a large skillet, over high heat. When very hot, add fish, skin side facing up, and sauté for 1½ minutes. With a spatula, turn fish over and sauté for a minute more. Transfer fish to the baking pan, placing them over the tomato sauce, skin side down. Bake for 10 to 15 minutes, depending on their thickness. Sprinkle cheese substitute over fish and sauce and bake 5 minutes more.

SERVING SIZE: ¼ recipe
CALORIES: 252
FAT: 8.96 grams

CHOLESTEROL: 56.94 milligrams
SODIUM: 352 milligrams

BROILED BLUEFISH WITH SPICY DRESSING

Makes 4 servings

The dressing gives a spicy and crunchy contrast to the rich flesh of the fish. For added color try using both red and green bell peppers. And if bluefish isn't available in your market, or you don't happen to enjoy it, salmon can be substituted. ■

1½ pounds bluefish **fillets, fresh or frozen, thawed**

1 **tablespoon olive oil**

2 **tablespoons wine vinegar**

½ **cup minced fresh parsley**

1 **red or green bell pepper, seeds and membranes removed, chopped fine**

2 **green onions, sliced thin**

Pepper

Preheat broiler.

Broil fillets for 6 to 9 minutes, depending on their thickness; take care not to overcook.

While fish is broiling, in a mixer or blender combine oil, vinegar, parsley, green bell pepper, and green onions; season to taste with pepper.

When fish is cooked through, spoon one-fourth of the dressing over each fillet and serve immediately.

SERVING SIZE: ¼ recipe
CALORIES: 303
FAT: 12.2 grams

CHOLESTEROL: 80 milligrams
SODIUM: 178 milligrams

■■

FISH PAELLA

Makes 6 to 8 servings

Many restaurants stake their claim to fame on their paella recipes. This dish is loved from coast to coast and around the world. Here's a variation on the theme, with salmon or bluefish substituting for the usual chicken, and rice bran supplying the creamy texture. Try it with a glass of Spanish wine, if you like. ■

1 onion, chopped fine

1 clove garlic, minced

1 red or green bell pepper, chopped fine

½ cup chopped pimientos

½ cup white wine

1½ cups long-grain rice

⅛–¼ teaspoon saffron threads

One 8-ounce can no-salt-added tomato sauce

½ cup pulverized Vita Fiber

One 10-ounce pack thawed petite peas

1½ pounds boneless salmon or bluefish fillets, cut into 1-inch cubes

Pepper

Spray a large skillet or saucepan with Pam or Baker's Joy; sauté the onion, garlic, and green bell pepper for 3 minutes, stirring continuously. Add pimientos and white wine and simmer 3 minutes more.

Stir in rice, saffron, and tomato sauce, along with 2 cups water. Bring to a boil and simmer, covered, for 15 minutes.

Stir in Vita Fiber, peas, and fish, and season to taste with pepper. Cover and simmer 5 minutes more or until fish is just cooked through and rice is just tender to the bite.

SERVING SIZE: ⅛ recipe
CALORIES: 237
FAT: 5.03 grams

CHOLESTEROL: 80 milligrams
SODIUM: 133 milligrams

■ ■

SIDE DISHES

BEANS AND LEGUMES

Refried Beans

Bean or Legume Pancakes

Easy Baked Beans

Spiced Baked Beans

Pinto Bean and Artichoke Casserole

Pinto Bean Succotash

Purée of Lima Beans and Carrots

Fava Bean and Garlic Purée

Scandinavian White Bean and Rice
    Stew

Baked Hominy or Chickpea Casserole

Chickpea, Garlic, and Thyme Purée

Black Bean Cakes

Black Beans and Rice Medley

Creole Red Beans and Rice

Braised Red Kidney Beans and
    Cabbage

Red Bean Stir-Fry

Red Beans with Garlic and Ginger

Barbecued Kidney Beans

Split Pea and Potato Purée

Pease Pudding

French Bean Casserole

Mixed Beans and Squash

Mixed Vegetable and Bean Pudding

Persian Rice and Lentils

Sweet Swedish Lentils

Sweet-and-Sour Lentils

RICE BRAN AND OAT BRAN

Artichoke and Chicken Risotto

Mushroom Risotto

Risotto Milanese

Indian Rice Pilaf

Rice and Carrot Pancakes

Chilled Tomato and Vegetable
    Purée

Scallion, Cornmeal, and Oat-Bran
    Johnnycakes

Carrot and Potato Pancakes

BARLEY

Barley and Green Pea Medley

Chinese Fried Barley

Mushroom Barley Pilaf

R EFRIED BEANS

Makes 4 to 6 servings

An absolute must when enjoying Mexican food, refried beans traditionally are made with lard. This basic recipe calls for healthful olive oil instead. You can further enhance the recipe by adding one or more of the following: two large garlic cloves, minced fine; one jalapeño pepper, minced fine; a dash or two of Tabasco; one teaspoon of salt (if your sodium limitations permit). If you add the garlic and/or peppers, sauté them along with the onion. ∎

2 tablespoons olive oil

1 small onion, or about ¼ cup chopped fine

Two 1-pound cans red or pink beans

Lime juice, optional

Chopped freshly cilantro, optional

In a large skillet, heat oil. When hot, add onion and sauté for 2 to 3 minutes. Drain one of the cans of beans.

Add to the skillet one can of beans with liquid and the drained beans. Turn heat up fairly high and begin to mash the beans, with the edge of a wooden spoon, until they are coarsely broken down.

Reduce heat to low and simmer gently, stirring continuously with a wooden spoon, for 5 to 10 minutes, or until the beans form a coarse purée, which begins to stick to the bottom of the skillet.

Serve as is or lightly seasoned with drops of lime juice and cilantro.

SERVING SIZE: ⅙ recipe
CALORIES: 160
FAT: 2.86 grams

CHOLESTEROL: 0
SODIUM: 494 milligrams

∎∎

BEAN OR LEGUME PANCAKES

Makes 12 pancakes

You can use this recipe as a blueprint for any dried-bean pancakes. They make an interesting appetizer or can be served as a side dish with dinner. Applesauce is a nice accompaniment. ■

2 cups cooked or drained canned chickpeas **or other** beans, lentils, or split peas

2 green onions, chopped

⅓ cup chopped red bell pepper

6 tablespoons flour

1 teaspoon cumin seeds or other spice of your choice

2 egg whites

Canola oil

Preheat oven to 250 degrees.

In a blender or food processor, combine chickpeas, green onions, red pepper, flour, and cumin. Add ⅓ cup or more water to make a somewhat loose dough.

Beat egg whites until stiff and fold into batter.

Heat a large skillet, preferably nonstick. Brush surface lightly with oil. Drop batter by ¼ cupfuls onto skillet. With the back of a spoon, gently spread the pancake until it is about ⅛ inch thick. Cook for 3 to 4 minutes per side.

Keep cooked pancakes warm in oven, while you make some more.

SERVING SIZE: 1 pancake
CALORIES: 57
FAT: .23 grams

CHOLESTEROL: 0
SODIUM: 147 milligrams

EASY BAKED BEANS

Makes about 6 servings

Baked beans come in many forms, from the Boston baked beans served in a ceramic pot to the kind heated over a campfire in the West. The kind you buy canned in the supermarket almost always are made with pork fat and are lacking in flavor. This recipe gives you all the flavor with none of the saturated fat. It calls for one of three kinds of beans, but you might also try using all three types in the same dish. ■

¼ **cup brown sugar**

2 **tablespoons molasses**

3 **tablespoons Dijon-style mustard**

⅓ **cup ketchup**

1 **teaspoon garlic powder**

Pepper

Three 1-pound-3-ounce cans navy, Great Northern, **or** white kidney beans, **or 6 cups cooked** white beans

Preheat oven to 350 degrees.

In a bowl combine brown sugar, molasses, mustard, ketchup, and garlic powder, and season to taste with pepper. Stir in beans and transfer to a baking dish. Cover and bake for 30 minutes; uncover and bake 15 minutes more.

SERVING SIZE: ⅙ recipe
CALORIES: 313
FAT: 1.543 grams

CHOLESTEROL: 0
SODIUM: 260 milligrams

■ ■

SPICED BAKED BEANS

Makes 8 servings

Someday when the weather is cold and the wind roaring, you might like to try an old-fashioned cook-all-day baked-bean recipe. This is the way your grandmother cooked, and it fills the house with the aromas that memories are made of. ■

2 cups (1 pound) navy, pea, or small white beans, soaked (see page 89) and drained

2 cups fat-free chicken broth or water

1 medium onion, chopped fine

¼ pound 96 percent fat-free ham, chopped

4 cloves garlic, minced

½ teaspoon ground cumin

¼ teaspoon ground cloves

¼ teaspoon mace

Pepper

¼ cup blackstrap molasses

Preheat oven to 300 degrees.

In a 3- to 5-quart flameproof casserole, combine all ingredients and stir until mixed. Add 4 cups water (6 cups liquid in all), bring to a simmer on top of the stove, cover, and bake for 6 hours.

Increase the oven heat to 350 degrees. Uncover the casserole and bake for 45 minutes to an hour more, or until the beans have absorbed all the liquid and formed a slight crust on top.

SERVING SIZE: ⅛ recipe
CALORIES: 115
FAT: 1.03 grams

CHOLESTEROL: 4.15 milligrams
SODIUM: 175 milligrams

■■■■■■■■■■■■■■■■■■■■■■■■■■■■■■■■■■■■■■

PINTO BEAN AND ARTICHOKE CASSEROLE

Makes 4 to 6 servings

Served with rice this can make a very attractive vegetarian meal. If you prefer, serve it as a side dish with a piece of broiled Dakota lean steak. ∎

Two 1-pound cans pinto or pink beans

One 1-pound can artichoke hearts, drained and chopped

⅛ **teaspoon each cayenne and ground cloves**

½ **teaspoon ground cumin**

2 **tablespoons chili sauce**

Preheat oven to 350 degrees.

Empty 1 can of beans and liquid into a 9-inch-square baking pan. Drain and rinse the other can of beans, then roughly chop the beans. Add chopped beans and artichokes to the whole beans. Add spices and chili sauce and mix together well.

Set pan in oven, uncovered, and bake for 30 minutes.

SERVING SIZE: ¼ recipe
CALORIES: 259
FAT: .72 grams

CHOLESTEROL: O
SODIUM: 80.2 milligrams

■ ■

PINTO BEAN SUCCOTASH

Makes 4 to 6 servings

The Indians introduced colonial American settlers to succotash, a medley of corn and lima beans. This version also delivers soluble fiber by way of the apple fiber, which thickens the sauce and adds a touch of sweetness. Try it with low-fat ham steaks. ∎

4 **tablespoons** apple fiber

½ **cup evaporated skim milk**

2 **tablespoons ketchup**

Pepper

2 **cups cooked or drained canned (1 pound) pinto beans**

1 **cup thawed corn kernels**

¼ **cup or one 3½-ounce jar cocktail onions**

In a medium saucepan, bring apple fiber, milk, ¼ cup water, and ketchup to a slow boil, stirring all the while, preferably with a whisk. Season to taste with pepper.

Stir in beans, corn, and onions, and simmer, uncovered, for 15 minutes or until the flavors come together and the sauce thickens a bit more.

SERVING SIZE: ⅙ recipe
CALORIES: 84
FAT: .669 grams

CHOLESTEROL: .85 milligrams
SODIUM: 79 milligrams

■■■■■■■■■■■■■■■■■■■■■■■■■■■■■■■■■■■■■■■

Purée of Lima Beans and Carrots

Makes 4 to 6 servings

You can find both dried and canned lima beans in the supermarket; canned beans may be labeled as butter beans, but avoid the kind packed with pork. This is an interesting and delicious side dish, with a creamy texture that goes well with turkey or ham. ∎

1 tablespoon vegetable oil

1 cup fine-chopped carrots

½ cup chopped onions

1 cup dried lima beans, **large or baby, soaked (see page 89) and drained**

¾ cup evaporated skim milk, **approximately**

¼ teaspoon ground nutmeg

Pepper

In a medium saucepan, heat oil. When hot, sauté carrots and onions for 1 minute, stirring frequently. Add lima beans, 2 cups water, ½ cup of the milk, and nutmeg. Bring to a simmer, reduce heat to very low, and cook, partially covered, for 45 to 50 minutes or until the beans are tender. If the mixture looks a little curdled, don't worry; this all works itself out in the mashing or puréeing.

While beans are cooking, stir them on occasion to prevent them from sticking; if the liquid is evaporating too quickly, add the extra ¼ cup of milk. When done, mash the beans with a wooden spoon or, if you prefer a smooth texture, purée in a blender or food processor. Season well with pepper.

SERVING SIZE: ⅙ recipe
CALORIES: 86.1
FAT: 2.501 grams

CHOLESTEROL: 1.275 milligrams
SODIUM: 58.2 milligrams

FAVA BEAN AND GARLIC PURÉE

Makes 4 to 6 servings

A less common bean, the fava has a sturdy, hefty flavor. Wine, garlic, and thyme complement that flavor nicely. You must use a drinking-quality wine rather than a cooking wine in this dish, or the flavor will become harsh and unpleasant. ■

Two **1-pound cans** fava beans

4 **cloves garlic, chopped**

1 **teaspoon dried thyme**

2 **cups drinking-quality dry red wine, such as Burgundy**

Pepper

Gently simmer fava beans and their liquid, garlic, thyme, red wine, and 2 cups water, partially covered, for 45 minutes or until the fava beans have just absorbed all the liquid.

Mash the beans against the sides of the pot until you form a purée. If you do not like the texture of their skins, pass the fava beans through a food mill to make a smoother purée. Season to taste with pepper.

SERVING SIZE: ⅙ recipe
CALORIES: 304
FAT: .732 grams

CHOLESTEROL: 0
SODIUM: 5.114 milligrams

■ ■

SCANDINAVIAN WHITE BEAN AND RICE STEW

Makes 8 servings

Combining beans and rice yields high-quality protein. Combining two, three, or four kinds of beans provides interesting taste and texture. And fresh herbs give this dish wonderful flavor; by all means try to use fresh dill rather than dried whenever possible. ■

1 cup long-grain rice

2 cups cooked or drained and rinsed canned navy, pea, or white kidney beans

2 tablespoons lemon juice

4 tablespoons minced fresh dill or 1 tablespoon dry dill weed

Pepper

Place rice, beans, lemon juice, and 2 cups water in a large saucepan and bring to a boil. Cover and simmer for 20 minutes. Stir in dill and season to taste with pepper.

SERVING SIZE: ⅛ recipe
CALORIES: 133
FAT: .453 grams

CHOLESTEROL: 0
SODIUM: .031 milligrams

■ ■

BAKED HOMINY
OR CHICKPEA CASSEROLE

Makes 6 generous portions

This dish combines the soluble fibers of oat bran and chickpeas, delivering enough for the entire day. You'll notice that at first the oat-bran sauce is very thick, but the spinach will thin it out, and then baking will thin it further. Use as a side dish or add diced ham or turkey breast to make it a main course. ■

¼ **cup evaporated skim milk**

¾ **cup** oat bran, **processed into flour**

2 **teaspoons cumin powder**

2 **teaspoons chili powder**

One 10-ounce package frozen **chopped spinach, thawed**

½ **cup chopped bell pepper**

2 **green onions, sliced thin**

One 16-ounce can (2 cups) hominy **or** chickpeas

Preheat oven to 375 degrees.

In a 3-quart saucepan, slowly bring evaporated milk, oat bran, and 1¾ cups water to a boil, stirring constantly with a wooden spoon. When the sauce has thickened, stir in cumin and chili powders and spinach. Mix until well blended—the sauce will be very thick, but it will thin out in the oven.

Mix in pepper and green onions. Mix in hominy and turn into a shallow baking dish. Bake for 15 minutes or until hot.

SERVING SIZE: ⅙ recipe
CALORIES: 136
FAT: 2.52 grams

CHOLESTEROL: .42 milligrams
SODIUM: 351 milligrams

■■■

CHICK PEA, GARLIC, AND THYME PURÉE

Makes 6 to 8 servings

Here's a welcome alternative to mashed potatoes as a side dish for virtually any main course. ■

1 onion, chopped fine	1 teaspoon dried thyme
2 carrots, chopped fine	Skim milk
6 cloves garlic, minced	Pepper
Two 19-ounce cans chickpeas, drained and rinsed	

Spray a medium saucepan with Pam or Baker's Joy, and sauté onion, carrots, and garlic. Cover and simmer gently for 3 to 4 minutes, or until onions begin to soften.

Add chickpeas, ½ cup water, and thyme. Cover and simmer for 20 minutes more. Purée in a food processor or blender. If mixture is too thick, thin with skim milk; season to taste with pepper.

SERVING SIZE: ⅛ recipe
CALORIES: 17.1
FAT: .91 grams

CHOLESTEROL: .125 milligrams
SODIUM: 11.2 milligrams

BLACK BEAN CAKES

Makes 6 servings

Black beans have a distinctive flavor that really comes through in this dish. You can use the cakes as a side dish, as I prefer, or as a main course if you're in the mood for a vegetarian meal. I like to make the cakes quite spicy, with lots of Tabasco and chili powder. When using it as a main dish, you may wish to hold back a bit on the spices. ■

1 cup chopped fresh tomatoes

One 4-ounce can green chilies

¼ cup chopped fresh cilantro or parsley

1 tablespoon lemon juice

Tabasco

2 cups freshly cooked or one 15- or 16-ounce can black beans, **drained and rinsed**

¼ cup oat bran

1 teaspoon ground cumin

1 teaspoon chili powder

1 green onion, sliced

Pepper

1–2 tablespoons olive oil

Additional oat bran

Nonfat yogurt

In a small mixing bowl combine tomatoes, green chilies, cilantro, and lemon juice. Season to taste with Tabasco and chill until ready to serve.

In a food processor or blender, purée black beans. Mix with oat bran, cumin, chili powder, and sliced green onions; season to taste with pepper. Shape mixture into 2-inch patties.

In a large skillet, preferably nonstick, heat olive oil. Dip each patty on both sides in oat bran and sauté olive oil. Dip each patty on both sides in oat bran and sauté for 2 to 3 minutes per side. Serve with chilled tomato-and-chili sauce and nonfat yogurt.

SERVING SIZE: ⅙ recipe
CALORIES: 86.4
FAT: 3.287 grams

CHOLESTEROL: 0
SODIUM: 167 milligrams

■ ■

BLACK BEANS AND RICE MEDLEY

Makes 4 to 6 servings

This recipe provides another example of how foods can be combined to give a full protein complement with no meat at all. Beans and rice are a staple in many parts of the world. But if you'd really enjoy some meat, you can add some diced smoked ham or turkey to round out the dish. ■

1 **tablespoon canola or olive oil**	1 **cup long-grain converted rice**
½ **small onion, chopped fine**	2 **cups cooked or canned (1 pound)** black beans, **rinsed**
1 **green bell pepper, chopped fine**	¼ **cup chopped fresh parsley or 4** teaspoons dried
1 **stalk celery, chopped fine**	**Pepper**
¼ **teaspoon garlic powder**	
½ **teaspoon thyme**	

In a medium saucepan heat oil. When hot, stir-fry onion, pepper, and celery for 1 minute. Cover saucepan and cook for 3 to 4 minutes, or until vegetables have softened. Add garlic powder and thyme and stir in rice. Add 2 cups water and bring to a boil. Cover pan and simmer gently for 10 minutes.

Add black beans, stir, cover, and simmer for another 10 minutes or until rice is cooked through. Stir in parsley and season to taste with pepper.

SERVING SIZE: ⅙ recipe
CALORIES: 105
FAT: 3.06 grams

CHOLESTEROL: 0
SODIUM: 375 milligrams

■ ■

CREOLE RED BEANS AND RICE

Makes 4 to 6 servings

This is a staple food throughout Louisiana, especially down around New Orleans. It's a tasty side dish along with some blackened salmon. ■

2 tablespoons olive or canola oil	½ teaspoon dried thyme
2 green onions, sliced thin	¼ teaspoon cayenne
1 green pepper, chopped fine	One 1-pound can red kidney beans, with liquid
1 stalk celery, chopped fine	
½ teaspoon garlic powder	1 cup long-grain rice

In a medium saucepan, heat oil. When hot, stir in green onions, pepper, and celery. Sauté for 2 to 3 minutes.

Add garlic, thyme, and cayenne, and sauté for 10 seconds. Add kidney beans and their liquid. Stir in rice and 1½ cups water. Cover and simmer gently for 20 minutes. Remove cover and fluff up with a fork.

SERVING SIZE: ⅙ recipe
CALORIES: 151
FAT: 5.03 grams

CHOLESTEROL: 0
SODIUM: 223 milligrams

■ ■

BRAISED RED KIDNEY BEANS AND CABBAGE

Makes 8 servings

This dish can be served as a side dish or main course, or you can serve it in place of salad, before the meal. If you use it as a main course, you might want to add some diced low-fat ham. Any way you choose, it's a treat. ■

One 1-pound can no-salt-added tomatoes, chopped

1½ teaspoons caraway seeds

½ medium cabbage, shredded

½ pound fresh mushrooms, sliced

Two 1-pound-3-ounce cans kidney beans, drained, or 4 cups cooked

Pepper

In a large saucepan, bring tomatoes and caraway seeds to a boil. Add cabbage and mushrooms, cover pot, and simmer, stirring every now and then, for 30 minutes or until cabbage is tender but still has some crunch to it. Add beans and simmer, uncovered, for 15 minutes longer. Season to taste with pepper.

SERVING SIZE: ⅛ recipe
CALORIES: 159
FAT: .79 grams

CHOLESTEROL: 0
SODIUM: 77.9 milligrams

■ ■

RED BEAN STIR-FRY

Makes 4 servings

Red beans are a particular favorite in Louisiana cookery, while water chestnuts are a staple in Chinese stir-fry dishes. In this dish the water chestnuts provide a fine textural contrast to the soft beans. While you can rely entirely on the canola oil, the sesame oil offers a distinct flavor. ∎

1 tablespoon soy sauce

½ teaspoon ground ginger

½ teaspoon sugar

2 teaspoons sesame oil

1 teaspoon canola oil

One 8-ounce can sliced water chestnuts

1 garlic clove, minced

One 1-pound can small red kidney or pink beans, well rinsed and drained, or 2 cups cooked

2 green onions, sliced thin

In a small dish, whisk together soy sauce, ginger, and sugar until well combined.

In a large skillet, preferably nonstick, heat sesame and canola oils, over high heat. When very hot, add water chestnuts and garlic and stir-fry for 30 seconds, stirring constantly. Add beans and stir-fry for another 1 to 2 minutes, or until very hot. Add green onions and soy-sauce mixture and simmer for another minute.

SERVING SIZE: ¼ recipe
CALORIES: 167
FAT: 3.89 grams

CHOLESTEROL: 0
SODIUM: 67.5 milligrams

■ ■

R ED BEANS WITH GARLIC AND GINGER

Makes 6 servings

T he flavors of both garlic and ginger are well absorbed by beans. Fresh ginger is preferable to powdered in this recipe, but for a real taste treat, look for crystallized ginger to use in this and other recipes calling for ginger. ■

1 tablespoon olive oil

1 tablespoon minced fresh garlic

1 tablespoon minced fresh or 2 teaspoons powdered ginger

½ cup chili sauce

4 cups cooked or drained and rinsed canned red or pink beans

Pepper

In a medium saucepan, heat oil. When very hot, add garlic and ginger. Cover and simmer very gently for 3 minutes, making sure garlic does not burn.

Add chili sauce and beans. Cover and simmer gently for 30 minutes. Season to taste with pepper.

SERVING SIZE: ⅙ recipe
CALORIES: 197
FAT: 2.93 grams

CHOLESTEROL: 0
SODIUM: 182 milligrams

■ ■

B ARBECUED KIDNEY BEANS

Makes 6 servings

These beans will give you a taste of the Old West. For an added zing, you might want to add a drop or two of liquid smoke to bring the campfire closer to home. Serve with grilled hamburgers made with low-fat beef. ■

1 small onion, chopped fine

1 cup ketchup

2 tablespoons Worcestershire sauce

2 teaspoons sugar

2 tablespoons red wine or cider vinegar

Two 1-pound cans red kidney beans, drained and rinsed

In a medium saucepan, combine onion, ketchup, ¼ cup water, Worcestershire, sugar, and vinegar. Bring to a boil, then simmer for 5 minutes. Add kidney beans and simmer, uncovered, for 10 minutes or until heated through.

SERVING SIZE: ⅙ recipe
CALORIES: 188
FAT: .61 grams

CHOLESTEROL: 0
SODIUM: 566 milligrams

■■■

SPLIT PEA AND POTATO PURÉE

Makes 6 servings

The combination of peas and potatoes yields a particularly rich and satisfying soup. Enjoy it as a prelude to dinner or along with a sandwich. ■

1 **cup** green split peas	½ **teaspoon rosemary**
1 **pound boiling potatoes, peeled and halved**	**Pepper**
1 **clove garlic**	½ **cup minced fresh parsley, optional**
1 **tablespoon olive oil**	

In a medium saucepan, bring peas, potatoes, garlic, oil, rosemary, and 3 cups water to a boil. Cover, then simmer gently for 45 minutes, or until peas are tender. Check on peas every now and then to see if they need a bit more water.

Purée through a food mill or in a food processor. Season to taste with pepper and fold in parsley if you wish.

SERVING SIZE: ⅙ recipe
CALORIES: 131
FAT: 2.48 grams

CHOLESTEROL: 0
SODIUM: 6.844 milligrams

■■■■■■■■■■■■■■■■■■■■■■■■■■■■■■■■■■■■■

PEASE PUDDING

Makes 8 servings

Pease porridge hot, pease porridge cold, pease porridge in the pot nine days old. Kids used to chant the words, but how many of us know what pease porridge is? Nothing more than a purée of cooked split peas, baked and set by egg whites, this dish can be eaten hot or cold. It only improves when kept in the refrigerator for a while. Season to your taste. But I guarantee this thickened pudding won't stay around anywhere near nine days. ■

1 **pound** green split peas

1 **carrot, chopped fine**

1 **onion, chopped fine**

1 **celery stalk, chopped fine**

2 **egg whites**

1 **teaspoon dried spices or herbs according to your taste, as marjoram, thyme, mint, dill, and/or parsley**

Pepper

Place peas, carrot, onion, and celery in a large pot. Cover with 8 cups water. Bring to a boil, cut back to a simmer, and cook gently, covered, for 45 minutes.

Preheat oven to 350 degrees.

Drain peas through a colander, reserving liquid for another soup if you wish. Purée peas and vegetables in a food processor, blender, or food mill, and blend in egg whites. Add herbs or spices and pepper according to taste.

Bake in a 6-cup baking pan for 45 minutes.

SERVING SIZE: ⅛ recipe
CALORIES: 77.4
FAT: .278 grams

CHOLESTEROL: 0
SODIUM: 21.3 milligrams

■■

FRENCH BEAN CASSEROLE

Makes 8 servings

Just about all the bean recipes in this book can be made with combinations of beans in the way this casserole uses them. For taste, texture, and visual appeal, the more kinds of beans the better. ■

One 19-ounce can chickpeas

One 19-ounce can red kidney or pink beans

One 19-ounce can white kidney or navy beans

One 6-ounce can pitted black olives, chopped

One 8-ounce can no-salt-added tomato sauce

½ teaspoon garlic powder

½ teaspoon thyme

2 tablespoons olive oil

½ cup chopped fresh basil or parsley

Pepper

Preheat oven to 350 degrees.

Drain all of the chickpeas and beans and rinse them with fresh water. Place them in a baking pan about 9 by 13 inches. Add the black olives, and toss together.

In a small mixing bowl combine tomato sauce, garlic powder, thyme, olive oil, and basil; season to taste with pepper. Toss this mixture with the beans and olives; bake uncovered for 20 minutes.

SERVING SIZE: ⅛ recipe
CALORIES: 265
FAT: 9.854 grams

CHOLESTEROL: 0
SODIUM: 129.7 milligrams

■■

MIXED BEANS AND SQUASH

Makes 6 servings

While vegetables of all sorts contribute some soluble fiber and a significant amount of insoluble fiber, any dish's soluble-fiber content can be boosted tremendously by adding some beans. ∎

1 **tablespoon olive oil**	½ **teaspoon celery seed**
1 **onion, chopped fine**	1 **small zucchini, cut into ¾-inch dice**
1 **red pepper, chopped fine**	1 **small yellow summer squash, cut into ¾-inch dice**
1 **cup each cooked or rinsed and drained canned** chickpeas, red beans, **and** white beans	**Pepper**
One 8-ounce can no-salt-added tomato sauce	

In a medium-large saucepan, heat olive oil. When hot, add onion and red pepper and sauté for 3 to 4 minutes. Add beans, tomato sauce, and celery seed. Cover the pot and simmer gently for 15 minutes.

Stir in squash and simmer, covered, for 5 minutes more, or until the squash is just tender; season to taste with pepper.

SERVING SIZE: ¼ recipe
CALORIES: 148
FAT: 4.83 grams

CHOLESTEROL: 0
SODIUM: 290 milligrams

∎■∎■∎■∎■∎■∎■∎■∎■∎■∎■∎■∎■∎■∎■∎■∎■∎■∎

MIXED VEGETABLE AND BEAN PUDDING

Makes 6 to 8 servings

This recipe will perk up even the most jaded tastebuds. ∎

1 tablespoon olive oil

½ cup chopped onions

2 cups freshly cooked or 1-pound can pink beans, drained and rinsed

½ cup no-salt-added tomato sauce

½ cup oat bran

One 10-ounce package frozen mixed vegetables, thawed

3 egg whites

Preheat oven to 350 degrees. Spray a 9-by-5-inch loaf pan with Pam or Baker's Joy and set aside.

In a medium skillet heat olive oil. When hot, reduce heat and sauté onions for 5 minutes or until softened; stir continuously so they do not burn.

Transfer onions, beans, tomato sauce, and oat bran to a food processor or blender and mix until smooth. Transfer mixture to a bowl and fold in the vegetables.

Beat egg whites until stiff, then fold them into the bean-and-vegetable mixture. Pour mixture into prepared loaf pan, then bake for 1 hour. Spoon out servings.

SERVING SIZE: ⅛ recipe
CALORIES: 128
FAT: 2.488 grams

CHOLESTEROL: 0
SODIUM: 38.9 milligrams

PERSIAN RICE AND LENTILS

Makes 6 to 8 servings

In this dish, rice cooks gently for so long that a wonderful crust develops on the bottom of the pot and gives the dish a deep, rich flavor. It's worth cleaning the pot at the end. ■

1 tablespoon canola oil	¼ teaspoon saffron
½ cup lentils	½ teaspoon honey
2 carrots, chopped fine	Pepper
1 cup long-grain rice	

Spread oil on the bottom of a medium-large pot. Add lentils, carrots, rice, saffron, honey, and 3 cups water. Season to taste with pepper.

Very slowly bring liquid to a boil, cover, and simmer very gently until rice and lentils have absorbed all the liquid; this may take as long as 35 minutes. You can eat this dish now, or you can try to form a rice crust in the following way.

Place a damp towel over the rice and lentils, cover again, and cook very slowly and gently for 30 minutes more or until the bottom crusts. When you serve the rice, simply break this dried crusty rice into the tender kernels for a wonderfully interesting textural contrast.

SERVING SIZE: ⅛ recipe
CALORIES: 66
FAT: 1.888 grams

CHOLESTEROL: 0
SODIUM: 10 milligrams

■■

SWEET SWEDISH LENTILS

Makes 6 servings

Preparing tasty dishes needn't mean elaborate preparation. This simple dish goes well with any number of meat or fish entrées. ■

1 **cup** lentils	2 **tablespoons white wine vinegar**
2 **tablespoons brown sugar**	Pepper

In a medium saucepan bring lentils and 3 cups water to a boil. Cover, then simmer gently for 30 minutes or until lentils are tender. Check on lentils every now and then to see if they need a bit more water.

Meanwhile, simmer sugar with vinegar just until sugar is dissolved. When lentils are tender, stir in sugar-and-vinegar mixture and simmer for 5 minutes. Season to taste with pepper.

SERVING SIZE: ⅙ recipe
CALORIES: 52.7
FAT: .7 grams

CHOLESTEROL: 0
SODIUM: 11.4 milligrams

■■

SWEET-AND-SOUR LENTILS

Makes 8 to 10 servings

Planning a picnic or tailgate party? This dish is a natural for any outdoor get-together. ∎

1 **pound dry** brown lentils	1 **teaspoon sugar**
¾ **cup white wine vinegar**	1 **teaspoon prepared mustard**
1 **cup tomato juice**	2 **tablespoons Worcestershire sauce**
1 **sour pickle, cut up**	½ **cup chopped parsley**
1 **stalk celery, cut up**	

Sort through and rinse lentils, place them in a pot, and cover with water. Bring to a boil, cut back to a simmer, and cook gently, partially covered, for 25 minutes or until lentils are just tender. Be sure they remain covered with water while they are cooking. Drain lentils and place in a mixing bowl.

Combine all remaining ingredients in a blender or food processor and purée until smooth. Toss this dressing over warm lentils. Cover, and marinate at room temperature for 2 hours.

SERVING SIZE: ⅛ recipe
CALORIES: 62.6
FAT: .015 grams
CHOLESTEROL: 0
SODIUM: 147 milligrams

∎ ∎

ARTICHOKE AND CHICKEN RISOTTO

Makes 4 to 6 servings

Rice bran comes through to give a creamy texture to this delicious dish. I recommend trying it with the Formagg Parmesan cheese; 1 ounce adds only 5 grams of fat, with no cholesterol. ∎

1 tablespoon olive oil

½ cup thin-sliced onions

1 cup chopped artichoke hearts (canned or frozen and thawed)

One 14½-ounce can no-salt-added stewed tomatoes

1 cup long-grain converted rice

¾ pound boneless, skinless chicken breast, cut into ¾-inch cubes

½ cup Vita Fiber, **pulverized**

Pepper

¼ cup Formagg grated Parmesan cheese substitute, optional

In a medium saucepan, heat olive oil. Add sliced onions and stir-fry for 2 to 3 minutes. Add artichoke hearts and stewed tomatoes, rice, and 2 cups water. Simmer, covered, for 10 minutes.

Add chicken and simmer for 5 minutes more, then stir in Vita Fiber and simmer 2 minutes. Season to taste with pepper and serve lightly sprinkled with cheese if you wish.

SERVING SIZE: ⅙ recipe
CALORIES: 194
FAT: 3.979 grams

CHOLESTEROL: 48.9 milligrams
SODIUM: 101 milligrams

MUSHROOM RISOTTO

Makes 4 to 6 servings

If you've never experienced it, you'll be surprised at the creamy texture of risotto. That creaminess comes from slowly simmering and stirring short-grain white rice for 35 minutes. This recipe takes a short cut, using the more common long-grain rice, without the need for continuous stirring. It's the rice bran mixed with the Parmesan cheese that give the dish its marvelous creaminess. If you'd like to cut the cholesterol and saturated fat a bit more, use Formagg Parmesan-flavored cheese substitute instead of regular Parmesan. ■

1 teaspoon olive oil

½ pound fresh mushrooms, cleaned and chopped fine

1 cup long-grain converted rice

¼ cup Vita Fiber, **pulverized**

¼ cup grated Parmesan

Pepper

In a medium saucepan heat olive oil. Add mushrooms and 2 tablespoons of water; cover and simmer gently for 10 minutes.

Add rice to the pan, along with 2½ cups water. Cover and simmer gently for 15 to 20 minutes, or until rice is just tender. Stir in Vita Fiber and Parmesan and cook for a minute or so longer. Season with pepper to taste and serve immediately, or the mixture will dry out and turn sticky.

SERVING SIZE: ⅙ recipe
CALORIES: 68.7
FAT: 1.945 grams

CHOLESTEROL: 1.646 milligrams
SODIUM: 39.9 milligrams

■■

RISOTTO MILANESE

Makes 4 servings

A classic risotto calls for long simmering of short-grain rice to provide the characteristic creaminess. This recipe is made with long-grain rice, to which is added Vita Fiber rice bran to give it the creaminess of the classic dish. ∎

1 teaspoon olive oil

¼ cup fine-chopped onion

⅛ teaspoon saffron

1 cup long-grain converted rice

⅓ cup Vita Fiber

Pepper

¼ cup grated Parmesan

In a medium saucepan heat olive oil. When hot, sauté onions for 1 minute. Add saffron and rice and cover with 2½ cups water. Bring to a boil, cut back to a simmer, and cook gently, covered, for 17 minutes.

Stir in Vita Fiber and cook a minute or so more or until rice is just tender to the bite. Season to taste with pepper and serve with Parmesan on the side.

SERVING SIZE: ¼ recipe
CALORIES: 94.1
FAT: 2.803 grams

CHOLESTEROL: 2.469 milligrams
SODIUM: 58.4 milligrams

■■

INDIAN RICE PILAF

Makes 6 servings

The sweetness of sugar and the zing of curry combine to give you a tasty side dish when serving a piece of broiled salmon or beef. ∎

1 teaspoon canola or olive oil	1 cup converted long-grain rice
1 small onion, chopped fine	¼ cup rice bran **or** Vita Fiber
1 teaspoon sugar	½ cup raisins
1 teaspoon curry powder	Pepper

In a medium saucepan, heat oil. When hot, stir in onion and sauté for 2 to 3 minutes. Stir in sugar and curry powder and sauté for 30 seconds more.

Add rice, Vita Fiber, and 2½ cups water. Bring to a boil, cut back to a simmer, and cook gently, covered, for 12 minutes.

Stir in raisins, cover, and cook for 3 to 5 minutes longer, or until rice is just tender. Season to taste with pepper, fluff up with a fork, and serve.

SERVING SIZE: ⅙ recipe
CALORIES: 86
FAT: .564 grams

CHOLESTEROL: 0
SODIUM: 7.235 milligrams

RICE AND CARROT PANCAKES

Makes 4 servings or 2 pancakes each

Remember that Vita Fiber rice bran delivers as much soluble fiber in two table-spoons as oat bran does in one-half cup. You can enjoy this cholesterol-lowering dish as an appetizer along with some nonfat yogurt or as a potato-substitute side dish. ■

½ **cup** Vita Fiber

2 **cups cooked long-grain rice**

1 **cup grated carrots**

2 **green onions, sliced thin**

½ **teaspoon curry powder**

2 **egg whites**

In a blender or food processor, pulverize Vita Fiber. Add cooked rice, carrots, green onions, curry powder, egg whites, and ½ cup water. Process until you have formed a thick mixture.

With your hands, shape the mixture into 8 patties. Heat a nonstick skillet or one sprayed with Pam or Baker's Joy. When hot, sauté the pancakes for about 4 minutes per side.

SERVING SIZE: 2 pancakes
CALORIES: 149
FAT: 1.278 grams

CHOLESTEROL: 0
SODIUM: 34.6 milligrams

■ ■

CHILLED TOMATO AND VEGETABLE PURÉE

Makes 6 servings

During the hot summer months, try this chilled dish along with a turkey sandwich for a complete meal without heating the kitchen. ∎

1 **cup** Vita Fiber	¼ **cup red wine vinegar**
2 **green onions**	**Three 6-ounce cans V-8 juice**
1 **red or green bell pepper, chopped**	2 **cups tomato juice**
	¼ **teaspoon garlic powder**
1 **cucumber, peeled and chopped**	**Pepper**

Purée all ingredients in a food processor or blender. Cover and chill, preferably overnight.

SERVING SIZE: ⅙ recipe
CALORIES: 57.3
FAT: .24 grams

CHOLESTEROL: 0
SODIUM: 317 milligrams

■ ■

S CALLION, CORNMEAL, AND OAT-BRAN JOHNNYCAKES

Makes 4 servings or 8 to 10 cakes

This dish makes an unusual breakfast, a nice lunch, or a side dish for dinner. For the main meal of the day I like the cakes with thick slices of low-fat ham and some vegetables. ■

½ **cup yellow or white cornmeal**	Tabasco
½ **cup** oat bran	**2 egg whites**
1 **teaspoon baking powder**	1–2 **tablespoons canola oil**
2 **green onions, sliced thin**	

Blend cornmeal and oat bran with baking powder; stir in green onions. (This can all be done in a food processor.)

Bring 1 cup water to a boil and mix it into the cornmeal mixture; season to taste with Tabasco. Transfer mixture to a bowl.

Whip egg whites until stiff and fold into batter.

Heat a griddle or nonstick skillet until very hot, or heat 1 table-spoonful of the oil in a regular cast-iron frying pan. When oil is hot, drop in the batter by ¼ cupfuls, and cook the johnnycakes for 2 minutes per side. If needed, use the remaining oil to fry the remaining johnnycakes.

SERVING SIZE: 1 cake
CALORIES: 66.2
FAT: 3.33 grams

CHOLESTEROL: 0
SODIUM: 44.1 milligrams

■ ■

CARROT AND POTATO PANCAKES

Makes 6 servings or 12 to 14 pancakes

Traditionally, potato pancakes are quite greasy. The recipe as it stands calls for only one to two tablespoons of canola oil. Or you can cut the fat drastically by using a spray of Pam or Baker's Joy and a nonstick pan and frying for a longer time over a lower heat. ■

4 **carrots, peeled and grated**	½ **cup** oat bran
2 **medium boiling potatoes, peeled and grated**	**Salt and pepper to taste**
2 **egg whites**	1–2 **tablespoons canola oil**

Preheat oven to 250 degrees.

In a large mixing bowl combine carrots, potatoes, egg whites, and oat bran. Season to taste with salt and pepper.

Heat 1 tablespoon of the oil in a large skillet, preferably nonstick. While oil is heating up, shape carrot-and-potato mixture into little pancakes, using about ⅓ cup of the mixture for each one. When shaping the pancakes squeeze the mixture tightly.

Sauté the pancakes, over low heat, for 5 minutes on the first side. With a spatula, turn the pancakes over, pressing down hard to flatten them out, and sauté for 10 minutes on the second side. Repeat procedure until all the carrot mixture has been used up. If you are working in several batches, put the first pancakes on a baking pan and set them, uncovered, in the oven to keep warm.

SERVING SIZE: 2 pancakes
CALORIES: 132
FAT: 5.31 grams

CHOLESTEROL: 0
SODIUM: 35.9 milligrams

BARLEY AND GREEN PEA MEDLEY

Makes 6 to 8 servings

You can cut the fat content of this dish considerably by using Pam or Baker's Joy to sauté the onions, omitting the olive oil completely. To get the onions nice and soft, cover the skillet while sautéing. This tip applies to many other recipes as well. ■

1 **tablespoon olive oil**	**Pepper**
1 **onion, chopped fine**	6 **tablespoons Parmesan cheese or substitute**
1 **cup** pearled barley	
1 **ten-ounce package frozen peas, preferably petite peas, thawed**	

In a medium saucepan heat olive oil. When hot, add onion and simmer, covered, for 5 minutes or until very soft. If onion begins to burn or stick, add a few teaspoons water and continue to cook.

Add barley and stir around for 30 seconds. Add 2½ cups water and simmer gently, partially covered, for 20 minutes. Add peas and pepper to taste, and simmer for another 5 minutes or until barley is just tender to the bite. Stir in Parmesan and serve immediately.

SERVING SIZE: ⅛ recipe
CALORIES: 145
FAT: 2.766 grams

CHOLESTEROL: 1.852 milligrams
SODIUM: 75.6 milligrams

■ ■

CHINESE FRIED BARLEY

Makes 4 servings

Traditional Chinese fried rice uses leftover rice. You can make this dish to use up any leftover barley you may have from time to time. You can make it either as a side dish or main course. ■

1 tablespoon canola oil	2 green onions, sliced thin
3 cups cooked pearled barley	2 tablespoons reduced-salt soy sauce
1 cup frozen petite peas, thawed	
8 ounces 96 percent fat-free ham, cut into ½-inch cubes	3 tablespoons rice or white wine vinegar
3 egg whites	Pepper

Heat oil in a large skillet over high heat. When very hot, add barley, peas, and ham, and stir-fry for 1 minute. Add egg whites, green onions, soy sauce, and vinegar, and stir-fry for 1 to 2 minutes more or until egg whites have formed long, thin white threads and the mixture is very hot. Season to taste with pepper and serve immediately.

SERVING SIZE: ¼ recipe
CALORIES: 687
FAT: 7.78 grams

CHOLESTEROL: 16.6 milligrams
SODIUM: 611 milligrams

■■■■■■■■■■■■■■■■■■■■■■■■■■■■■■■■■■■■■■■

MUSHROOM BARLEY PILAF

Makes 6 servings

Many of us get stuck in a rut when it comes to side dishes. Here's a wonderful alternative you and your family will love. ■

½ ounce dried mushrooms

2 tablespoons olive oil

1 bell pepper, chopped fine

4 cloves garlic, minced

8–10 ounces fresh mushrooms, chopped fine

1 cup barley, pearled or whole

Pepper

Soak dried mushrooms in 2 cups hot water for 30 minutes or until rehydrated. Cut off any parts of mushrooms that remain tough. Chop mushrooms and reserve soaking water.

In a medium saucepan heat olive oil. When hot, add bell pepper, garlic, fresh mushrooms, and chopped rehydrated mushrooms. Sauté for about 3 to 4 minutes.

Add barley and 4 cups water. Cover and simmer gently for 25 to 45 minutes, depending on what type of barley you are using. Check on barley every now and then to make sure bottom is not burning and that you have enough liquid to cover. If water level has gone down before barley is tender, simply add ½ cup more and simmer until done.

SERVING SIZE: ⅙ recipe
CALORIES: 153
FAT: 2.854 grams

CHOLESTEROL: 0
SODIUM: 2.918 milligrams

SAUCES
AND TOPPINGS

Onion Raisin Sauce

Tomato Sauce

Tomato, Chickpea, and Turkey Sauce

Curried Split Pea Sauce

Seasoned Crumbs

ONION RAISIN SAUCE

Makes 2 cups, or 4 servings

A meal of ham, Brussels sprouts, and mashed potatoes sounds pretty good. But when you ladle this sauce over the ham and sprouts you have a real taste treat. The sauce alone provides half the soluble fiber you need for the day. ■

1 tablespoon canola oil

1 onion, sliced thin

1 tablespoon wine vinegar

¼ cup raisins

¼ cup rice bran

½ cup evaporated skim milk mixed with 1½ cups fat-free chicken broth or water

Pepper

In a medium saucepan heat oil. When hot, add onion and stir-fry for 1 to 2 minutes. Add vinegar, raisins, and a couple of tablespoons water. Cover and simmer gently for 10 to 12 minutes, or until onions are very soft. Be sure to stir every now and then to make sure the onions are not sticking; if they are, add a tablespoon or two of water.

Stir in rice bran, add milk and broth, and bring to a boil. Stir and simmer for 2 minutes; season to taste with pepper.

VARIATIONS. This makes a thin sauce—good when served over something that will absorb it, like mashed potatoes. To thicken it, one can add 1 scant teaspoon **guar gum** and whisk it in, off heat (the texture works, although the flavor of the guar gum always comes through). One could also purée the sauce to make it thicker.

To make the flavor more buttery, when you add the rice bran, stir in 2 teaspoons Butter Buds.

SERVING SIZE: ¼ cup
CALORIES: 126
FAT: 5.37 grams

CHOLESTEROL: 1.275 milligrams
SODIUM: 38.6 milligrams

■ ■

TOMATO SAUCE

Makes about 5 cups

The characteristic sweetness of truly authentic Italian tomato sauces usually comes from the plum tomatoes. Here you can get the sweetness, along with extra body and soluble fiber from apple fiber. Use the sauce with pastas of all sorts. ■

1 tablespoon olive oil

2 onions, chopped fine

4 cloves garlic, minced

2 carrots, chopped fine

One 2-pound-3-ounce can Italian plum tomatoes

2 tablespoons minced fresh or 1 teaspoon dried basil

½ teaspoon oregano

Pepper

¼–½ cup apple fiber

In a medium-large saucepan heat olive oil. When hot, stir in onions, garlic, and carrots, and sauté for 3 to 4 minutes. Add tomatoes and their juice. Add herbs and pepper, cover, and simmer gently for 45 minutes.

Purée sauce in a blender or food processor. Add apple fiber to thicken it. (Add the maximum amount for a thicker sauce.) Return sauce to the saucepan and simmer 5 minutes.

SERVING SIZE: ½ cup

CALORIES: 50.9

FAT: 1.913 grams

CHOLESTEROL: 0

SODIUM: 166 milligrams

■ ■

Tomato, Chickpea, and Turkey Sauce

Makes enough for 6 servings of pasta

This sauce offers a tasty change of pace for pastas. It works particularly well with pasta shapes that can catch the sauce, such as fusilli, penne, and shells. ∎

2 tablespoons olive oil

1 onion, sliced thin

1 teaspoon minced garlic

Four 8-ounce cans no-salt-added tomato sauce

2 cups cooked or drained canned chickpeas

8 ounces fine-chopped turkey breast

½ cup chopped basil leaves

¼ cup chopped black olives

Pepper

Spray a large skillet with Pam or Baker's Joy, and sauté onion for 3 to 4 minutes. Stir in garlic and sauté for 30 seconds more. Add tomato sauce and chickpeas and cover. Simmer for 10 minutes.

Add remaining ingredients, cover, and simmer 10 minutes longer.

SERVING SIZE: ⅙ recipe
CALORIES: 236
FAT: 4.397 grams

CHOLESTEROL: 31.5 milligrams
SODIUM: 139 milligrams

CURRIED SPLIT PEA SAUCE

Makes 3 cups or 4 servings

You don't have to work very hard to prepare Indian-style curry. As you see, three ingredients do the trick. Pour the curried peas over rice and serve with a piece of broiled fish. Or, if you prefer, you can add the fish to the peas during the last ten minutes of cooking. I enjoy a glass of beer with Indian food. ■

½ **cup** green split peas   1 **teaspoon garlic powder**
1 **tablespoon curry powder**

Bring split peas and 3 cups water to a boil. Simmer for 15 minutes, skimming off froth as it rises to the top. Add curry and garlic powders and continue to simmer, partially covered, for 30 to 45 minutes or until peas are soft. Leave the split peas as is—there should be some texture to this sauce. Serve over 2 cups cooked rice or barley.

SERVING SIZE: ¼ recipe   CHOLESTEROL: 0
CALORIES: 28   SODIUM: .5 milligrams
FAT: .1 grams

■■■■■■■■■■■■■■■■■■■■■■■■■■■■■■■■■■■■■■

SEASONED CRUMBS

Makes about 2 cups

I prepare a lot of oven-fried foods since everyone in my family enjoys them. We save a lot of fat cooking chicken, scallops or shrimp by coating them with seasoned crumbs, spraying with Pam or Baker's Joy, and then baking. Chicken takes about 30 minutes in a preheated 400-degree oven; seafood requires less time. You can make a batch of the crumbs to keep on hand whenever the mood for oven-fried foods strikes. ■

1 **cup** oatmeal

1 **cup** oat bran

¼ **cup cornmeal**

1 **tablespoon dry** *fines herbes,* **or** ¾ **teaspoon each dry basil, oregano, marjoram, thyme, sage, and rosemary**

2 **egg whites**

Preheat oven to 400 degrees.

In a mixing bowl combine oatmeal, bran, cornmeal, and dried herbs. Mix in egg whites and, with your hands, squeeze the mixture together as best you can. The egg whites should help the herbs adhere to the oat mixture, which should fall together now in small clumps; some of the mixture will remain dusty-looking.

Transfer mixture to a 9-by-13-inch baking pan and bake for 30 to 45 minutes, stirring every 15 minutes or so or until the mixture smells toasty and looks slightly yellow.

SERVING SIZE: ¼ cup
CALORIES: 84.8
FAT: 1.519 grams

CHOLESTEROL: 0
SODIUM: 84.4 milligrams

CEREALS, PANCAKES, BREADS, AND MUFFINS

Toasted Rice and Oat-Bran Hot Cereal
Barley Maple Porridge
Sweet Sprinkles Topping or Cold Cereal
Date and Raisin Granola Bars
Three-Grain Pancakes
Oat-Bran and Rice-Fiber Pancakes
Oatmeal and Oat-Bran Bread
Barley Bread
Onion-Rye and Oat-Bran Bread
Oatmeal Sweet Bread
Boston Brown Bread
Pumpkin Bread
Jalapeño Cornbread
Fruit Bread
Banana Date-Nut Bread
Baking-Powder Biscuits

Italian Dinner Rolls
Bannocks
English Muffin Loaf
Oatcakes
Oat-Bran and Apple-Fiber Muffins
Cranberry Oat-Bran Muffins
Orange Oat-Bran Muffins
Lemon-Glazed Oat-Bran Muffins
Maple and Spice Oat-Bran Muffins
Strawberry Muffins
Gingerbread Rice-Bran Muffins
Raisin Rice-Bran Muffins
Orange Rice-Bran Muffins
Blueberry Corn-Bran Muffins
Apple-Fiber Raisin Muffins

Toasted Rice
AND OAT-BRAN HOT CEREAL

Makes 1 serving

Here's a way to get even more soluble fiber into your breakfast bowl than from oat bran alone. But don't limit this to the morning; it makes a great evening snack as well. ∎

3 **tablespoons** oat bran	¼ **cup raisins**
3 **tablespoons** Vita Fiber	**Brown sugar**
¼ **cup evaporated skim milk, mixed with ¾ cup water**	**Ground cinnamon**

Heat a small saucepan. When hot, add oat bran and Vita Fiber and stir continuously with a wooden spoon for about a minute, or until the oat bran gives off an aroma of popcorn. Be careful to stir all the time as you do this or some of the bran could burn.

Add milk and water and raisins and bring to a boil. Simmer for 1 minute, and serve, dusted with brown sugar and cinnamon.

SERVING SIZE: 1 recipe
CALORIES: 304
FAT: 5.788 grams

CHOLESTEROL: 2.55 milligrams
SODIUM: 79.1 milligrams

■ ■

BARLEY MAPLE PORRIDGE

Makes about 1 breakfast serving

I get bored pretty quickly with breakfast cereals, and this mixture offers a nice alternative. Try it with some fresh fruit in season. ■

¼ **cup** pearled barley

2 **tablespoons** Vita Fiber rice bran

⅛ **teaspoon ground cinnamon**

1 **tablespoon maple syrup**

1 **tablespoon evaporated skim milk**

In a medium saucepan bring barley, 1 cup water, Vita Fiber, cinnamon, and maple syrup to a boil. Lower heat, cover the pot, and simmer gently for 10 minutes. Add evaporated milk and continue to simmer 5 to 10 minutes more, or until enough liquid has evaporated to suit your taste and the barley is tender. You'll have to watch the pot as it simmers, once the milk is added, as the barley and milk tend to boil over.

SERVING SIZE: 1 bowl
CALORIES: 267.3
FAT: 3.027 grams

CHOLESTEROL: .64 milligrams
SODIUM: 19.81 milligrams

■■

SWEET SPRINKLES TOPPING OR COLD CEREAL

Makes about 2 cups

This is a delightful topping to sprinkle over nonfat frozen yogurt. You get the sweetness and crunch of the Vita Fiber rice bran with the extra zing of the spices. This mixture also makes a delicious cold cereal or dry snack. Even desserts can be a wonderful source of soluble fiber. ■

2 **cups** Vita Fiber

2–4 **tablespoons honey**

½ **teaspoon each of cinnamon and cardamon**

¼ **teaspoon ground nutmeg**

Preheat oven to 350 degrees.

In a mixing bowl combine Vita Fiber, honey according to taste, and spices. Mix with a fork or your fingers.

Transfer mixture to a 9-by-13-inch baking pan and bake 5 to 10 minutes only. Watch the mixture carefully, as it tends to burn quickly.

SERVING SIZE: ¼ cup

CALORIES: 41

FAT: 1.2 grams

CHOLESTEROL: 0

SODIUM: .25 milligrams

■■■

DATE AND RAISIN GRANOLA BARS

Makes 16 to 20 squares

Just take a quick glance at the ingredients list on store-bought granola bars and you'll know you don't want to buy them. Here's a healthful alternative that's low in fat and high in fiber. ■

3 cups oatmeal	¾ cup chopped pitted dates
1 cup Vita Fiber	¾ cup evaporated skim milk
½ teaspoon baking soda	6 tablespoons honey
½ teaspoon cinnamon	3 egg whites
¾ cup raisins	½ cup sugar

Preheat oven to 350 degrees. Spray a 9-inch-square baking pan with Pam or Baker's Joy.

In a mixing bowl, with a fork or whisk, blend oatmeal, Vita Fiber, baking soda, cinnamon, raisins, and dates.

In a small bowl combine milk and honey.

Beat egg whites until almost stiff. Slowly, about ¼ cup at a time, add the sugar to the whites and continue to beat until stiff and glossy.

Stir the liquid ingredients into the dry ones. Fold half the egg whites into the oatmeal batter to lighten and moisten it, then add the other half. Spoon the batter into the prepared baking pan, and bake for 35 minutes or until a toothpick, when inserted into the center of the batter, comes out dry. It will be easier to cut this into squares if you let the granola bars sit overnight at room temperature.

SERVING SIZE: 1 bar
CALORIES: 118
FAT: .834 grams

CHOLESTEROL: .382 milligrams
SODIUM: 106 milligrams

■■■

THREE-GRAIN PANCAKES

Makes about eight 3-inch pancakes

All three grains supply soluble fiber and together make delicious and unusual pancakes. You might even consider having this as a "backward breakfast" in the evening, along with an omelet made with Egg Beaters and Formagg cheddar-cheese substitute. ■

⅓ **cup cornmeal**

⅓ **cup** oat bran

⅓ **cup** Vita Fiber

2 **tablespoons sugar**

½ **teaspoon baking powder**

1¼ **cups boiling water**

2 **egg whites**

Preheat a griddle or nonstick skillet.

In a food processor or blender, combine cornmeal, oat bran, Vita Fiber, sugar, and baking powder, and process until smooth. Add boiling water and transfer batter to a mixing bowl.

Beat egg whites until stiff, and fold them into the batter.

Drop the pancakes by ¼ cupfuls onto the hot griddle, and cook them about 4 minutes on each side.

SERVING SIZE: 1 pancake
CALORIES: 46
FAT: .722 grams

CHOLESTEROL: 0
SODIUM: 38.1 milligrams

■■

OAT-BRAN
AND RICE-FIBER PANCAKES

Makes about 12 pancakes

As with all baked goods, this recipe tastes best if you first beat the egg whites and then fold them into the batter, rather than just combining all the ingredients. That little extra step makes all the difference in the world. ■

1½ cups oat bran

½ cup Vita Fiber

2 tablespoons sugar

2 teaspoons baking powder

1 cup skim milk, evaporated or fresh

½ cup water

¼ cup egg substitute or 2 egg whites

Preheat a griddle or nonstick skillet.

In a mixing bowl, combine oat bran, Vita Fiber, sugar, and baking powder. Combine skim milk and water, and stir into the dry ingredients. Stir in the egg substitute. If you are using egg whites, beat them until stiff and then fold them into the batter.

Drop batter by ¼ cupfuls onto a hot griddle, and cook 5 minutes on each side. These pancakes need to be cooked thoroughly or they will taste very heavy.

SERVING SIZE: 1 pancake
CALORIES: 63.6
FAT: 1.183 grams

CHOLESTEROL: .33 milligrams
SODIUM: 75.7 milligrams

OATMEAL AND OAT-BRAN BREAD

Makes one 8½-by-4½-inch loaf

Instead of muffins one morning, try this bread, either fresh from the oven or toasted. Spread with a little honey, jam, or marmalade, it's a wonderful treat. ∎

2 **cups quick-cooking** oatmeal	1 **teaspoon sugar**
½ **cup** oat bran	2 **tablespoons canola oil**
1 **package yeast**	About 1½ **cups flour**
1 **teaspoon salt**	

Soak oatmeal and bran for 2 hours in 1½ cups water. The mixture will be sticky-looking.

Dissolve yeast in ¼ cup warm water.

With a wooden spoon, beat, as best you can, salt, sugar, and 1 tablespoon of the oil into the oatmeal mixture. Stir in the dissolved yeast and water and mix as well as possible.

Add ½ cup of the flour to the mixture; if too stiff to stir, switch to your hands and squeeze the oatmeal and flour together; this is messy but it all works out well in the end. Try to work in ½ cup more flour.

Then sprinkle ¼ cup of the flour onto a lightly floured work surface. Turn the shaggy oatmeal-and-flour mixture onto the flour and knead the flour into the dough. Knead for 6 or 7 minutes, working in as much of the remaining ¼ cup of flour as you need to make a smooth but not too stiff dough. Set dough in a lightly oiled mixing bowl; cover surface of dough with some oil so that it does not crust. Cover the bowl with a damp towel and set in a warm, draft-free place. It should take about 1½ to 2 hours for this bread to rise. When sufficiently risen, the dough will look puffy, although it will never double in volume.

Punch dough down and knead for a minute more. Spray an 8½-by-4½-inch bread pan with Pam or Baker's Joy. Shape the dough into a sausage and place in the prepared bread pan. Cover the bread pan with a damp cloth and let rise for 45 minutes.

Preheat oven for 20 minutes to 400 degrees. Bake for 45 to 50 minutes. To test if the bread is done, insert a straw into center; it should come out dry. Or you could turn the bread out from its pan and tap the bottom; if it sounds hollow, the bread is done. This loaf will always look pale and whitish, because of the color of the oatmeal.

SERVING SIZE: ⅛ recipe

CALORIES: 105

FAT: 4.725 grams

CHOLESTEROL: 0

SODIUM: 317 milligrams

■■

BARLEY BREAD

Makes two 9-by-5-inch loaves (about 10 slices per loaf)

Granted, baking with yeast takes a bit of time and effort. But it's worth it at dinnertime. On the other hand, you might want to consider buying one of those Auto Bakeries I spoke about earlier on page 62 to be able to enjoy this freshly baked bread without any trouble at all. ∎

1 **package yeast**

2 **cups reserved barley cooking water, if you have it, or 2 cups warm water**

1 **tablespoon molasses**

2 **tablespoons canola oil**

2 **cups cooked** pearled barley

1 **cup** oat bran

1 **teaspoon salt**

About 5½ **cups flour**

In a large bowl, dissolve the yeast in the warm barley water or plain water.

With a wooden spoon stir the molasses and oil, cooked barley, oat bran, and salt into the yeast. Stir in 3 cups of the flour.

Sprinkle ½ cup flour onto a working board and dump the bread batter onto it; sprinkle ½ cup flour on top. With your hands work the flour in. Again sprinkle ½ cup flour on the board and ½ cup over the dough and knead it in.

Then sprinkle ¼ cup of flour onto the same surface. Dip your hands in the remaining ¼ cup flour and knead the dough for 6 or 7 minutes, dipping your hands lightly in flour if the dough becomes too sticky, but using only what is necessary.

Place dough in a lightly oiled mixing bowl; cover surface of dough with a little oil so that it does not crust, then cover the bowl with a damp towel and set in a warm, draft-free place. It should take about 2 hours for this bread to rise; when sufficiently risen, the dough will look puffy and should have doubled in volume.

Punch dough down and knead for a minute more. Spray two 9-by-5-inch bread pans with Pam or Baker's Joy. Divide the dough in half, shape each loaf into a sausage, and place in the prepared bread pans. Cover the bread pans with a damp cloth and let rise for 45 minutes.

Preheat oven for 15 minutes to 375 degrees. Bake loaves for 1 hour. To test if the bread is done, insert a straw or toothpick into center; it should come out dry. Or you could turn the breads out of the pans and tap the bottoms; if they sound hollow, they are done. These loaves will always look pale and whitish, because of the color of the oat bran.

SERVING SIZE: 1 slice
CALORIES: 164
FAT: 1.028 grams

CHOLESTEROL: 0
SODIUM: 101 milligrams

■■■

ONION, RYE, AND OAT-BRAN BREAD

Makes two 9-by-5-inch loaves (about 10 slices per loaf)

Breads made with oat bran typically do not rise very well because oats lack the gluten that makes wheat rise. Even mixing wheat flour with oat bran may not be enough. The answer is to use high-gluten wheat flour such as that made by Arrowhead Mills and found in health-food stores. Without the high-gluten flour you have to give the dough more time to rise. No doubt baking bread takes a lot of time and effort, but the aromas filling the house make it worthwhile. Of course you can cut hours into minutes by acquiring an Auto Bakery (see page 62). ■

4 **packages yeast**	1 **tablespoon canola oil**
4 **tablespoons honey**	½ **cup fine-chopped onions**
2 **cups nonfat yogurt**	3 **cups** oat bran
2 **teaspoons each caraway, dill, and fennel seed**	1½ **teaspoons salt**
2 **cups rye flour**	About 2 **cups all-purpose flour**

Dissolve yeast in 1 cup warm water in a large bowl and stir in honey.

In a small saucepan, gently heat yogurt with seeds until warm to the touch. Stir this into yeast and stir in the rye flour. Cover mixture and let it sit in a warm place for 2 hours, or until it becomes spongy; this process will help the bread rise later on.

Meanwhile, heat canola oil in a small skillet and sauté onions until brown; remove and set aside.

With a wooden spoon stir the spongy mixture down. Stir in oat bran, ½ cup at a time, then stir in salt and cooked onions.

Sprinkle ½ cup flour on a working board and scrape the rye-and-oat-bran dough over it; sprinkle ½ cup flour on top of the dough. With your hands work the flour in. Then sprinkle ¼ cup flour underneath the dough and ¼ cup over and knead in the flour, working the dough for about 5 minutes. If the dough becomes sticky, keep on dusting its surface and your hands with more flour. Do not overdo this step, however, as you want to keep the dough moist.

Place dough in a lightly oiled mixing bowl; cover surface of dough with some oil so that it does not crust. Then cover the bowl with a damp towel and set in a warm, draft-free place to rise, for about 2 hours. The dough will look puffy but will not have doubled in volume.

Punch dough down and knead for a minute. Spray two 9-by-5-inch bread pans with Pam or Baker's Joy. Divide the dough in half and shape each loaf into a sausage. Place in the prepared bread pans. Cover the bread pans with a damp cloth again and let rise for 1 hour longer.

Preheat oven to 375 degrees 20 minutes before you will bake the bread.

Spray the tops of the loaves lightly with water and set in oven. Bake for 1 hour, spraying the tops with more water every 20 minutes. To test if the bread is done, insert a straw or toothpick into center; it should come out dry. Or you could turn the loaves out of the pans and tap the bottoms; if they sound hollow, they are done. These loaves will always look grayish because of the color of the rye flour and oat bran.

SERVING SIZE: 1 slice
CALORIES: 163
FAT: 2.258 grams

CHOLESTEROL: .4 milligrams
SODIUM: 165 milligrams

■■

OATMEAL SWEET BREAD

Makes one 9-by-5-inch loaf (about 10 slices)

Quick to make, but long to bake! ■

1 **cup** oat bran	1 **teaspoon baking powder**
1 **cup** oatmeal	¼ **teaspoon powdered cardamom**
1 **cup flour**	1 **cup raisins**
⅓ **cup sugar**	2 **cups 1 percent fat buttermilk**
½ **teaspoon baking soda**	3 **egg whites**

Preheat oven to 350 degrees. Spray a 9-by-5-inch loaf pan with Pam or Baker's Joy.

In a large mixing bowl, whisk together oat bran, oatmeal, flour, sugar, baking soda and powder, cardamom and raisins; mix thoroughly.

Stir buttermilk into the dry ingredients.

Beat egg whites until stiff. Fold half of the egg whites into the batter to lighten it, then fold in the remaining half. Spoon the batter into the prepared loaf pan.

Bake for 1 hour and 20 minutes. Turn bread out from pan onto a cake rack and thoroughly cool to room temperature before slicing.

SERVING SIZE: 1 slice
CALORIES: 173
FAT: 1.275 grams

CHOLESTEROL: .8 milligrams
SODIUM: 71.2 milligrams

BOSTON BROWN BREAD

Makes one 9-inch-square pan of bread (or nine 3-inch squares)

This hearty bread goes especially well with stews and casseroles. Don't be shy about dipping the bread into sauce to get every last drop. ∎

1 **cup flour**	2 **cups 1 percent fat buttermilk**
2 **cups** oat bran	½ **cup light corn syrup**
½ **cup cornmeal**	½ **cup molasses**
1 **teaspoon each baking powder and baking soda**	

Preheat oven to 350 degrees. Spray a 9-inch-square baking pan with Pam or Baker's Joy and set aside.

In a big bowl, whisk together flour, oat bran, cornmeal, baking powder, and baking soda. Stir in buttermilk, corn syrup, and molasses; mixture will be wet. Turn mixture into the prepared baking pan and cover pan tightly with foil. Place baking pan in a larger one. Fill the larger one with enough hot water to come three-quarters of the way up the sides of the baking pan filled with batter.

Bake for 1½ hours. Let bread sit in pan until cool before cutting into squares.

SERVING SIZE: one 3-inch square
CALORIES: 254
FAT: 2.264 grams

CHOLESTEROL: .889 milligrams
SODIUM: 58.1 milligrams

■ ■

PUMPKIN BREAD

Makes one 8½-by 4½-inch loaf

Why don't people think about eating pumpkin except at Thanksgiving and Christmas? You can buy canned pumpkin all year, and it tastes just as good—especially in a recipe like this one—in the summer as it does in the fall. Pumpkin also provides a wealth of vitamin A in the form of beta carotene. ∎

1 cup raisins, soaked in warm water for 15 minutes

1 cup canned unsweetened pumpkin purée

1 cup brown sugar

1 tablespoon vanilla

2 tablespoons canola oil

2 cups oat bran

½ teaspoon baking powder

¼ teaspoon baking soda

¼ teaspoon each ground allspice and cloves

3 egg whites

Preheat oven to 350 degrees; spray an 8½-by-4½-inch loaf pan with Pam or Baker's Joy.

In a mixing bowl or food processor, blend the pumpkin purée, ¾ cup of the brown sugar, vanilla, and oil; mix until well combined. Drain the raisins and stir in.

In another large mixing bowl, whisk together the oat bran, baking powder, soda, and spices until thoroughly mixed.

Blend the wet ingredients into the dry ones; the batter will be somewhat dry.

Beat the egg whites until stiff, gradually adding the remaining ¼ cup of brown sugar. Fold this into the batter and spoon the batter into the prepared loaf pan.

Bake for 50 to 55 minutes; cool in pan for 10 minutes before unmolding.

SERVING SIZE: 1 slice (¹⁄₁₆ recipe)
CALORIES: 102
FAT: 1.79 grams

CHOLESTEROL: 0
SODIUM: 25.9

JALAPEÑO CORNBREAD

Makes about 16 servings

Some call it Southwestern cooking, others refer to it as Santa Fe cuisine. Whatever the term used, interesting combinations of sweet and spicy ingredients mark this new approach to cooking, which has become very popular in restaurants across the country but especially in the West. Give this hearty bread a try. Beating and folding in the egg whites rather than simply mixing them into the batter makes the bread lighter. ∎

½ cup yellow cornmeal

½ cup all-purpose flour

½ cup oat bran

½ cup rice bran or apple fiber

2 teaspoons baking powder

½ teaspoon baking soda

¾ cup low-fat buttermilk mixed with ½ cup water

1 tablespoon vegetable oil

2 tablespoons minced jalapeño peppers

½ cup frozen corn kernels, thawed

3 egg whites

Preheat oven to 400 degrees. Spray an 8-inch-square baking pan with Pam or Baker's Joy.

In a large bowl, stir together cornmeal, flour, brans, baking powder, and soda.

In a small mixing bowl, combine buttermilk and water, vegetable oil, jalapeño peppers, and corn. Stir into the dry ingredients and mix thoroughly. Beat egg whites until stiff and fold gently into the batter. Pour into the prepared pan and bake for 25 minutes. Cool in pan for 10 minutes before serving.

SERVING SIZE: 1 slice (¹⁄₁₆ recipe)
CALORIES: 63
FAT: 1.64 grams

CHOLESTEROL: .188 milligrams
SODIUM: 31.3 milligrams

FRUIT BREAD

Makes 2 oval loaves

This delicious, not-too-sweet bread can be made with any kind of dried fruit. ∎

1 package yeast

2 cups warm skim milk

⅓ cup sugar

2 tablespoons canola oil

2 cups dried fruit, such as raisins or prunes or apricots cut into ½-inch pieces

2 cups oat bran

1 teaspoon salt

About 3–3½ cups flour

Pam or Baker's Joy

Honey

In a large mixing bowl, dissolve yeast in warm milk. With a wooden spoon stir sugar, oil, dried fruit, oat bran, and salt into the yeast and milk. Stir in 2 cups of the flour.

Sprinkle ½ cup flour on a working board and dump the batter onto it; sprinkle ½ cup flour on top. With your hands work the flour in, squeezing and working the dough as best you can; it will be sticky and hard to manage.

Then sprinkle ¼ cup flour onto the working board. Dip your hands in the remaining ¼ cup flour and knead the dough for 6 or 7 minutes, dipping your hands lightly in flour if the dough becomes too sticky. You may not use all of the flour.

Place dough in a lightly oiled mixing bowl. Cover surface of dough with some oil so that it does not crust, then cover the bowl with a damp towel and set in a warm, draft-free place. It should take about 2 hours for this bread to rise; when sufficiently risen, the dough will look puffy, although it never will double in volume.

Punch dough down and knead for a minute more. Spray a large cookie sheet with Pam or Baker's Joy. Divide the dough into 2 parts and shape into two oval loaves, about 6 inches long. Set the loaves on the baking sheet, cover with a damp cloth again, and let rise for 45 minutes to 1 hour.

Preheat oven for 20 minutes to 375 degrees. Bake for about 1 hour. To test if the bread is done, insert a straw or toothpick into center; it should come out dry. Or you could turn the breads out and tap the bottoms; if they sound hollow, they are done. While breads are still warm, lightly brush the tops with honey to give them a glaze and a softer texture.

SERVING SIZE: 1 slice (⅟₁₅ recipe)

CALORIES: 223

FAT: 1.615 grams

CHOLESTEROL: .533 milligrams

SODIUM: 151 milligrams

■ ■

BANANA DATE-NUT BREAD

Makes one 8½-by-4½-inch loaf

Oat bran is a natural for a dense, satisfying bread such as this one. With this recipe in mind, save overripe bananas and store them in the freezer until you're ready to use them. ■

2 very ripe bananas, puréed (this should measure 1 cup)	½ cup chopped walnuts
¾ cup sugar	2 cups oat bran
1 tablespoon vanilla	2 teaspoons baking powder
1 tablespoon canola oil	½ teaspoon ground cinnamon
½ cup chopped pitted dates	3 egg whites

Preheat oven to 350 degrees. Spray an 8½-by-4½-inch loaf pan with Pam or Baker's Joy.

In a mixing bowl or food processor, blend puréed bananas with ½ cup of the sugar, vanilla, and oil; mix until well combined. Stir in dates and nuts.

In another large mixing bowl, whisk together oat bran, baking powder, and cinnamon until thoroughly mixed.

Blend the wet ingredients into the dry ones.

Beat egg whites until stiff, gradually adding the remaining ¼ cup sugar; fold into the batter and spoon the batter into the prepared loaf pan.

Bake for 50 to 55 minutes; cool in pan for 10 minutes before unmolding.

SERVING SIZE: 1 slice (1/12 recipe)
CALORIES: 112
FAT: 2.517 grams
CHOLESTEROL: 0
SODIUM: 13.6 milligrams

BAKING-POWDER BISCUITS

Makes about eighteen 1 ½-inch biscuits

Biscuits like these taste best hot out of the oven. Plan on them to give a nice touch to your dinner as well as a lot of soluble fiber. I like mine with honey, but you might prefer to spread on a bit of margarine and let it melt into the hot biscuit. ■

1 **cup all-purpose flour**	½ **cup** apple fiber
1 **tablespoon baking powder**	¼ **teaspoon salt**
½ **cup** rice bran	¾ **cup evaporated skim milk**

Preheat oven to 450 degrees.

In a mixing bowl, stir together flour, baking powder, rice bran, apple fiber, and salt. Or you could do this in a food processor. Add milk all at once and stir until ingredients are just combined; if you are doing this in a food processor, pulse the machine a few times just until dough is combined. If the dough seems a little dry, sprinkle on a tablespoon of water, and work it in.

With lightly floured hands, knead the dough for 30 seconds. Then pat and push it out until it is ½ inch thick. With a 1½-inch biscuit cutter, cut dough into about 18 rounds. Set rounds on an ungreased baking sheet. Bake for 16 minutes or until cooked through.

VARIATIONS.   To make herbed biscuits, add 1 teaspoon dried herbs of your choice to the dry ingredients, before adding the milk.

To make buttermilk biscuits, use 1 percent fat buttermilk instead of the evaporated milk and substitute 2 teaspoons baking powder, mixed with ½ teaspoon baking soda, for the baking powder.

To make oat-bran biscuits, substitute 1 cup oat bran for the rice bran and apple fiber.

SERVING SIZE: 1 biscuit
CALORIES: 53.7
FAT: 1.217 grams

CHOLESTEROL: .43 milligrams
SODIUM: 121 milligrams

■ ■

ITALIAN DINNER ROLLS

Makes 12 to 16 rolls

While you can use either rice bran or apple fiber in this recipe, it comes out a lot better if you use half of each. The apple fiber gives a bit of sweetness and the rice bran offers a nutty flavor. Both supply a lot of soluble fiber. I really don't think these rolls need any margarine at all. ■

1 package dry yeast	About 2 cups all-purpose white flour
1 cup warm water (not hotter than 115 degrees)	1 teaspoon salt
2 tablespoons sugar	1 teaspoon crumbled rosemary or oregano
2 cups rice bran **or** 1 cup **each** rice bran **and** apple fiber	½ cup nonfat yogurt
½ cup whole-wheat flour	2 tablespoons olive oil

Place yeast in a small mixing bowl, add warm water, and stir with a fork. Add sugar, and set aside.

Although this is not a crucial step, if you toast the rice bran first, the flavor of the bread will be nice and toasty; you should not, however, toast the apple fiber. To give the rice bran a nutty popcorn flavor, heat a large skillet over high heat, add the bran and stir continuously, with a wooden spoon, for 2 minutes or until it smells nutty; it will turn a deeper shade of brown.

Transfer rice bran to a bowl, and add whole-wheat flour and 1½ cups of all-purpose flour, salt, and rosemary. With a whisk or fork, stir to combine thoroughly.

To the yeast in the small mixing bowl add yogurt and olive oil. Add the liquid to the dry ingredients and beat with a wooden spoon until dough is combined.

Turn dough onto a well-floured board and knead about ¼ cup flour into the dough. Knead the dough for about 8 minutes, dusting your hands with flour as you work. Try not to incorporate all the remaining ¼ cup flour into the dough, so that the dough remains as moist as possible. Turn dough around in an oiled bowl and cover well. Set in a draft-free place and let the dough rise for 1½ hours.

Punch dough down and divide into 12 or 16 pieces. Roll each piece into a neat ball and set on a baking sheet; cover and let rise for 40 to 45 minutes.

Preheat oven to 400 degrees. Bake rolls for 18 to 20 minutes. Remove from oven and cool 20 minutes before eating.

SERVING SIZE: 1 roll

CALORIES: 139

FAT: 4.453 grams

CHOLESTEROL: .125 milligrams

SODIUM: 129 milligrams

■ ■

BANNOCKS

Makes about 24

This simple recipe is baked on a griddle, but is more like a biscuit than a griddlecake. You can serve bannocks for breakfast, lunch, dinner, or snacks. Enjoy them with preserves or honey. ■

2 **cups** oat bran

2½ **cups** oatmeal, **chopped or pulverized in a blender**

1 **teaspoon baking soda**

2 **cups boiling water**

¼ **cup canola oil**

Flour

Preheat a griddle or large nonstick skillet.

In a mixing bowl, combine oat bran, oatmeal, and baking soda. Combine water and oil and stir into the batter, which will be somewhat stiff.

Dip your hands in flour, then take about 2 tablespoons of the dough and pat it into a round, about ¼ inch thick.

Cook 10 minutes on each side on low heat; these bannocks need to be cooked thoroughly or they will taste very heavy—their texture should be somewhat like a cracker.

SERVING SIZE: 1 bannock
CALORIES: 69.2
FAT: 3.25 grams

CHOLESTEROL: 0
SODIUM: 59.8 milligrams

ENGLISH MUFFIN LOAF

Makes 2 loaves, 10 slices per loaf

This is an unusual recipe for breakfast, a kind of cross between oat-bran muffins and English muffins. It's particularly good sliced and toasted, with a bit of marmalade or preserves. ∎

2½ cups oat bran

2½ cups whole-wheat flour

1 cup nonfat dry milk

2 packages rapid-rise yeast

1 tablespoon granulated sugar

½ teaspoon salt

¼ teaspoon baking soda

2½ cups warm water

1 tablespoon cornmeal

Preheat oven to 400 degrees. In a large mixing bowl combine all ingredients except water and cornmeal. Add water and mix thoroughly. Cover with wax paper and let rise till double in bulk, about 35 minutes. Spray 2 bread pans on bottom and sides with Pam or Baker's Joy and sprinkle on cornmeal so a little sticks to the bottom and sides of the pans. Divide dough and place into the prepared pans. Bake 25 minutes.

SERVING: 1 slice
CALORIES: 99.2
FAT: 1.22 grams

CHOLESTEROL: .2 milligrams
SODIUM: 7.059 milligrams

■ ■

Oatcakes

Makes 2½ dozen 2-inch crackers

Because these cakes have so little oil, they tend to harden and dry out rather quickly. Enjoy them right out of the oven, spread with jam or preserves. ▪

2⅔ **cups** oatmeal	2 **tablespoons canola oil**
¾ **cup high-gluten flour**	6 **tablespoons skim milk**
¼ **cup** oat bran	4 **tablespoons water**
½ **teaspoon salt**	Flour

Preheat oven to 350 degrees.

In a food processor or blender combine oatmeal, flour, oat bran, and salt, and mix until oatmeal is somewhat broken up. Transfer dry ingredients to a mixing bowl.

Stir liquid ingredients into the dry ones and knead for 2 minutes. The dough will be somewhat resistant.

On a floured board, with lightly floured rolling pin, roll the dough out until ⅛ inch thick. With a 2-inch cookie cutter, cut into rounds. Gather scraps of dough into a ball, roll out the dough, and cut into rounds. Do this until all the dough has been cut out.

Place crackers on an ungreased cookie sheet and bake for 45 minutes.

SERVING SIZE: 1 cake
CALORIES: 30.4
FAT: 1.173 grams

CHOLESTEROL: .017 milligrams
SODIUM: 26 milligrams

▪▪

O AT-BRAN
AND APPLE-FIBER MUFFINS

Makes 12 muffins

The French eat croissants for breakfast regularly from cradle to grave and don't get tired of them. I prefer a bit more variety. Here oat bran and apple fiber combine to deliver more soluble fiber than oat bran alone, and with a nice flavor twist. You can further modify the recipe with some chopped nuts, dried fruit bits, or little pieces of fresh fruit or berries. ■

2 **cups** oat bran

½ **cup** apple fiber

½ **teaspoon baking soda**

2 **tablespoons canola oil**

1½ **cups skim milk**

½ **cup raisins**

2 **egg whites**

⅓ **cup white or brown sugar**

Spray 12 muffin cups with Pam or Baker's Joy or use paper cups. Preheat oven to 400 degrees.

In a large mixing bowl, combine oat bran, apple fiber, and baking soda.

In another mixing bowl, combine oil, milk, and raisins; set aside.

Beat egg whites until stiff, gradually beating in the sugar.

Stir the liquid ingredients into the dry ones, and immediately thereafter fold the egg whites into the batter. You should not stir the liquid ingredients into the dry ones before you are ready to fold in the egg whites because the batter will become stiff and it will be hard to work in the egg whites.

Scoop the batter into the prepared muffin cups and bake for 18 minutes or until a toothpick inserted in the center of a muffin comes out clean.

SERVING SIZE: 1 muffin
CALORIES: 101
FAT: 4.118 grams

CHOLESTEROL: 4 milligrams
SODIUM: 92.6 milligrams

CRANBERRY OAT-BRAN MUFFINS

Makes 24 muffins

I like these muffins so much that I keep a supply of cranberries in my freezer so I can enjoy them throughout the year, not just during the autumn and winter. Using a food processor to render the oat bran to a flourlike consistency gives the muffins a lighter, cakier texture. You can, of course, cut the recipe in half to make only 12 muffins, but I think you'll like them so much you'll want the full two dozen. ■

One 1-pound box oat bran

½ **cup granulated sugar**

2 **tablespoons baking powder**

1½ **cups (12 ounces) frozen white-grape-juice concentrate**

1½ **cups (12 ounces) skim milk**

1 **container Egg Beaters (8 ounces = 4 eggs)**

¼ **cup canola or rice-bran oil**

1 **cup fresh or frozen whole cranberries**

¼ **cup chopped walnuts**

Preheat oven to 425 degrees. Combine oat bran, sugar, and baking powder in food processor with large metal blade. Allow the food processor to grind the oat bran as you combine the moist ingredients in a separate bowl or blender. Add whole cranberries to the oat bran in the food processor and pulse the mixture for a few seconds to break up the berries. Combine all ingredients, including chopped walnuts, in a large bowl and mix gently. Pour batter into muffin pans lined with paper baking cups. Bake 17 minutes. Test for doneness with a toothpick; it should come out moist but not wet.

You don't have to use a food processor for this recipe. Just omit the grinding of the oat bran and cut the cranberries into small pieces with a paring knife.

SERVING SIZE: 1 muffin
CALORIES: 154
FAT: 4.775 grams

CHOLESTEROL: .25 milligrams
SODIUM: 23 milligrams

■ ■

ORANGE OAT–BRAN MUFFINS

Makes 24 muffins

You can create a wide variety of tasty muffins merely by changing the type of liquid used as a sweetener. Here concentrated orange juice, with a little grated orange rind, provides an extra zing. You can also use a spritz of club soda to give additional lightness to any of the recipes for muffins or other baked goods.

This recipe uses a whole one-pound box of oat bran, making two dozen muffins. You can adapt all your oat-bran muffin recipes accordingly, to give you a full week's supply or to allow you to freeze a dozen for future use. ■

One 1-pound box oat bran

½ cup chopped walnuts

1 cup granulated sugar

2 tablespoons baking powder

3 tablespoons grated orange peel

One 12-ounce can (1½ cups) frozen concentrated orange juice

1½ cups skim milk

2 tablespoons canola or rice-bran oil

2 tablespoons light corn syrup

1 container Egg Beaters (8 ounces = 4 eggs)

Club soda

Preheat oven to 425 degrees. In a large bowl combine oat bran, nuts, sugar, baking powder, and orange peel. Mix all moist ingredients except club soda and blend together with dry ingredients. Add a spritz of club soda and gently fold into batter; not too much, just about an ounce or two, and you'll see the batter puff up. Pour batter into muffin pans lined with paper baking cups. Bake 17 minutes. Test for doneness with a toothpick; it should come out moist but not wet.

SERVING SIZE: 1 muffin
CALORIES: 151
FAT: 2.88 grams

CHOLESTEROL: .25 milligrams
SODIUM: 23.7 milligrams

LEMON-GLAZED OAT-BRAN MUFFINS

Makes 12 muffins

Here we give oat-bran muffins a little extra touch by way of the glaze topping. You can do the same thing with orange or lime juice for a variety. ∎

2½ **cups** oat bran	2 **tablespoons canola oil**
½ **teaspoon baking soda**	1 **cup skim milk**
1 **cup sugar**	¼ **cup lemon juice + 3 tablespoons**
¼–½ **cup chopped walnuts, optional**	2 **egg whites**

Spray a 12-cup muffin tin with Pam or Baker's Joy or use paper cups. Preheat oven to 400 degrees.

In a large mixing bowl, combine oat bran, baking soda, ¾ cup of the sugar, and walnuts, if you are using them.

In another mixing bowl, combine oil, milk, ¼ cup lemon juice, and ¼ cup water.

Beat egg whites until foamy. Gradually beat in the rest of the sugar, and beat until the mixture is stiff and glossy.

Beat the liquid ingredients into the dry ones, and immediately thereafter fold the egg-white mixture into the batter. You should not beat the liquid ingredients into the dry ones before you are ready to fold in the egg-white mixture. The longer the oat bran sits, the stiffer this batter becomes and the harder it is to work in the egg whites.

Scoop the batter into the prepared muffin cups and bake for 18 minutes. While the cupcakes are baking, stir together the remaining 3 tablespoons lemon juice and ¼ cup sugar.

When cupcakes are done, poke each one, while still hot, with a toothpick, making about 5 holes in each. Spoon the lemon-juice-and-sugar glaze over the cupcakes while they are still warm. Cool to room temperature.

WITHOUT NUTS
SERVING SIZE: 1 muffin
CALORIES: 160
FAT: 3.87 grams

CHOLESTEROL: .333 milligrams
SODIUM: 19.7 milligrams

WITH WALNUTS (¼ CUP)
SERVING SIZE: 1 muffin
CALORIES: 223
FAT: 9.758 grams

CHOLESTEROL: .333 milligrams
SODIUM: 19.8 milligrams

■ ■

M APLE
AND SPICE OAT–BRAN MUFFINS

Makes 12 muffins

J ust a simple thing like changing the sweetening agent and the spices can make an entirely different muffin. Here we've used maple syrup along with allspice, cardamom, cinnamon, and nutmeg. I think you'll really like the result. ■

2¼ **cups** oat bran

1 **teaspoon baking powder**

⅛ **teaspoon each ground allspice, cardamom, cinnamon, and nutmeg**

½ **cup chopped walnuts**

½ **cup maple syrup**

1 **cup evaporated or fresh skim milk**

2 **egg whites**

Spray a 12-cup muffin pan with Pam or Baker's Joy or use paper cups. Preheat oven to 400 degrees.

In a large mixing bowl, combine oat bran, baking powder, spices, and walnuts.

In another mixing bowl, combine maple syrup and milk.

Beat egg whites until stiff.

Beat the liquid ingredients into the dry ones and immediately thereafter fold in the beaten egg whites.

Spoon the batter into the prepared muffin cups and bake for 18 minutes.

SERVING SIZE: 1 muffin
CALORIES: 150
FAT: 4.54 grams

CHOLESTEROL: .333 milligrams
SODIUM: 42.9 milligrams

■ ■

STRAWBERRY MUFFINS

Makes 12 muffins

You can use frozen berries in this recipe, but fresh ones make it so much better. For dessert, try the muffins spread with some strawberry preserves. ∎

1½ **cups** oat bran	¼ **cup sugar**
1 **cup** apple fiber	**Skim milk, if needed**
1 **teaspoon baking soda**	2 **tablespoons canola oil**
2 **cups strawberries, fresh or frozen, preferably unsweetened**	3 **egg whites**

Preheat oven to 425 degrees. Line 12 muffin cups with paper cups or spray them with Pam or Baker's Joy.

In a large mixing bowl or in the food processor, combine oat bran, apple fiber, and baking soda. Stir until thoroughly mixed.

Place in a blender or food processor 1 cup of the strawberries with the sugar and purée until smooth. Measure the strawberry purée; if it does not measure 1 cup, add enough skim milk to bring it to that level. Dice remaining strawberries.

In a small mixing bowl combine the strawberry purée and oil, and stir this into the dry ingredients to combine thoroughly. Stir in the chopped strawberries.

Beat egg whites until stiff and fold them into the batter. Spoon the batter into the prepared muffin cups and bake for 20 minutes.

SERVING SIZE: 1 muffin
CALORIES: 142
FAT: 4.076 grams

CHOLESTEROL: 0
SODIUM: 14.2 milligrams

■ ■

GINGERBREAD RICE–BRAN MUFFINS

Makes 12 muffins

Because there's more soluble fiber per ounce in rice bran than in oat bran, you can combine the rice bran with flour to make muffins that are a potent source of soluble fiber. This recipe shows how you can use the Vita Fiber rice bran like flour by pulverizing it by hand or with a food processor or blender. ■

1½ **cups** Vita Fiber rice bran **ground into "flour"**

¾ **cup all-purpose flour or whole-wheat flour**

1½ **tablespoons baking powder**

¾ **teaspoons each ginger and cinnamon**

¼ **cup raisins**

½ **cup hot water**

¾ **cup molasses**

2 **tablespoons canola or rice-bran oil**

2 **egg whites**

Preheat oven to 425 degrees. Mix dry ingredients, including raisins, together in a large bowl. Mix moist ingredients in a blender and then add to dry ingredients. Pour batter into muffin pans lined with paper baking cups. Bake 15 to 17 minutes.

SERVING SIZE: 1 muffin
CALORIES: 152
FAT: 4.905 grams

CHOLESTEROL: 0
SODIUM: 26.9 milligrams

■ ■

R AISIN RICE-BRAN MUFFINS

Makes 12 muffins

While oat-bran muffins have been my breakfast staple for years, it's nice to have a change now and then. These muffins provide all the soluble fiber I need from the rice bran and apple fiber. As with all muffin recipes, you can use 2 egg whites mixed into the batter, 2 egg whites beaten until fluffy and then folded into the batter, or ¼ cup of egg substitute. The beaten and folded egg whites yield the lightest muffins. ■

1 **cup** rice bran	½ **cup** raisins
½ **cup** apple fiber	¾ **cup** 1 percent buttermilk mixed with ½ **cup** water
¾ **cup** flour	2 **tablespoons** canola oil
¾ **teaspoon** baking soda	2 **tablespoons** honey
¼ **cup** sugar	2 **egg whites**

Preheat oven to 425 degrees. Line 12 muffin cups with paper cups or spray them with Pam or Baker's Joy.

In a large mixing bowl or a food processor, combine oat bran, apple fiber, flour, baking soda, and sugar. Stir until thoroughly mixed; stir in the raisins.

In a small mixing bowl, combine buttermilk and water, oil, honey, and egg whites. Stir this into dry ingredients and mix thoroughly. Spoon batter into the prepared muffin cups and bake for 18 minutes or until a toothpick inserted into the center of a muffin comes out clean.

SERVING SIZE: 1 muffin
CALORIES: 157
FAT: 5.299 grams

CHOLESTEROL: .25 milligrams
SODIUM: 18 milligrams

■ ■

ORANGE RICE-BRAN MUFFINS

Makes 12 muffins

Vita Fiber rice bran can be used to boost the soluble-fiber content of practically any recipe. There are some recipes that just don't lend themselves to oat bran in place of wheat flour. In these you can just add some Vita Fiber. ∎

1 **cup all-purpose flour**

1¼ **cups pulverized** Vita Fiber

⅓ **cup sugar**

1 **tablespoon fresh grated orange zest**

1 **tablespoon baking powder**

2 **tablespoons canola oil**

1¼ **cups orange juice**

¼ **cup egg substitute, made from powdered or frozen mix, or 2 egg whites, or ¼ cup equivalent made from powdered mix**

Spray 12 muffin cups with Pam or Baker's Joy or use paper cups. Preheat oven to 400 degrees.

In a large mixing bowl, combine flour, Vita Fiber, sugar, orange zest, and baking powder.

In another mixing bowl, combine oil, orange juice, and egg substitute.

Beat the liquid ingredients into the dry ones, and scoop the batter into the prepared muffin cups. Bake for 18 to 20 minutes.

SERVING SIZE: 1 muffin
CALORIES: 137
FAT: 4.985 grams

CHOLESTEROL: 0
SODIUM: 8.844 milligrams

■ ■

BLUEBERRY CORN–BRAN MUFFINS

Makes 12 muffins

I think you're going to really like the combination of oat bran with cornmeal. And the blueberries—heaven! These taste especially good hot out of the oven, so plan to make them on a leisurely Sunday morning. ∎

1½ **cups** oat bran

1 **cup yellow cornmeal**

¼ **cup sugar**

1 **tablespoon baking powder**

1 **cup skim or evaporated skim milk**

2 **tablespoons canola oil**

½ **cup blueberries, fresh or frozen**

3 **egg whites**

Preheat oven to 425 degrees. Line 12 muffin cups with paper cups or spray them with Pam or Baker's Joy.

In a large mixing bowl or in the food processor, combine oat bran, cornmeal, sugar, and baking powder. Stir until thoroughly mixed.

In a small mixing bowl combine milk and oil, and stir into the dry ingredients to combine thoroughly; stir in the blueberries.

Beat egg whites until stiff and fold them into the batter. Spoon the batter into the prepared muffin cups and bake for 20 minutes.

SERVING SIZE: 1 muffin
CALORIES: 137
FAT: 3.69 grams

CHOLESTEROL: .85 milligrams
SODIUM: 37 milligrams

APPLE–FIBER RAISIN MUFFINS

Makes 12 muffins

Now and then I like to take a break from oat-bran muffins, and then I turn to muffins made with another source of soluble fiber. Apple fiber in these muffins and in almost any baked-goods recipe adds a bit of sweetness and a whole lot of fiber. ∎

1 **cup** apple fiber	½ **teaspoon ground cinnamon**
1 **cup flour**	1 **cup raisins**
⅔ **cup brown sugar**	1 **cup skim milk**
½ **teaspoon baking soda**	1 **cup 1 percent fat buttermilk**
2 **teaspoons baking powder**	3 **egg whites**

Spray a 12-cup muffin pan with Pam or Baker's Joy or use paper cups. Preheat oven to 400 degrees.

In a large mixing bowl, combine apple fiber, flour, sugar, baking soda, baking powder, and cinnamon; whisk thoroughly. Add raisins and stir in milk and buttermilk.

Beat egg whites until stiff and fold them into the batter, working in one-third of the egg whites at a time.

Scoop the batter into the prepared muffin cups and bake for 20 minutes.

SERVING SIZE: 1 muffin
CALORIES: 153
FAT: 1.109 grams

CHOLESTEROL: .667 milligrams
SODIUM: 38.8 milligrams

■ ■

DESSERTS
AND SWEETS

Applesauce Oat-Bran Cake
Zucchini Cake
Mocha Torte
Cranberry Orange Cake
Ginger Cake
Rum Torte
Carrot Cake
Apricot Cake
Dried-Fruit Oatmeal Crisp
Apple-Fiber and Oatmeal Cookies
Gingersnaps
Honey Oatmeal Drop Cookies

Oatmeal "Smacks"
Chocolate, Chocolate Brownies
Raspberry Fool
Prune and Date Bars
Mocha Pudding
Berry Pudding
Indian Barley Pudding
Rice Pudding
Fruit and Fiber Gelatin
Chocolate Milkshake
Orange Guarius
Orange Guar Smoothie

APPLESAUCE OAT-BRAN CAKE

Makes one 9-by-13-inch cake (about 12 squares)

It's really easy to convert just about any cake into a heart-healthy dessert. First replace half the flour with oat bran or apple fiber. Next use egg substitute or egg whites instead of whole eggs. Finally, replace the butter or margarine with canola or rice-bran oil. This is a terrific snack cake that needs no topping at all. ∎

1¼ cups all-purpose flour

1¼ cups oat bran **or** apple fiber

2 cups granulated sugar

1 cup raisins

¼ cup chopped walnuts

1 teaspoon baking soda

1 tablespoon baking powder

¾ teaspoon ground cinnamon

¼ teaspoon ground cloves

¼ teaspoon ground allspice

1½ cups applesauce

¼ cup light corn syrup

¼ cup canola oil

4 ounces egg substitute (equal to 2 whole eggs)

½ cup club soda

Preheat oven to 350 degrees. Spray a baking pan 13 by 9 by 2 inches with Pam or Baker's Joy. Mix all dry ingredients in a large bowl, then mix together all moist ingredients except club soda. Blend moist ingredients with the dry. Add club soda and gently fold into batter; you'll see the batter puff up. Bake about 60 minutes. Test with toothpick to determine doneness.

Sprinkle top of cake with half-and-half mixture of cinnamon and granulated sugar, if you wish.

SERVING SIZE: one 3-inch square
CALORIES: 341
FAT: 7.27 grams

CHOLESTEROL: 0
SODIUM: 21.4 milligrams

ZUCCHINI CAKE

Makes one 9-inch-square cake

Zucchini must be one of the easiest vegetables to grow in the world; everyone I know who's ever planted it has had a bumper crop. If you become a zucchini farmer, or know someone who is, you'll be looking for ways to use it. Here's a perfect application. ■

½ **cup flour**

½ **cup pulverized** Vita Fiber

1 **cup** apple fiber

1 **teaspoon baking soda**

½ **teaspoon allspice**

2 **cups grated zucchini**

1 **cup raisins**

One 12-ounce can evaporated or 2 cups fresh skim milk

5 **egg whites**

1 **cup sugar**

Preheat oven to 375 degrees. Spray a 9-inch-square pan with Pam or Baker's Joy.

In a large mixing bowl, whisk together flour, Vita Fiber, apple fiber, baking soda, and allspice, and mix thoroughly. Stir in zucchini and raisins.

Blend milk into the dry ingredients and mix well.

Beat egg whites until stiff. Slowly and gradually add the sugar to the egg whites and continue to beat until thick and glossy.

Fold half of the egg whites into the batter to lighten it, then fold in the remaining half. Spoon the batter into the prepared cake pan.

Bake for 1 hour; cool in pan to room temperature before slicing into squares. This is a very moist cake.

SERVING SIZE: one 3-inch square
CALORIES: 215
FAT: 1.685 grams

CHOLESTEROL: .89 milligrams
SODIUM: 58.7 milligrams

■■

MOCHA TORTE

Makes one 9-inch torte

Here's a way to enjoy chocolate flavor without chocolate's fat. ∎

1 **cup** oat bran	2 **teaspoons instant coffee**
¼ **cup flour**	5 **egg whites**
6 **tablespoons unsweetened cocoa**	1 **cup sugar**
½ **teaspoon baking soda**	

Preheat oven to 350 degrees. Spray one 9-inch round cake pan with Pam or Baker's Joy.

In a mixing bowl, combine oat bran, flour, cocoa, baking soda, and coffee.

With an electric mixer, beat egg whites until foamy. Tablespoon by tablespoon, beat sugar into the whites until they become very stiff and shiny.

Sprinkle one-quarter of the dry ingredients onto the egg whites and, with a rubber spatula, fold them into the egg whites. Add one-quarter more of the dry ingredients and fold, and so on until the ingredients are completely homogenized. When you are folding the whites and dry ingredients together, work swiftly but gently, taking care to deflate the egg whites as little as possible. Spoon the batter into the prepared pan.

Bake for 30 minutes. Lower heat to 325 degrees and bake for 15 minutes longer. Remove from oven and let cool in cake pan for 15 minutes. With a knife, loosen edges and gently loosen cake from bottom. Turn upside down onto a cake rack and cool. When completely cool, serve as is or dusted with confectioners' sugar.

SERVING SIZE: ⅙ torte
CALORIES: 349
FAT: 4.65 grams

CHOLESTEROL: 0
SODIUM: 43.4 milligrams

■ ■

CRANBERRY ORANGE CAKE

Makes one 8½-by-4½-inch loaf

Remember that it's best to spread your intake of soluble fiber throughout the day rather than having it all at one time. Cakes like this one make it easy and delicious to do just that. A muffin in the morning and some cake at night—not a bad way to stay heart-healthy! ■

1 cup cranberries, frozen or fresh	2 teaspoons baking powder
1 cup sugar	2 teaspoons vanilla
2 tablespoons grated orange peel	¾ cup orange juice
1½ cups oat bran	2 tablespoons canola oil
½ cup apple fiber	3 egg whites

Preheat oven to 350 degrees; spray an 8½-by-4½-inch loaf pan with Pam or Baker's Joy.

With a sharp knife or in a food processor, chop cranberries with ¼ cup of the sugar and blend in orange peel; set aside.

In a large mixing bowl, whisk together oat bran, apple fiber, and baking powder, and mix thoroughly.

In another smaller mixing bowl, combine vanilla, orange juice, 1 cup water, and the oil. Blend the liquid ingredients into the dry ones.

Whip egg whites until stiff. Slowly and gradually add the remaining ¾ cup sugar to the egg whites and continue to beat until very stiff and glossy.

Fold half of the mixture into the batter to lighten it, then fold in the remaining half. Spoon the batter into the prepared loaf pan.

Bake for 1 hour; cool in pan for 10 minutes before unmolding.

SERVING SIZE: ⅛ cake	CHOLESTEROL: 0
CALORIES: 221	SODIUM: 105 milligrams
FAT: 5.496 grams	

■ ■

GINGER CAKE

Makes two 8-inch cakes

Beating the egg whites helps makes this cake light and airy. The flavor is wonderful and the orange glaze a perfect topper. A dollop or two of nonfat frozen vanilla yogurt melting over the cake makes this a real treat, but it's terrific as is. ∎

½ **cup** rice bran

½ **cup** apple fiber

½ **cup flour**

1 **teaspoon baking powder**

1 **teaspoon ground ginger**

½ **teaspoon grated orange zest**

1 **cup evaporated skim milk mixed with** ½ **cup water**

5 **egg whites**

⅔ **cup sugar**

OPTIONAL ORANGE GLAZE

2 **tablespoons frozen orange-juice concentrate, thawed**

6 **tablespoons confectioners' sugar**

Preheat oven to 350 degrees. Spray two 8-inch cake pans with Pam or Baker's Joy.

In a mixing bowl, combine rice bran, apple fiber, flour, baking powder, ginger, and orange zest. Stir milk and water into the dry ingredients and mix to form a wet batterlike dough.

With an electric mixer, beat egg whites until foamy. Tablespoon by tablespoon, beat sugar into the egg whites, and beat until the egg whites becomes very stiff and shiny.

With a rubber spatula, fold half of the egg whites into the bran batter, then fold in the remaining half. When you are folding the whites into the batter, work swiftly but gently, taking care not to deflate the egg whites too much; they are what will lighten the cake.

Bake for 30 minutes. Lower heat to 325 degrees and bake for 15 minutes longer. Remove from oven and let cool in cake pan for 15 minutes. With a knife, loosen edges and gently loosen cake from bottom. Turn upside down on a cake rack and cool. When completely cool, serve as is or dusted with confectioners' sugar.

If you wish, mix the ingredients for the glaze and spread half on top of one cake. Set second cake on top of first and spread remaining glaze over the top; some may drip down the sides of the cake, and that will make it look pretty. Let glaze set for half an hour before serving.

WITHOUT GLAZE

SERVING SIZE: ⅙ cake
CALORIES: 91.3
FAT: .16 grams

CHOLESTEROL: .85 milligrams
SODIUM: 47 milligrams

WITH GLAZE

SERVING SIZE: ⅙ cake
CALORIES: 159
FAT: .22 grams

CHOLESTEROL: .85 milligrams
SODIUM: 48 milligrams

■ ■

RUM TORTE

Makes one 9-inch torte, or 8 servings

Puréed beans give this torte a body and flavor reminiscent of chestnuts—perfect for the holiday season. Use freshly cooked beans rather than canned ones for the best results. ■

1½ **cups cooked or canned** navy **beans, drained and rinsed**	1 **tablespoon vanilla**
	¼ **cup** apple fiber
⅔ **cup sugar**	5 **egg whites**
4 **tablespoons rum**	3–4 **tablespoons fruit jelly, optional**

Preheat oven to 350 degrees. Spray a 9-inch round cake pan with Pam or Baker's Joy.

In a blender or food processor, purée beans, ⅓ cup of the sugar, and the rum and vanilla until smooth. Add apple fiber and purée. If the mixture seems dry, add 2 to 3 tablespoons water to make a thick batter.

Beat egg whites until stiff, then gradually beat in the remaining ⅓ cup of sugar. Fold gently into the bean-and-fiber mixture. Spoon into prepared cake pan and bake for 50 minutes, or until a toothpick, when inserted into center of cake, comes out dry.

Serve warm as is. Or, when cake has cooled to room temperature, cut it into two thin horizontal layers with a serrated knife. Spread the bottom layer with the jelly and place the second layer on top. Let torte sit for a couple of hours before serving.

SERVING SIZE: ⅛ torte
CALORIES: 136
FAT: .492 grams

CHOLESTEROL: 0
SODIUM: 33.8 milligrams

■■

CARROT CAKE

Makes one 9-inch-square cake

Oat bran is a natural for heavy cakes such as a carrot cake. Port is my favorite choice, though Sherry works well also, to give the cake a real flavor boost. This cake is a winner. ■

1½ cups raisins	1 cup brown sugar
¼ cup Port or Sherry	¼ cup canola oil
1¼ cups oat bran, **processed into flour**	¼ cup evaporated skim milk
¾ cup all-purpose flour	¼ cup corn syrup
1 tablespoon baking powder	2 teaspoons vanilla
2 teaspoons ground cinnamon	1 cup egg substitute
	2 cups grated fresh carrots

Preheat oven to 400 degrees. Spray a 9-inch-square baking pan with Pam or Baker's Joy.

In a small mixing bowl, soak raisins in Port and set aside.

In a mixing bowl, sift together oat bran, flour, baking powder, and cinnamon.

Place in another bowl brown sugar, oil, milk, corn syrup, vanilla, and egg substitute, and mix with an electric beater for a minute or two. Add carrots to the liquid mixture, then stir in the flour mixture, then the raisins and Port. Pour mixture into prepared baking pan and bake for 40 to 45 minutes, or until a toothpick, when inserted in center of cake, comes out dry. Let cool to room temperature, then cut into squares.

SERVING SIZE: ⅑ cake
CALORIES: 368
FAT: 7.434 grams

CHOLESTEROL: .283 milligrams
SODIUM: 69.9 milligrams

■■■

A PRICOT CAKE

Makes one 9-by-9-inch cake

T his cake recipe calls for half high-gluten flour and half apple fiber. You can turn virtually any cake recipe into a source of soluble fiber simply by replacing half the flour with the apple fiber. Spoon a bit of apricot preserves over the cake as a topping. ■

1 cup chopped pitted dates	2 teaspoons baking soda
1½ cups (about 1-pound–1-ounce can) canned apricots, drained and chopped coarse	1½ cups canned apricot nectar
	1 cup apple fiber
1 cup sugar	1 cup flour
4 tablespoons canola oil	4 egg whites

Preheat oven to 350 degrees. Spray a 9-inch-square pan with Pam or Baker's Joy.

In a mixing bowl, combine dates and apricots. Add ½ cup of the sugar, the oil, and baking soda. Heat nectar to boiling point and pour over ingredients; let mixture cool.

Beat egg whites until stiff. Slowly and gradually add the remaining ½ cup sugar to the egg whites and continue to beat until very stiff and glossy.

With a wooden spoon beat apple fiber and flour into the fruit mixture.

Fold half of the egg whites into the batter to lighten it, then fold in the remaining half. Spoon the batter into the prepared cake pan.

Bake for 1 hour or until a toothpick inserted into center of cake comes out clean. Cool in pan to room temperature before slicing into squares.

SERVING SIZE: ⅑ cake
CALORIES: 301
FAT: 7.552 grams

CHOLESTEROL: 0
SODIUM: 26 milligrams

DRIED-FRUIT OATMEAL CRISP

Makes 6 servings

This is delicious and flavorful, and even tastier with a topping of some sort—a few dollops of nonfat frozen yogurt or the whipped topping YoWhip, which is made with nonfat yogurt. ∎

6 ounces dried apricots	¼ teaspoon cinnamon
6 ounces dried pitted prunes	¼ teaspoon cloves
4 ounces raisins	½ cup Port or red wine
4 ounces dried figs, chopped	2 tablespoons apple fiber

TOPPING

2 tablespoons brown sugar	¼ cup apple fiber
¼ cup rolled oats	¼ cup chopped walnuts, optional
¼ cup oat bran	1 tablespoon canola oil

Preheat oven to 350 degrees.

Combine all the fruit in a 9-by-9-inch baking pan. In a small mixing bowl, combine cinnamon, cloves, wine (or substitute orange juice or water if you wish) and apple fiber. Mix until well combined, and blend with the dried fruit.

In another mixing bowl, combine sugar, oats, oat bran, apple fiber, and nuts if desired, and sprinkle this on the dried fruit. Drizzle the oil over the top and bake for 35 to 40 minutes, or until fruit has softened somewhat and topping has browned.

SERVING SIZE: ⅙ crisp
CALORIES: 328
FAT: 3.48 grams

CHOLESTEROL: 0
SODIUM: 58.8 milligrams

APPLE-FIBER AND OATMEAL COOKIES

Makes 3 dozen cookies

I got this recipe from the makers of Tastee Apple Fiber. You can get more recipes using apple fiber by calling the company at (800) 262-2957 in Ohio or (800) 262-7753 outside. When my wife and kids tried these cookies, they couldn't believe they're good for you. ∎

½ cup all-purpose flour	½ cup chopped nuts
½ cup apple fiber	2 egg whites
½ teaspoon baking soda	1 cup brown sugar
¼ teaspoon cinnamon	½ cup oil
½ teaspoon salt, optional	½ cup skim milk
1½ cups quick-cooking oatmeal	1 teaspoon vanilla
1 cup seedless raisins	

Preheat oven to 350 degrees. Sift together flour, apple fiber, baking soda, cinnamon, and salt, if you wish. Stir in oatmeal, nuts, and raisins. Combine egg whites, sugar, oil, milk, and vanilla. Add to flour mixture and mix well. Drop by tablespoons onto cookie sheet sprayed with Pam or Baker's Joy. Bake 10 to 12 minutes.

SERVING SIZE: 1 cookie
CALORIES: 80.9
FAT: 4.323 grams

CHOLESTEROL: .056 milligrams
SODIUM: 41.7 milligrams

■ ■

GINGERSNAPS

Makes 24 to 28 cookies

Crisp gingersnaps, along with a glass of cold skim milk, will wake up the child in you. If no one's looking, you might even want to dunk the cookies in the milk. But remember what happens if you hold the cookie in the milk too long; timing is everything! ∎

1 cup oat bran

¾ cup flour

1 teaspoon baking powder

¾ teaspoon each ground cinnamon and ginger

½ teaspoon ground cloves

¼ cup canola oil

¼ cup light corn syrup

2 egg whites

½ cup sugar, white or brown

Preheat oven to 375 degrees. Spray two cookies sheets with Pam or Baker's Joy.

In a mixing bowl, with a fork or whisk blend oat bran, flour, baking powder, cinnamon, ginger, and cloves.

In a small bowl combine oil and corn syrup.

Beat egg whites until almost stiff. Slowly, about ¼ cup at a time, add sugar to the whites and continue to beat until stiff and glossy.

Stir the liquid ingredients into the dry ones—the two won't homogenize at all and will remain crumbly, but that is all right. Stir half of the egg whites into the oat-bran batter to lighten and moisten it, then stir in the other half. Stir until the oat bran and spice mixture and egg whites are well mixed.

Drop the batter by teaspoonfuls, onto the prepared cookie sheets and bake for 10 to 12 minutes. If you are using two racks, switch the cookie sheets around halfway during baking. Keep your eye on the cookies as they will burn quickly.

SERVING SIZE: 1 cookie
CALORIES: 63.2
FAT: 3.59 grams

CHOLESTEROL: 0
SODIUM: 6.07 milligrams

■ ■

HONEY OATMEAL DROP COOKIES

Makes 22 two-inch cookies

Here's a variation on oatmeal cookies with added soluble fiber from oat bran. They're on the chewy side and not too sweet. Depending on your tastes, you might want to add a bit more sugar. ■

½ **cup** oat bran	2 **tablespoons canola oil**
1½ **cups** oatmeal	2 **egg whites**
¼ **cup flour**	1 **teaspoon vanilla**
¼ **teaspoon baking powder**	¼ **cup honey**
⅛ **teaspoon allspice**	½ **cup brown sugar**

Preheat oven to 350 degrees. Spray 2 large cookie sheets with Pam or Baker's Joy.

In a large mixing bowl combine oat bran, oatmeal, flour, baking powder, and allspice.

In a blender or food processor, combine oil, egg whites, vanilla, honey, and brown sugar. Blend these liquid ingredients into the dry ones.

By tablespoons, drop the batter onto the prepared cookie sheets and bake for 12 to 14 minutes.

SERVING SIZE: 1 cookie
CALORIES: 69.1
FAT: 1.66 grams

CHOLESTEROL: 0
SODIUM: 45.3 milligrams

■ ■

OATMEAL "SMACKS"

Makes 16 squares

These morsels got their name because they are so delicious one needs to "smack" one's lips after eating them. This revised "healthy" version is still good enough to "smack" ones lips! ■

1 **cup** oat bran, **pulverized into flour**

½ **cup all-purpose flour**

½ **cup** oatmeal

½ **cup brown sugar**

2 **teaspoons baking powder**

½ **cup chopped pitted dates**

4 **egg whites or** ½ **cup egg substitute, made from frozen or dried eggs**

2 **tablespoons canola oil**

1 **teaspoon vanilla**

2 **egg whites**

½ **cup brown sugar**

Preheat oven to 350 degrees. Spray an 8-inch-square baking pan with Pam or Baker's Joy.

In a food processor or electric mixer combine oat bran, flour, oatmeal, brown sugar, and baking powder; stir in chopped dates.

In a small mixing bowl combine the 4 egg whites or egg substitute, oil, and vanilla. Add to the dry ingredients. With your hands mix and squeeze the ingredients together until you have formed a dough that just holds together.

Pat the dough into the prepared baking pan. Beat the 2 egg whites until stiff, then gradually add the brown sugar, a tablespoon at a time, until all of it has been incorporated. Spread this over the dough and bake for 45 minutes. Cool to room temperature and cut into 16 squares.

SERVING SIZE: 1 square
CALORIES: 128
FAT: 2.37 grams

CHOLESTEROL: 0
SODIUM: 83.6 milligrams

CHOCOLATE, CHOCOLATE BROWNIES

Makes about 18 brownies

One of my favorite recipes in *The 8-Week Cholesterol Cure* is my oat-bran brownies. I've enjoyed them for years to satisfy my chocolate cravings. Here's another version I think you'll like. You'll find they're easier to cut into squares if left to sit overnight. That is, if you can stay away from them that long! ■

2 **cups** oat bran	1 **tablespoon vanilla**
12 **tablespoons unsweetened cocoa**	6 **egg whites**
½ **teaspoon baking soda**	1 **cup brown sugar**
½ **cup evaporated skim milk**	1 **cup white sugar**
2 **very ripe bananas, mashed**	

Preheat oven to 375 degrees. Spray a 9-by-13-inch baking pan with Pam or Baker's Joy and set aside.

In a food processor, or in a mixing bowl using a fork, blend oat bran, cocoa, and baking soda. Transfer to a bowl.

In a small bowl combine milk, bananas, and vanilla.

Whip egg whites until almost stiff. Slowly, about ¼ cupful at a time, add the sugars to the whites and continue to beat until they are thick.

Stir the liquid ingredients into the dry ones; the batter will be crumbly. Stir one-quarter of the egg-white mixture into the oat-bran batter to lighten and moisten it, then add another quarter of the whites. Fold the last half of the egg whites into the lightened batter and spoon into the prepared baking pan. Bake for 30 minutes.

SERVING SIZE: 1 brownie
CALORIES: 240
FAT: 3.111 grams

CHOLESTEROL: .28 milligrams
SODIUM: 238 milligrams

R ASPBERRY FOOL

Makes 4 servings

A classic raspberry fool calls for puréed fruit blended into whipped cream. In this version we purée the fruit with apple fiber to thicken it and fold the purée into a meringue. You can make it especially festive by putting a few fresh raspberries on top and drizzling a bit of Chambord raspberry liqueur over it. ■

Two 10-ounce packages frozen raspberries in light syrup, thawed

⅓ **cup** apple fiber

3 **egg whites**

¼ **cup sugar**

Purée frozen raspberries and their syrup in a food processor or blender. To eliminate the seeds, push the raspberries through a sieve, mashing down on the purée with a spoon. Discard the seeds.

Blend apple fiber into the raspberry purée and simmer over low heat for 3 minutes. Cool the mixture to room temperature, then chill. About 1 hour before serving, beat the egg whites until stiff, gradually adding the sugar. Fold into the raspberry purée and apple fiber. Spoon into 4 serving dishes or large wine glasses and chill for an hour.

SERVING SIZE: ¼ recipe
CALORIES: 221
FAT: .983 grams

CHOLESTEROL: 0
SODIUM: 38 milligrams

PRUNE AND DATE BARS

Makes 16 bars

While most baked goods are best straight out of the oven, these are better if left to stand for a day. They keep well for up to a week, and are welcome treats in a lunch bag at school or work. ■

FILLING

¼ cup brown sugar

½ cup apple fiber

1 cup fine-chopped pitted prunes

½ cup fine-chopped pitted dates

DOUGH

1 cup oatmeal, **not quick-cooking kind**

1 cup oat bran

1 cup apple fiber

¼ teaspoon ground cinnamon

1 cup brown sugar

1 cup all-purpose flour, sifted with ½ teaspoon baking powder

1 cup Egg Beaters

2 very ripe bananas, mashed

Preheat oven to 350 degrees. Spray an 8-inch-square baking pan with Pam or Baker's Joy.

To make filling, combine brown sugar and 1 cup water in a small saucepan; bring to a boil. Stir in apple fiber, prunes, and dates, and simmer 3 to 5 minutes; mixture should be thick. Set aside.

In a large mixing bowl, combine oatmeal, oat-bran, apple fiber, cinnamon, brown sugar, and flour. With a whisk or your hands, combine ingredients until thoroughly mixed.

Add Egg Beaters and bananas. With your hands, squeeze ingredients together; dough should just hold together and be quite crumbly. If dough is too dry and some particles do not adhere, sprinkle a tablespoon of water over the dough and mix again. Divide dough in half.

Pat half of the dough into the prepared cake pan. With a spatula, spread the prune-and-date filling over dough. Between two pieces of waxed paper, roll the dough into a square the size of your baking pan, and lay this dough over the filling, trying to cover the entire surface. Bake for 35 to 40 minutes. Cool to room temperature before cutting.

SERVING SIZE: 1 bar
CALORIES: 205
FAT: 1.87 grams

CHOLESTEROL: 0
SODIUM: 62 milligrams

■■

M OCHA PUDDING

Makes 1 serving

Y ou can make a single serving of this cholesterol-lowering pudding, or a batch to keep in the refrigerator. Use more or less cocoa and coffee to taste. ∎

1 **heaping teaspoon** guar gum	½ **teaspoon instant coffee**
3 **tablespoons sugar**	¼ **cup evaporated skim milk**
2 **tablespoons unsweetened cocoa**	½ **teaspoon vanilla**

In a small saucepan mix together, with a wire whisk, guar gum, sugar, cocoa, and instant coffee. Whisk until well blended. Gradually beat in the skim milk, vanilla, and ¾ cup water. Mix until well blended and smooth.

Bring mixture to a slow boil, stirring constantly with a wooden spoon. Be sure to get into the corners of the pan, where the guar gum tends to settle and lump. Stir well so that the pudding is lump-free. When the mixture comes to a boil, remove from heat and cool to room temperature. Refrigerate for 3 hours at least or until well chilled.

SERVING SIZE: 1 recipe
CALORIES: 214
FAT: 1.92 grams

CHOLESTEROL: 2.55 milligrams
SODIUM: 75.15 milligrams

■■

BERRY PUDDING

Makes 2 servings

This pudding is good enough to serve to company. Be sure to tell your guests the added benefit you're giving them in terms of cholesterol lowering! Put a few pieces of fresh fruit on top for a stunning presentation. ■

3 **heaping teaspoons** guar gum

2 **tablespoons sugar**

One 10-ounce package frozen raspberries or strawberries, in light syrup, thawed

½ **teaspoon vanilla**

½ **cup nonfat yogurt**

In a blender or food processor, mix guar gum, sugar, raspberries and their syrup, vanilla, and yogurt. Blend thoroughly. (You can, if you wish, first pass this mixture through a strainer to remove the raspberry seeds.)

Transfer the mixture to a small saucepan and slowly bring to a boil, stirring constantly with a wooden spoon (be sure to get into the corners of the pan, where the guar gum tends to settle and lump). Stir well so that the pudding is lump-free. When the mixture comes to a boil, simmer for 2 minutes, then remove from the heat. Transfer mixture to 2 dishes and cool to room temperature. Refrigerate for 3 hours at least or until well chilled. You can serve with sweetened whipped evaporated skim milk if you wish.

SERVING SIZE: ½ recipe
CALORIES: 239
FAT: .7 grams

CHOLESTEROL: 1 milligram
SODIUM: 44.3 milligrams

■■

INDIAN BARLEY PUDDING

Makes 6 to 8 servings

Barley has cholesterol-lowering ability and this pudding is a really delicious way to enjoy it. You can jack up the soluble-fiber content of the dish more by sprinkling Vita Fiber rice bran on top. ■

1 **cup barley,** pearled **or** whole	2 **tablespoons rum**
1 **can evaporated skim milk**	½ **cup egg substitute**
⅓ **cup molasses**	1 **cup raisins**
¼ **teaspoon each powdered cloves, cinnamon, and nutmeg**	**Sour-cream substitute**

Preheat oven to 325 degrees. Spray with Pam or Baker's Joy a wide, shallow ovenproof glass or ceramic baking pan, about 9 by 13 inches; set aside.

In a large saucepan bring barley, milk, 2½ cups water, molasses, spices, and rum to a boil and simmer 3 minutes. Remove from heat and cool 10 minutes. In a small mixing bowl combine egg substitute with raisins, and after 10 minutes, stir this into the barley-milk mixture. Pour the mixture into the prepared baking pan and bake for 1½ hours.

Serve warm or at room temperature with chilled sour-cream substitute, if you wish.

SERVING SIZE: ⅛ recipe
CALORIES: 207
FAT: .61 grams

CHOLESTEROL: 1.35 milligrams
SODIUM: 61.4 milligrams

■ ■

RICE PUDDING

Makes six ½-cup servings

Traditional rice pudding might taste good, but it contains virtually no fiber and is high in fat. Here we've added back the fiber in the form of either Vita Fiber rice bran or apple fiber. Each will give the dish a distinctive flavor. You can also make the pudding richer and creamier by using only evaporated milk instead of the milk-water combination. Serve the pudding at room temperature, since rice tends to be tough when chilled. ■

One 12-ounce can evaporated skim milk

½ cup sugar

1 cup raisins

1 teaspoon vanilla or ½ teaspoon almond extract

1 cup converted long-grain rice

4–6 tablespoons pulverized Vita Fiber **or** apple fiber

Cinnamon or sliced strawberries

In a medium saucepan, bring skim milk, 2 cups water, sugar, raisins, and vanilla to a slow boil. Gently, in a steady stream, add rice and stir a couple of times. Lower heat and simmer, partially covered, for 25 minutes, or until rice is very tender.

When rice is soft, stir in Vita Fiber and cook for 1 minute more. Transfer rice pudding to a 3-cup dish or to six ½-cup ramekins or glass pudding dishes.

Serve at room temperature garnished with a dusting of cinnamon or sliced fresh berries.

SERVING SIZE: ⅙ recipe
CALORIES: 294
FAT: .42 grams

CHOLESTEROL: 2.27 milligrams
SODIUM: 69.4 milligrams

■ ■

FRUIT AND FIBER GELATIN

Makes 6 to 8 servings

Everyone has room for at least a light dessert to end a meal sweetly. This recipe fills that need perfectly. Have a few servings prepared in the refrigerator for when the snack craving hits later in the evening. ■

One 3-ounce package gelatin dessert, strawberry- or raspberry-flavored	**One 8-ounce can fruit, such as apricots, drained and chopped**
	3 egg whites
½ **cup** apple fiber	¼ **cup sugar**

Dissolve gelatin dessert in 1 cup boiling water and set aside.

In a small bowl dissolve apple fiber in 1 cup warm water, then stir in cut-up fruit. Whisk dissolved gelatin into fiber and fruit.

Whip egg whites until they form stiff peaks, then gradually beat in sugar. Fold this into gelatin, fiber, and fruit.

Spoon into 6 or 8 glass or ceramic ramekins (1-cup size) and chill for 3 hours.

SERVING SIZE: ⅛   CHOLESTEROL: 0
CALORIES: 90.9   SODIUM: 31.6 milligrams
FAT: .638 grams

■ ■

CHOCOLATE MILKSHAKE

Makes 1 serving

Many people think they can't enjoy the flavor of chocolate when watching their cholesterol counts. The truth is that cocoa powder has no fat or cholesterol; it's only when cocoa powder gets mixed with butterfat to make chocolate that it becomes an artery clogger. This milkshake offers not only a chocolate fix but also a good dose of soluble fiber by way of the guar gum. ■

1 **heaping teaspoon** guar gum

2 **tablespoons unsweetened cocoa**

2 **tablespoons sugar**

½ **cup evaporated skim milk, preferably chilled**

In a food processor or blender, combine guar gum, cocoa, and sugar; mix until well blended. In a measuring cup, combine skim milk and ¼ cup water. While blender or food processor is running, pour in the liquid and mix for about a minute or until thickened. Drink as is or on ice. You could also mix this with seltzer to make an unorthodox version of an egg cream.

VARIATIONS. To make a mocha shake, use 1 tablespoon cocoa and 1 teaspoon instant coffee.

To make a coffee shake, omit cocoa and use 1 to 1½ teaspoons instant coffee.

To make a vanilla shake, use 1 tablespoon vanilla extract, and use ¾ cup evaporated skim milk instead of ½ cup milk and ¼ cup water.

SERVING SIZE: 1 shake
CALORIES: 215
FAT: 2.03 grams

CHOLESTEROL: 5.1 milligrams
SODIUM: 147 milligrams

ORANGE GUARIUS

Makes 1 serving

A West Coast original, the Orange Julius has sprouted at stands all over the country. When you're in the mood for a tasty fiber-packed alternative, try this orange guarius made with guar gum. You can get guar gum in any health-food store, and one teaspoon has as much soluble fiber as an oat-bran muffin. ∎

1 **heaping teaspoon** guar gum, **preferably orange-flavored**

2 **tablespoons sugar**

2 **tablespoons frozen orange-juice concentrate, thawed**

1 **teaspoon vanilla**

½ **cup evaporated skim milk, preferably chilled**

In a blender or food processor combine guar gum and sugar; mix until blended. In a measuring cup, mix orange-juice concentrate, vanilla, skim milk, and ¼ cup water. While blender or food processor is running, pour in the liquid. Mix for a minute or until thickened and well homogenized. Serve as is or on ice.

SERVING SIZE: 1 recipe
CALORIES: 189
FAT: .53 grams

CHOLESTEROL: 2 milligrams
SODIUM: 64.27 milligrams

ORANGE GUAR SMOOTHIE

Makes 1 serving

Remember the Dreamsicles and Creamsicles you enjoyed as a child? This creamy orange concoction will bring all those memories back. And the guar gum adds soluble fiber while it thickens the drink. ∎

2 heaping tablespoons frozen
orange-juice concentrate

1 heaping teaspoon orange-flavored
guar gum

6 ounces plain nonfat yogurt

Sugar or sugar substitute to
taste

Place all ingredients in a blender for a few seconds, then pour and enjoy.

SERVING SIZE: 1 recipe
CALORIES: 245
FAT: .48 grams

CHOLESTEROL: 2.99 milligrams
SODIUM: 133.27 milligrams

Index

Chinese fried barley, 249
Chinese stir-fried beef, 174
Chocolate. *See also* Cocoa
  chocolate brownies, 310
  milkshake, 319
Cholesterol (cholesterol levels)
  dietary, 19–21
  heart disease and, 4–5
  kinds of, 5–6
  label terms referring to, 24
Cholesterol-lowering drugs, 6–7
Cholesterol-lowering foods, 7, 27–50
  apple fiber, 35–36
  barley, 33–34
  dried beans and peas, 32–33
  fish and fish oils, 40–50
  guar gum, 36–38
  oat bran, 27–32
  rice bran, 38–40
Cholestyramine, 6, 29
Chowder, salmon, 126
Citrus pectin, 35–36
Cock-a-leekie soup, Scottish, 120
Cocoa
  chocolate milkshake, 319
  mocha milkshake, 319
  mocha pudding, 314
  mocha torte, 298
Coconut oil, 14
  percentages of saturated,
    monounsaturated, and
    polyunsaturated fatty acids in,
    16
Coffee, 25
  milkshake, 319
Coffee creamers, 54
Colestipol, 6, 29
Colon cancer, 12
Conner, William, 45
Cookies
  apple-fiber and oatmeal, 306
  gingersnaps, 307
  honey oatmeal drop, 308
Corn
  and chili soup, 122
  and mackerel salad, 139
  in pinto bean succotash, 219
  salad with chickpeas and pimiento,
    135
Cornbread, jalapeño, 273

Cornmeal
  blueberry corn-bran muffins, 293
  johnnycakes with scallions and oat
    bran, 246
  pancakes, three-grain, 262
Corn oil: percentages of saturated,
  monounsaturated, and
  polyunsaturated fatty acids in,
  16
Cottage cheese, 51
Cottonseed oil: percentages of
  saturated, monounsaturated,
  and polyunsaturated fatty acids
  in, 16
Crackers, oatcakes, 282
Cranberry
  oat-bran muffins, 284
  orange cake, 299
Cream, evaporated skim milk as
  substitute for, 54
Creamers, coffee, 54
Creole red-bean patties, 153
Creole red beans and rice, 227
Crumbs, seasoned, 256
Cucumber(s)
  and barley salad, 131
  dressing, creamy, 145
Curried pea-bean and
    Brussels-sprouts soup, 96
Curried split pea sauce, 255
Curry, bean and eggplant, 165

Dairy industry, 52–53
Dairy products, 10
  shopping for, 51–55
Dakota lean meats, 56. *See also under*
    Beef *for recipes*
Date(s)
  apricot cake with, 304
  -nut banana bread, 276
  and prune bars, 312
  and raisin granola bars, 261
Davidson, Dennis, 28
Desserts and sweets, 295–321
  apple-fiber and oatmeal cookies,
    306
  applesauce oat-bran cake, 296
  apricot cake, 304
  berry pudding, 315
  carrot cake, 303

Fish oils, 43
Fish oil supplements, 46
Flatulence, oat bran and, 30
Fonnebo, V., 11–12
Food groups, 9–11
Food processors, 61
Formagg cheeses, 10, 53, 54
"Fortified," meaning of, 22
Fraser, Gary, 11
French bean casserole, 234
Fruit(s), 10–13
    bread, 275
    dried. *See also specific dried fruits*
        -oatmeal crisp, 305
    fiber content of (table), 41
    and fiber gelatin, 318
    shopping for, 59–60

Galaxy Cheese Company, 10, 54
Garbanzo beans. *See* Chickpeas
Garbure: a French soup of beans and
        cabbage, 101
Garlic
    and bean soup, Provençal, 112
    and chickpea and thyme purée, 224
    and fava bean purée, 221
    red beans with ginger and, 230
Gastric emptying, oat bran and, 29
Gelatin, fruit and fiber, 318
Ginger
    cake, 300
    red beans with garlic and, 230
Gingerbread rice-bran muffins, 290
Gingersnaps, 307
Ginter, Emil, 36
Grain group (breads and cereals
        group), 13
Grains, fiber content of (table), 41
Granola bars, date and raisin, 261
Great Northern white beans
    baked, easy, 216
    in cassoulet with ham, 188
    in garbure: a French soup of beans
        and cabbage, 101
Greek pastitsio with lentils, 163
Greek-style chicken lemon soup, 121
Green beans
    in mackerel and bean Niçoise salad,
        140
    in Provençal bean and garlic soup,
        112

Green beans *(cont.)*
    salad
        spicy rice, ham, and, 142
        three-bean salad, 133
Green hummus, 85
Green onions. *See* Scallions
Green peas (sweet peas)
    and barley medley, 248
    in fish paella, 212
    salad with rice and black beans,
        134
    split. *See* Split peas, green
Greens and chickpea soup,
        Portuguese, 108
Green sauce, poached salmon with,
        194
Green split peas. *See* Split peas, green
Grundy, Scott, 14–15
Guacamole, fat-free, 90
Guar gum, 36–38
    in chocolate milkshake, 319
    cholesterol-lowering effects of,
        37–38
    forms of, 38
    in mocha pudding, 314
    in orange guarius, 320
    orange smoothie, 321
Gumbo, chicken and bean, 109

Ham, 56
    Chinese fried barley with, 249
    entrées
        black-eyed pea casserole with
            ham and carrots, 186
        cassoulet, 188
        Hungarian bean and sauerkraut
            with ham, 187
        Spanish lentil, barley, and ham
            casserole, 185
    hoppin' John with, 166
    in pot au feu, 184
    salad of rice, green bean, and, spicy,
        142
    in soup
        barley, carrot, and ham, 116
        chickpea soup with ham, hearty,
            107
        lentil, potato, and, 114
        navy-bean and, one-cup, 97
        Portuguese chickpea and greens
            soup, 108

Oatmeal *(cont.)*
  in date and raisin granola bars, 261
  dried-fruit crisp, 305
  honey drop cookies, 308
  and oat-bran bread, 264
  oatcakes, 282
  in prune and date bars, 312
  in seasoned crumbs, 256
  "smacks," 309
  sweet bread, 270
Oils. *See also* Vegetable oils
  monounsaturated, 18–19
Olive oil, 15, 19
  percentages of saturated,
    monounsaturated, and
    polyunsaturated fatty acids in,
    16
Olives, 11
Omega-3 fatty acids, 42–43, 44
  in 3½-ounce servings of fish
    (table), 45
Onion(s)
  and black bean soup, 100
  green. *See* Scallions
  -raisin sauce, 252
  and rye and oat-bran bread, 268
Orange
  cranberry cake, 299
  glaze for ginger cake, 300
  guarius, 320
  guar smoothie, 321
  oat-bran muffins, 285
  rice-bran muffins, 292
"Organic," meaning of, 23

Paella, fish, 212
Palmitic acid, 15
Palm kernel oil, 14
  percentages of saturated,
    monounsaturated, and
    polyunsaturated fatty acids in,
    16
Palm oil, 14
  percentages of saturated,
    monounsaturated, and
    polyunsaturated fatty acids in,
    16
Pam, 19
Pancakes
  bean or legume, 215
  carrot and potato, 247

Pancakes *(cont.)*
  oat-bran and rice-fiber, 263
  rice and carrot, 244
  three-grain, 262
Parsley and lentil salad, Italian, 130
Pasta, 59
  black-eyed peas and macaroni, 164
  e fagioli, 111
  Greek pastitsio with lentils, 163
  lasagna with chickpeas, 148
  tomato sauce for, 253
    with chickpeas and turkey, 254
Pasta maker, 62
Pâté, bean, three-color, 82
Pea bean(s). *See also* White beans
  baked, spiced, 217
  and broccoli stew, 156
  in pot au feu, 184
  and rice stew, Scandinavian, 222
  soup
    Brussels-sprouts and, curried, 96
    garlic and, Provençal, 112
    mushroom, barley, and, 118
  in three-bean salad, 133
  and turkey skillet dinner, 189
Peanut butter, 20
Peanut oil: percentages of saturated,
    monounsaturated, and
    polyunsaturated fatty acids in,
    16
Peas, 32–33, 58. *See also* Black-eyed
    peas; Green peas; Split peas
  cholesterol-lowering effects of, 33
  fiber content of (table), 41
  in Scotch broth, 117
Pease pudding, 233
Pectin, 35–36. *See also* Apple fiber
Peppers, sweet
  green, in chickpea and
    four-vegetable salad, 136
  red
    in black bean chili, 157
    roasted, black and white bean
      salad with, 137
    sauté with barley and bean curd,
      169
    stuffed with barley and raisins, 150
Persian rice and lentils, 237
Peterson, David, 34
Pickled sardine and beet salad, 141
Pie, sardine and potato, 209

White beans (cont.)
in three-bean soup with celery and
lemon, 105
Wild game, 57
Wine, beef stew with, 173

Yellow split peas. See Split peas, yellow
Yogurt
cheese, 62

Yogurt (cont.)
cucumber dressing, creamy,
145
frozen, 60
and herb dip, 87
nonfat, 52
YoWhip, 60

Zucchini cake, 297